REVOLUTION IN OUR TIME

THE BLACK PANTHER PARTY'S PROMISE TO THE PEOPLE

REVOLUTION
THE BLACK PANTHER PARTY'S

CANDLEWICK PRESS

IN OUR TIME

PROMISE TO THE PEOPLE

KEKLA MAGOON

For all of us,
that tomorrow may be better
than yesterday

 First edition 2021. Library of Congress Catalog Card Number pending. ISBN 978-1-5362-1418-5. This book was typeset in Bayard, Franklin Gothic, and Redaction. Candlewick Press, 99 Dover Street, Somerville, Massachusetts 02144. www.candlewick.com Printed in Heshan, Guangdong, China. 21 22 23 24 25 26 LEO 10 9 8 7 6 5 4 3 2 1

A JUNIOR LIBRARY GUILD SELECTION

THE REVOLUTION HAS ALWAYS BEEN IN THE HANDS OF THE YOUNG.

HUEY P. NEWTON

CONTENTS

When people talk about the Black Panthers,

sometimes they speak in hushed tones, as if history itself could overhear. As if the Panthers are a secret no one should talk about. For many years, Americans have looked away from the Black Panthers' legacy, and because people have looked away, many have forgotten who and what the Panthers really were.

The Black Panther Party was a nation-wide organization that existed in Black[1] communities in the United States from 1966 until 1982. The Panthers played several roles: they were civil rights and human rights activists, militant revolutionaries, and community organizers, and they were also a political party. They taught Black Americans how to fend for themselves in a country that treated them like second-class citizens, where police officers and politicians often failed to protect people but abused their power instead. The Panthers committed to defending Black people—with weapons, but also with education and with services designed to raise families out of abject poverty. They were one manifestation of a widespread belief that the passive resistance tactics of the civil rights movement were no longer effective.

[1] **Black communities, Black people:** It is standard practice today to capitalize Black when referring to Black people, Black communities, and Black culture. This was not always the case historically. I've left any direct quotes as they were written, so the capitalization will appear inconsistent at times within the text.

The Panthers' decision to advocate self-defense was controversial at the time, and it remains controversial. But one thing cannot be denied: in the midst of one of the most turbulent times their country had ever faced, the Panthers took a stand. Their actions drew thousands of followers and brought the attention of the entire nation to their movement, making them the target of one of the most sustained and organized repression efforts ever made by the U.S. government against its own citizens.

The Panthers fought a revolution in their time, just as we are fighting one in ours.

They were called troublemakers, terrorists, and branded as anti-American, but the truth of their work belies these labels. They boldly claimed their place at the vanguard of a centuries-old fight for equality, and their legacy continues to lead the way forward. The story of the Black Panther Party is one of violence and heartbreak and struggle and conviction. It is the story of a group of young people who set out to change the world around them—in very radical ways. ■

SPARK

May 2, 1967

The moment that speaks to everything before . . . and everything to come

SHATTERING THE STATUS QUO

Radical simply means "grasping things at the root."

—ANGELA DAVIS

Early in the morning on May 2, 1967, a group of thirty Black people piled into cars in Oakland, California, and struck out on the highway, headed for the state capitol in Sacramento. The group was made up of twenty-four men and six women. Among them were members of the Black Panther Party for Self-Defense, other community residents, and the family members of Denzil Dowell, a young Black man who had been shot and killed by police officers about a month earlier. The trunks of the cars were filled with pistols, shotguns, and semiautomatic weapons.

Everyone was nervous. But the eighty-mile drive from Oakland to Sacramento gave them plenty of time to think and to remember why they were going to the capitol: because they did not want what happened to Denzil Dowell to happen to anyone else. Denzil was a Black teen accused of robbing a local liquor store. Police officers shot him multiple times, although he was unarmed and possibly in the act of surrendering. Then they left him to die without even calling an ambulance.

Panthers speaking with a state police lieutenant on the steps of the capitol

Previous spread: **Members of the Black Panther Party inside the state capitol, accompanied by police and press**

It wasn't the first time that area police had shot a Black suspect in questionable circumstances. Police officers rarely gave Black citizens the benefit of the doubt. Far beyond Oakland, throughout the nation, Black Americans struggled with similar issues. An entire movement for civil rights was underway, one goal of which was to protect Black people from race-based violence. Young people led peaceful public protests aimed at calling attention to racism, changing unjust laws, and demanding equal treatment. Unfortunately, those changes hadn't come in time to save Denzil Dowell. So for the past few months, the Panthers had been leading armed community patrols that monitored police officers at work, in hopes of preventing more senseless violence.

Now they were headed to the state legislature to protest a bill called the Mulford Act, which would make it illegal for citizens to carry guns in public. This piece of legislation had been introduced specifically to prevent the Panthers from carrying the weapons they used to protect citizens from such police brutality. As American citizens, they knew they had a right to protest a law they disagreed with, so they were headed to Sacramento to publicly share their views in front of elected officials.

When they arrived at the state capitol, the Panthers parked their cars right in front of the building. They got out, retrieved their guns, and began loading them with live ammunition. The guns hadn't been loaded during the long drive because it was illegal to carry loaded weapons (except pistols) in a car. The Panthers had carefully studied California gun laws, and they followed them to the letter. It was still legal to carry unconcealed weapons in public places, and the Panthers planned to do so as part of their protest against the Mulford Act.

At that moment, California governor Ronald Reagan was standing out in front of the capitol, speaking to a group of students and members of the press. The Black Panthers gathering their weapons nearby frightened him. He abruptly ended his talk and left the scene.

The journalists turned around to see what had startled the governor and saw a fresh story coming at them. They turned their microphones and cameras toward the Panthers, capturing their approach on the capitol.

The chairman of the Black Panther Party, Bobby Seale, led the way up the courthouse steps. He had a .45-caliber pistol holstered at his hip. Right behind him, toting a twelve-gauge shotgun, was sixteen-year-old Lil' Bobby Hutton, the youngest Panther.

The Panthers knew they might be arrested, even though they were not breaking the law. They knew that police or security guards in the capitol might even shoot at them. They were prepared to shoot back if they had to. They were willing to go to jail if they had to. But no matter what happened, they intended to deliver their message.

The Panthers approached the front doors and came face-to-face with a security guard standing at the entrance. The guard may have been uncomfortable at the sight of the Panthers, but he knew the law, too. "Well, you aren't violating anything with your gun, so if you want to, you can go inside," he said.

The Panther delegation in the halls of the state capitol

The Panthers entered the capitol rotunda, a high-ceilinged, clean, and shiny space. People turned to stare at them. In their black leather jackets and berets, with guns boldly displayed, the Panthers seemed shockingly out of place in the halls of government. Most of the group had never set foot in a legislative building before. Bobby Seale looked around, trying to figure out which way led to the visitors' gallery, where citizens could go to watch the state assembly proceedings. "Anybody here know where you go in and observe the Assembly making these laws?" he called out.

"Upstairs on the next floor," someone answered. So the Panthers went upstairs, looking for the visitors' room. The reporters surrounded them the whole way, shouting questions and jockeying to get in the best camera position to document the Panthers walking through the capitol.

Following signs for the Assembly Chambers, Bobby Seale walked through a door on the second floor—and found himself standing not in the visitors' gallery, but right on the Assembly floor! Members of the press—on purpose or not—had misdirected the Panthers, and they had ended up somewhere regular citizens weren't supposed to be.

The Panthers were surprised to end up on the floor of the legislature.

Frightened legislators began shouting for the Panthers to leave the room. Security guards approached the Panthers in the doorway. One reached out and took Lil' Bobby Hutton's shotgun away from him. Lil' Bobby cried out in protest, "Am I under arrest? What the hell you got my gun for? If I'm not under arrest you give me my gun back!" He knew he wasn't breaking the law by carrying the weapon and was within his rights to ask for it back.

The security guards escorted the Panthers out of the Assembly Chambers. They went willingly. The Panthers had not come to the state capitol to shoot anyone. They had come to read a statement, which Bobby Seale presented on the capitol steps, amid the chaos created by frightened politicians and journalists:

> The Black Panther Party for Self-Defense calls upon the American people in general and the Black people in particular to take careful note of the racist California Legislature which is now considering legislation aimed at keeping the Black People disarmed and power-less at the very same time that racist police agencies throughout the country are intensifying the terror, brutality, murder and repression of Black People.

He launched into reading Executive Mandate #1, a brief summary of the Panthers' beliefs and goals, which included demands for equal treatment:

> Black people have begged, prayed, petitioned, demonstrated and everything else to get the racist power structure of America to right the wrongs which have historically been perpetrated against Black people. . . . The Black Panther Party for Self-Defense believes that the time has come for Black people to arm themselves against this terror before it is too late. . . . A people who have suffered so much for so

long at the hands of a racist society must draw the line somewhere. We believe that the Black communities of America must rise up as one man to halt the progression of a trend that leads inevitably to their total destruction.

The event made news far beyond Sacramento. It had been an honest mistake, barging directly into the legislative session, but it worked out just fine for the Panthers. After all, they had wanted to be noticed and to have their message heard. Networks all over the country aired Bobby Seale's statement. But the greater impact came from the sight of those rows of Black people with guns, dressed like a small army behind him as he spoke such fiery words. People around the country wondered, *Who are these Panthers?*

The powerful image of Black men with guns on the steps of the California legislature put the Panthers on the map. For most of white America, that image defined the Black Panther Party. But to freeze the Panthers in this moment is to do them a disservice—it is to overlook the fact that the Panthers went to Sacramento that day not to commit violence but to speak a difficult truth about racism directly to the power structure of the government. They went as law-abiding citizens and yet were treated as an inherent threat because of the color of their skin. Twenty-three Panthers were arrested that day, despite not having broken the law.

Black Americans watching from around the country recognized the deeper promise of social transformation that the Panthers offered. In Seattle, eighteen-year-old Aaron Dixon felt "a tinge of pride and amazement" at the sight of the Panthers on television. "The image stayed in the back of my mind," he said. And fifteen-year-old Jamal Joseph, looking on from the Bronx, in New York City, thought, "Look at those dudes. . . . They've got black leather coats and berets, carrying guns, scaring white people. . . . I [want] to join."

Soon he would have the opportunity. After their march on the state capitol, the Black Panther Party for Self-Defense would not remain a small Oakland-based organization much longer.

May 2, 1967, marked a significant turning point—the moment when the Black Panthers' posture of armed self-defense became a matter of national awareness. This new militancy rolled across the American landscape like an earthquake, trembling the foundation of the republic.

On the surface, such an earthquake seems quite sudden. It catches people off guard. The ground begins to roll, and it is all too easy to lose footing. Solid things, things designed to be immovable, tilt suddenly, casting all confidence askew.

In moments of nervousness and fear, when the ground is shaking and it feels as if the world might come crashing down, sometimes people forget that earthquakes are, in fact, not sudden. Nor do serious political movements arise in one fell swoop. Nothing happens overnight. The major turning points of history are seismic, born of eons of slightly shifting geologic plates. They do not emerge from nowhere. They are born of deep unrest.

The front page of the *Sacramento Bee* the following day

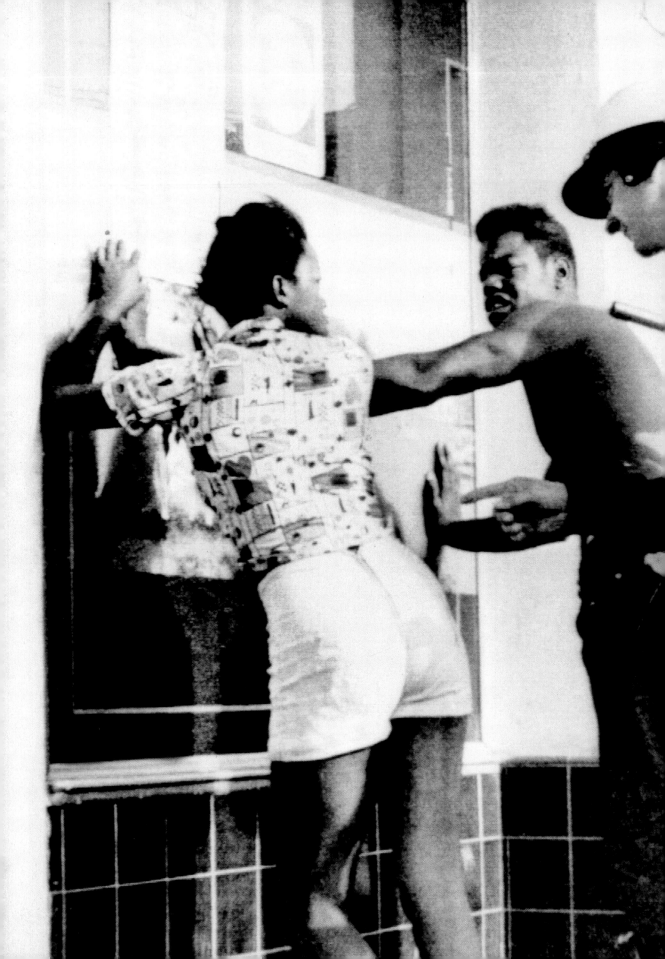

KINDLING

1619–1965

A legacy of uncountable wrongs

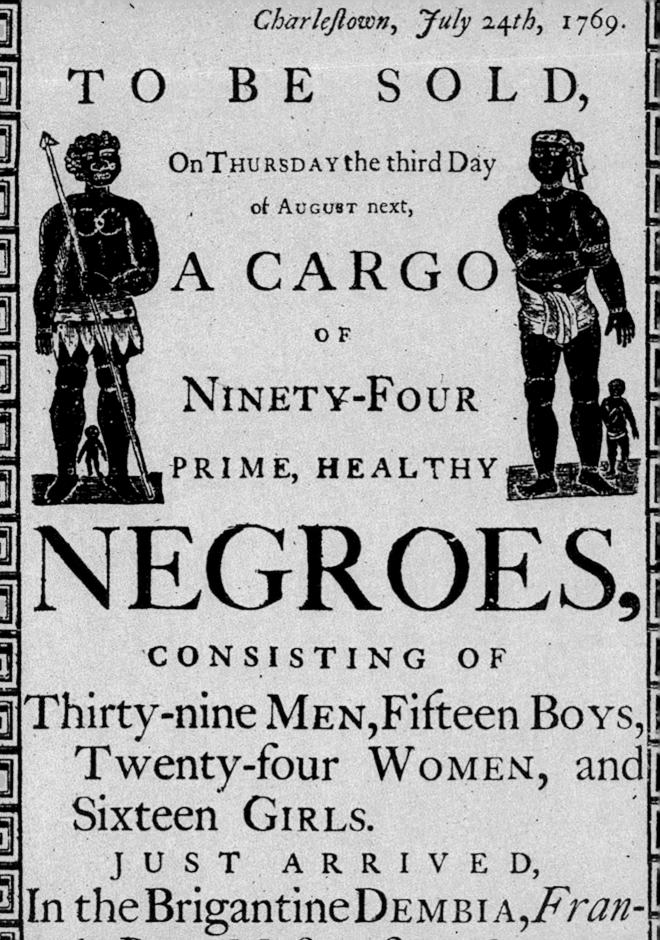

Charlestown, July 24th, 1769.

TO BE SOLD,

On THURSDAY the third Day
of AUGUST next,

A CARGO

OF

NINETY-FOUR

PRIME, HEALTHY

NEGROES,

CONSISTING OF

Thirty-nine MEN, Fifteen BOYS,
Twenty-four WOMEN, and
Sixteen GIRLS.

JUST ARRIVED,

In the Brigantine DEMBIA, *Fran-*
cis Bare Master from SIERRA

THE DARK PAST

For most of us whose ancestors were dragged ashore, shackled, bewildered, and despairing, it is difficult to tell where our stories begin or end.

—AARON DIXON

ANCESTORS IN CHAINS

The first Black people to set foot on North American soil were brought to these shores unwillingly. As early as the fourteenth century, European powers including Britain, France, Spain, Germany, Portugal, the Netherlands, and Belgium sent explorers around the world to trade goods and to acquire land. They traveled to Asia and Africa, planted their flags, and claimed those shores as their own colonies. The Europeans considered their culture and language and laws more advanced, more civilized, and just plain better than that of the brown-skinned people already living in these places, so they took forcible rule over the Indigenous people and began treating the land as an extension of their own nations, governed by their laws and injected with their languages and culture.

The Indigenous people did not give up their land without a fight. For example, Queen Nzinga led the Ndongo and Matamba people in successful

◀ White colonists bought and sold enslaved Black people in auctions such as the one described in this ad.

Previous spread: Los Angeles police detaining and searching a woman and man suspected of looting

rebellion against the Portuguese for decades (in what is now part of Angola). But few societies were able to match the firepower, cruelty, and economic domination of the European invaders.

White European colonists came to the place now called North America in great ships, prepared to build another colonial civilization in the "New World." Again, they forcibly displaced and murdered millions of Indigenous people, and after claiming the land, they brought over more ships full of Black people they had kidnapped from the African continent.

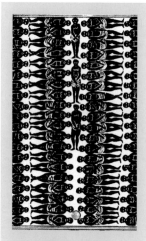

Slave traders treated kidnapped Africans as cargo to maximize profits.

Each ship carried hundreds of people, who were kept chained belowdecks and stacked practically on top of one another, like sardines in a can. They were barely fed and rarely allowed to exercise or breathe fresh air. There was no bathroom—they were forced to relieve themselves where they lay. All the captives became very weak during the passage, most became very sick, and many died.

Still, they found ways to resist. Africans on as many as one out of ten ships rose up in rebellion against the crew, likely hoping to take over the ship and get themselves back home. Weakened by hunger, unarmed, and trapped belowdecks, the prisoners were always at a disadvantage. Of the over one million kidnapped Black people who died in the course of these excruciating journeys across the Atlantic, an unknown number died fighting for their freedom.

Eleven million survived, traumatized by the horror of the passage. Once they arrived in North America, the Europeans kept the Black Africans in bondage, forcing them to work for no wages and providing them with only the most basic food and shelter in return for their labor. The European settlers regarded the Africans not as people, but as property, and bought and sold them like farm animals.

Amid these acts of cruelty and degradation, geologic plates began to shift. The first seeds of racial unrest were sown.

QUEEN NZINGA: PROTECTING HER PEOPLE

In 1624, Nzinga Mbande was elected ruler of the Mbundu Kingdom of Ndongo, an African state located within the area that makes up present-day Angola. Nzinga negotiated an alliance with the Portuguese to protect her kingdom from slave raiders and maintain political and economic control over her land. The alliance lasted only a short time before the Portuguese betrayed Nzinga, seeking to conduct their slave trade within her kingdom. Nzinga led armed resistance against the Portuguese within Ndongo for over a decade, then she took her people west and established a new state, Matamba. Nzinga's state provided a safe refuge for those who escaped capture and were willing to fight for their freedom, and also even offered sanctuary to African soldiers who had been trained and enlisted by the Portuguese. She built an army of young people, called *kilombo*, to defend Matamba, and they worked from afar to incite further rebellion within Ndongo.

ANN ZINGHA,
Queen of Matamba.

The original of this picture, painted on parchment, is to be found in Portugal in a convent of Coimbra.

Under Nzinga's leadership, Matamba remained independent, building economic power and trade capabilities to rival the colonial influence in the region. The culture of self-sufficiency, economic participation, and anti-colonial resistance that Nzinga fostered in her people did not fade over the centuries. In 1961, the people of Angola rose up in anti-colonial struggles that led to actual independence for the nation as a whole.

The majority of Black people in America remained enslaved for the next two hundred years. A small number of Black people earned or purchased their freedom, and some escaped from bondage. Slavery persisted as a bedrock of colonial culture, even as the European settlers from Great Britain, France, and Spain fought repeatedly over the land and the laws that governed it.

By the 1770s, Great Britain had claimed most of the eastern coast of North America. The land was divided into thirteen colonies, each governed by British citizens. Enslaved Black workers helped build and strengthen the colonies, and the British colonists grew very wealthy. White landowners sold crops that the enslaved people had planted, tended, and harvested. They lived in large fancy homes built from lumber that enslaved people had chopped and carried on their backs. And as generations passed, the enslaved population grew larger and larger.

The British colonists, unhappy with being ruled from afar by a ruthless king, began organizing to form their own government. In 1774, the First Continental Congress established goals for this new nation, and one goal was to abolish slavery in the colonies. In 1776, the American colonists drafted a Declaration of Independence and began fighting to create a new nation.

The colonists' fight succeeded. After eight years of the Revolutionary War, King George III of Great Britain withdrew his soldiers from the battlefield. The United States had won its independence. Delegates from all corners of the new United States of America came together in Philadelphia to create a constitution, the core set of laws that would govern the new nation. The delegates drafted the Constitution, which declared as its highest values the right of all citizens to elect their leaders, live in freedom, and pursue happiness.

Black Americans, however, were excluded from the rights and privileges of full American citizenship. The framers of the Constitution cast aside the intentions they had set in the First Continental Congress about ending the slave trade.

Slavery would continue, and the framers debated whether to count enslaved people as citizens. Black people would not be able to vote either way, but each state would receive government representation based on the number of citizens living there, so southern slaveholders wanted their enslaved people counted. Northern representatives thought that was unfair. As a compromise, they wrote in the Constitution that they would count each free person, but "all other persons" (which would mean non-free, or enslaved, people) would be counted as three-fifths of a person. Thus, the founders of the new America enshrined in the most integral document of the land the notion that Black people were less valuable—indeed, less *human*—than white people.

The framers may not have viewed this as a broken promise, but to enslaved Black people throughout the South, it was a crushing blow. Plates shifted. The seeds of unrest sprouted roots.

This 1850 lithograph depicts the Fugitive Slave Act being enforced through violence. The print was created to protest the act, which allowed for the creation of fugitive-hunting posses and introduced new strategies for law enforcement—the effects of which can still be seen today in the structures of modern policing.

WHO IS A CITIZEN?

When the British colonists-turned-Americans said "person" or "citizen," they were typically talking exclusively about white men. White women were fully counted as people for census purposes, but they were denied many of the rights that the Constitution promised to men, such as the right to own property, the right to vote, and the right to manage money. Black men gained some of these rights before women of any race did, although few were in a position to exercise them. Native people were also denied citizenship rights, and the United States repeatedly broke treaties and territory agreements with Indigenous nations. Many Native people were enslaved alongside (or in place of) Black people, and those individuals would have been counted based on the three-fifths clause.

The brand-new United States of America thrived as an independent nation, gaining economic power largely due to the strength of this unpaid labor force. But in the northern states, a growing movement for the abolition of slavery took hold. Abolitionists believed slavery was morally wrong, and they wanted to see the practice outlawed. There had always been abolitionists among free Black citizens, but the number of white people joining the cause increased. One by one the northern states outlawed slavery, turning their Black population free. Soon there was controversy about whether new states admitted to the Union would be slave states or free states.

For the millions of enslaved people, abolition in the North opened up new possibilities for escape. White abolitionists, free Black people, and some who had escaped slavery formed a network known as the Underground Railroad to help folks from the South escape to the North and, in some cases, all the way to Canada.

Fleeing slavery was extremely perilous—being captured could mean severe punishment, such as vicious beatings that might leave someone disfigured or wounded for life. It was also very frightening because those who escaped had no idea what they were running toward. Out of about three million enslaved people in the southern states, only about 100,000 managed to successfully escape.

Sojourner Truth escaped slavery and became a noted abolitionist and women's rights advocate. She traveled around the country giving powerful speeches that challenged embedded notions of racism and sexism.

Some did not want to flee—they wanted to fight. In 1800, an enslaved man named Gabriel¹ planned to take over the state capitol in Richmond, Virginia, intending to spark a widespread rebellion among Black people. The plot failed

---

¹ Gabriel is often referred to with the last name Prosser, which is the name of the family that enslaved him.

The Declaration of Independence states that "all men" are endowed with "inalienable rights," but to the drafters and signers, "all men" meant only landowning white men.

because weather delayed the attack, and Gabriel was caught and hanged before he could try again.

Denmark Vesey, a free Black man in Charleston, South Carolina, organized a similar rebellion in 1822 that would have been the most massive slave revolt in history. He, too, was caught and hanged before the rebellion could occur.

Discovery of Nat Turner, October 30, 1831

Nat Turner succeeded in rallying about seventy-five fellow enslaved people to attack plantation owners in 1831. They revolted against bondage, killing about fifty-five white people and confiscating their horses and weapons. Soon they also were caught and killed for rebelling. Each of these men hoped his actions would inspire all enslaved Black people in the South to rise up against the system and demand freedom.

Some enslaved people tried to earn their freedom through the law. Dred Scott sued for his freedom in 1847, in a case that went all the way up to the U.S. Supreme Court. The Supreme Court struck down Dred Scott's request in 1857, saying that because he was Black, he was not a citizen and had no right to sue. Other courts later held up the *Dred Scott* decision as a precedent for denying Black people any legal rights.

The abolitionist movement continued to grow, to a point where the U.S. government began considering a nationwide law banning slavery. In 1860, Abraham Lincoln was elected president, and southerners grew worried that anti-slavery laws would soon affect the entire country.

Black troops who served in the
Massachusetts 54th Regiment ▶

White southerners knew that the American economy would not continue to thrive without slavery. Enslaved people had been providing free labor for decades—if landowners suddenly had to start paying these Black workers, what would happen to the profits? Wealthy landowners got together to protest President Lincoln's election. If being part of the United States of America meant giving up their enslaved workers, they would rather withdraw from the Union and form their own nation. They called it the Confederate States of America and elected their own president.

Between December 1860 and the following summer, eleven southern states seceded from the Union and joined the Confederacy. Soon the nation was embroiled in a full-blown civil war, with the Confederates fighting for independence while Lincoln's army fought to preserve the full Union. In 1863, amid the war, President Lincoln signed the Emancipation Proclamation, a document that would free enslaved people throughout the South—if the Union won the war.

Thousands of Black soldiers joined the Union army, believing that they were fighting not just for their own freedom but for the freedom of all Black people in the country. They proudly took up arms alongside their white countrymen, willing to risk their lives for that freedom.

Black Americans celebrated when the Union proved victorious in the war against the Confederacy. They were free! But much as the previous generations of enslaved people had learned after the American Revolution, wartime promises quickly faded. As the Civil War concluded, the government began a process of reconstruction to bolster the ailing South, but those efforts were centered around white southerners. Southern Blacks, now legally free, had no place to go. Some rushed to the North, but most stayed on in the South and worked as sharecroppers.

Sharecropping meant working on someone else's land in exchange for a share of the profits, and it sounded like a good deal at first, but most Black people found it all too similar to slavery in the end. The landowners were all white,

This mural depicts Black civil war soldiers in battle at Fort Wagner, South Carolina.

and the sharecroppers' portion of the profits offered them little more than basic subsistence. Many found sharecropping worse than slavery, in fact, because the landowner no longer felt any obligation to keep the workers fed or clothed. Land-owners came up with all sorts of tricks to keep Black sharecroppers from making any profits—they charged for the seeds planted on the sharecroppers' portion of the land and for use of farm equipment, deducted high rental fees for living on the land, and sometimes even flat-out refused to pay the Black workers the percentage of profits they had earned. Many landowners got away with paying almost nothing to keep their labor force, even though the Black workers were no longer technically enslaved.

Abolitionists, along with members of the national government, called for aid to help the newly freed people. They held a meeting with twenty Black leaders (some freeborn men and some formerly enslaved), and asked them what they wanted most for the Black people of the South. This gathering was utterly unprecedented in American history, with white government leaders sitting down at the negotiating table alongside Black leaders, concerned for the future and the prosperity of Black Americans.

The Black leaders' request was simple but bold: "The way we can best take care of ourselves is to have land, and turn and till it by our own labor," said Rev. Garrison Frazier, the group's spokesperson. "We want to be placed on land until we are able to buy it and make it our own." They proposed that each formerly enslaved family be given a small plot of this land to farm. The gift of land would

The Freedmen's Bureau was created to facilitate the distribution of land to freed Black families. This 1868 drawing depicts a Bureau representative mediating conflict between white men and freed Black men.

represent a sort of back pay for all the years they had worked for no wages. This idea of back pay would come to be known as reparations. Black people had literally built the United States of America, but they had yet to share in the abundant profits.

The white officials accepted the Black leaders' proposal. The government agreed to reserve 400,000 acres of confiscated plantation land for Black families. They granted forty-acre parcels of this land to Black families, who were eager to get to work. The government even agreed to loan work animals to the freed Black farmers to help get them started. "Forty acres and a mule" became a slogan to describe the goods promised to the Black people.

It seemed like a promising way forward. Land ownership would give Black people a chance to build wealth of their own, instead of toiling for free. It would be a source of pride and something of value to pass on to future generations. But within a year, the American government reneged on these promises, returning the land to the white landowners and leaving the newly freed Black citizens to fend for themselves in a broken economy.

Geologic plates shifted once again. The seeds of unrest began to sprout.

SEPARATE
BUT EQUAL

The chasm between the principles upon which this Government was founded, in which it still professes to believe, and those which are daily practiced under the protection of the flag, yawn so wide and deep.

—MARY CHURCH TERRELL

Fear is a powerful motivator. The entire story of Black people in America is one that is built on fear. Afraid of losing their power and money, white landowners tormented, shamed, and abused their enslaved workers. Afraid of losing their lives, Black people submitted to the landowners' will. Those who did not submit were treated even worse or killed outright. In the midst of such violence, all this fear became twisted. It delved bone deep.

No one let go of their fear in the wake of Emancipation. White southerners continued to seek power at the expense of free Black people, who trembled in the shadows of this cruelty. Lessons long learned are hard to unlearn, even in the course of a generation.

Geologic plates trembled beneath this fear. The seedlings of unrest fed upon it.

◀ **Man drinking from segregated water fountain**

BLACK CODES

Slavery had long kept white people in a formal position of power over Black people, and the feelings of racial superiority ran deep in white southerners. They feared that freed Black people would rise up and gain economic advantages, so they did everything possible to limit Black folks' opportunities, through unlawful intimidation and violence, and even by enshrining segregation rules into law.

Leaders throughout the South implemented new laws informally known as black codes. Each state had separate laws, but most included restrictions on

Soon after the Civil War, several Black men were elected to serve in Congress, including (*portrayed above, left to right*) Senator Hiram Revels, Representatives Benjamin Turner, Robert De Large, Josiah Walls, Jefferson Long, Joseph Rainey, and Robert Elliott. Reconstruction-era backlash like the black codes ended this opportunity.

where Black people could work and what jobs they could hold. Many states required Black workers to sign a yearly employment contract in a labor position and either arrested or taxed Black men who did not secure contracts to work as farmers or servants. In other words, Black people who wanted to be artists, teachers, business owners, salesmen, or professionals could not afford to pursue their interests.

The black codes limited the types of property Black citizens could own and prohibited Black people from owning firearms, among other restrictions. Failing to follow the codes led to imprisonment or forced labor in exchange for no wages. And since Black people could not vote, they had no legal way of fighting against the black codes.

In 1867, the Reconstruction Acts passed by the U.S. Congress granted "equal protection" to Black citizens, including the right to vote, under the Fourteenth Amendment to the Constitution in 1868. (Specifically, this meant Black men— women of any race would not be able to vote until the twentieth century.) But despite the new amendment, white southerners found many ways to restrict Black men from voting, too.

WHITE SUPREMACY

Laws restricting Black life did not seem strong enough to some southern whites. Some formed white supremacist organizations, such as the Ku Klux Klan, the White Brotherhood, and the Knights of the White Camelia. These groups used racial violence to keep Black people in an inferior social standing.

The Ku Klux Klan became the most widespread and well-known white supremacist group. Klansmen wore white hoods and roamed the countryside at night, terrorizing Black citizens. Lynchings, or vigilante murder of Black citizens by white supremacists, happened often throughout the South. All a white man had to do was claim that a Black man had stolen something, or been rude, or even just looked too long at a white woman. The Klan would take the Black man from his house and beat him or even kill him, without any hint of a courtroom trial. When such violence happened, law enforcement officers and the courts almost always sided with the white murderers. Black people lived in constant fear of violence, knowing that the American democratic system, which was supposed to protect law-abiding citizens, would not punish white people for harming them.

For a long while, these intimidation tactics worked. Most Black people were too afraid to speak up for their rights because of what might happen to them if they did.

Ku Klux Klan members at a cross burning

Black and white citizens lived by totally different rules during Reconstruction. They lived in separate communities. Signs that read WHITES ONLY forced Black people out of many public spaces. Restrictions on where they could go meant Black people were being offered less freedom, a kind of second-class citizenship. Segregation—the practice of having separate spaces in society for Black people and white people—remained a matter of law for decades.

In 1892, a light-skinned Black man named Homer Plessy purposefully sat in a whites-only train car in Louisiana. He was light enough to "pass" for white, but he told the conductor he was Black and got arrested. In court, he argued that it was wrong to have separate cars for people of different races, but the court did not agree. The New Orleans Comité des Citoyens (Citizens' Committee), a Black civil rights organization, helped carry Homer Plessy's case all the way to the U.S. Supreme Court in a case known as *Plessy v. Ferguson*. Seven out of the nine justices decided that as long as the public provisions for Black and white people were equal, these segregation laws were acceptable under the Constitution.

In other words, the highest court in the land believed, at that time, that it was all right to legally separate Black people and white people in society. Justice John Marshall Harlan did not agree with the majority decision. He wrote:

> Our Constitution is color-blind, and neither knows nor tolerates classes among citizens. In respect of civil rights, all citizens are equal before the law. . . . The present decision . . . will not only stimulate aggressions . . . [toward] colored citizens, but will encourage the belief that it is possible [to make laws that undermine] the Constitution.

Justice Harlan was right. The Supreme Court's ruling in the *Plessy* case granted states permission to create more and more laws that suppressed Black freedom. Black people attended separate schools, ate at separate restaurants, and occupied separate seating in train cars. Even though these separate spaces for Black people were supposed to be equal, most of the time they were not.

Black citizens were already at a disadvantage because they'd come out of slavery with nothing and had more taken away during Reconstruction. Under segregation, those disadvantages compounded and pushed Black people further and further to the fringes of American society, especially in the southern states.

The Green Book was a travel guide published between 1936 and 1966 that listed hotels, restaurants, bars, and gas stations where Black travelers could stop safely within the segregated South.

HEADING NORTH

Frustrated by the sharecropping life and tired of being kicked around by racist white southerners, thousands of Black workers and their families headed north. Around the turn of the twentieth century, Black people poured into northern cities, looking for work and better opportunities. All their lives, they had been told about the mysterious, magical North, where dreams came true and people were treated as equals.

Nothing could have been further from the truth. While race relations in the North were indeed quite different from those in the South, there were still plenty of problems. Jobs were not as plentiful as everyone hoped, and Black people found themselves crowded into urban ghettos where the cost of living was high and there never seemed to be enough space for everyone. If life had improved much for Black people since slavery, it was hard for most of them to tell exactly how.

For a few, though, opportunities did arise. Against all odds, some Black people had begun to get their education. Religious communities, white liberals, and the few Black Americans with wealth helped develop Black colleges and universities, where those who had long been denied education could access it. In the halls of these institutions, a new social class of Black people was born—Black folks who had the formal education, financial resources, and intellectual training to begin to organize on a broad, national level.

Black migrants traveling North during Reconstruction

NEGRO IMPROVEMENT

In the early 1900s, Black intellectuals emerged who desperately wanted to lift Black people as individuals, and Black communities on the whole, out of pain and poverty.

One such intellectual, Booker T. Washington, believed that education and opportunities were the key to changing Black people's circumstances. Washington

Booker T. Washington

W. E. B. DuBois

Marcus Garvey

Constance Baker Motley

founded the Tuskegee Institute, the first higher-education institution specifically for Black students, which offered vocational training programs and teacher education. He felt that Black people needed to be as prepared as possible to enter the workforce and to fill the types of jobs available to them.

Another leading scholar, W. E. B. DuBois, disagreed with Washington's tactics. He believed that Black people should strive for intellectual growth, aspire to professions, and celebrate their own culture. He thought Black Americans could do better than simply folding into the place white Americans offered them. DuBois helped found the National Association for the Advancement of Colored People (NAACP), an organization whose purpose was to break down legal barriers to Black advancement, mainly by expanding education and voting rights.

Around the same time, Marcus Garvey's Universal Negro Improvement Association proclaimed a "Back to Africa!" message. Garvey proposed the creation of a Black nation, a place where Black people could come together in their own land and govern themselves, no longer enslaved in a white man's world.

These leaders sought to gain followers and to unite Black people around the common cause of bettering their lives. They did not always agree on the best path to freedom for Black people, but they all began to talk seriously about the deep wrongs that had been committed against Black Americans. But while these conversations went on in the "elite" Black communities, most Black folks were just struggling to survive, in communities concentrated in the rural South and urban North.

Through World War I, the economic prosperity of the 1920s, and the Great Depression, it appeared that the seeds of unrest had been beaten too deep into the ground by decades of fear and oppression. Strong voices called for Black people to rise up, and Black people longed to change their circumstances, but they were fearful. The time was coming, but it had not yet arrived.

SOLDIERS' VIEW

In 1939, Germany began invading other European nations, with the intent to take over the world. Japanese planes bombed the U.S. Navy's base at Pearl Harbor, in Honolulu, Hawaii, on December 7, 1941, and the United States entered World War II. Amid the war effort, the tides began to turn for Black Americans.

The war helped spur the American economy, with new jobs opening up for war production workers building ships, planes, tanks, guns, and more. Thousands

BLACK WALL STREET

Some Black communities thrived in spite of segregation. This law office (*above*) in Ardmore, Oklahoma, was one of many successful businesses. Across the state, in Tulsa, the similarly thriving Greenwood District (*below*) became known as Black Wall Street, due to its affluence. Racial tensions were high as a result. On May 31, 1921, two armed, angry crowds surrounded the local courthouse after a Black man was arrested for allegedly interacting with a white woman—the Black crowd hoping to stave off a lynching, and the white crowd eager to see consequences enacted. Shots were fired. The much larger white crowd chased the Black Tulsans back to the Greenwood District, then proceeded to loot, attack, and set fire to the area. The entirety of Black Wall Street (35 city blocks) was burned to the ground, and perhaps as many as 300 people died in what is now known as the Tulsa Race Massacre.

of young white men left to go fight in the war, leaving jobs on the home front open to Black men (as well as both Black and white women)—jobs in industries that had never been open to them before. The United States once again benefited from a robust Black workforce.

However, Black men who joined the military served in segregated units, which were often assigned menial or ultra-dangerous tasks because Black soldiers were perceived as less talented and less important.

"Here we were as a nation involved in a war to make the world safe for democracy, and one of the embarrassing features was that blacks were segregated in our armed forces, and they resented it," said Constance Baker Motley, an attorney with the NAACP's Legal Defense and Educational Fund. "People became more aware that black servicemen were overseas dying for this country, [yet] they would be coming home to a situation that said, in effect, You're a second-class citizen."

The visibility of Black servicemen during and after World War II led communities across the nation to reconsider the circumstances of segregation. After the risks and the sacrifices they had made to serve, and after so many of their brothers had been lost in the same fight, the returning soldiers felt more than ever that they deserved equality.

"There was extreme resentment among the Black veterans when they came back, because they felt, 'I paid my dues over there and I'm not going to take this anymore over here,'" said James Hicks, a Black officer who served in the war.

The nation tried to return to business as usual. Many Black men who had been able to take on jobs previously unavailable to them, and who had performed well in those roles, were forced to give those jobs back to white servicemen returning home. This was patently unfair.

Black people in America had had about enough. The seeds of unrest were now in full bloom.

SHALL WE OVERCOME?

You can resist—you can fight back with your mind, with your wit, with your courage, and that fight will be more effective than if you swung your fist at them.

—**JAMES LAWSON**

Black Americans grappled with the knowledge that their country would fight a dangerous and costly war to defend freedom and democracy worldwide, all the while denying full citizenship rights to many of its own people. Wartime propaganda posters proclaimed, "Americans will <u>always</u> fight for liberty." Yet Black citizens lived in oppression and fear, with very little control over their own lives. Despite a century of so-called liberty, they did not feel very free.

Racism, the great foundation and bedrock of the United States, was as strong as ever. In the hearts of Black America, geologic plates shifted. Things needed to be shaken up.

◁ **The March on Washington for Jobs and Freedom, 1963**

JIM CROW HAS GOT TO GO

Decades of legal efforts had already been underway to change segregation laws. The NAACP employed attorneys—some Black, some white—who worked full time to bring legal cases forward. In 1953, one of these cases made it to the U.S. Supreme Court. The court's unanimous decision in *Brown v. Board of Education of Topeka, Kansas*, delivered on May 17, 1954, declared that "separate educational facilities are inherently unequal" and that schools must be integrated "with all deliberate speed." Unfortunately, the court didn't say exactly how fast that should be, so it took several years for integration to get rolling throughout the South.

Black Americans weren't going to wait. The *Brown v. Board of Education* decision was merely the first wave in a great tide of integration efforts. As the legal battles continued, Black people began organizing to change the law through other means of protest.

In Montgomery, Alabama, riding the city's segregated buses was a source of daily frustration and humiliation for Black people. The front of the bus was reserved for white people. Black people couldn't even enter there; they had to pay their fare at the front and then walk outside the bus to enter from the back door, hoping that the driver didn't choose to drive off with their dime before they had time to board. No matter how crowded the back of the bus got, no one could move forward, even if the whites-only section was entirely empty.

Claudette Colvin, age 13

On March 2, 1955, a high school junior named Claudette Colvin lost patience with the system. When the driver demanded that Claudette and her three classmates stand up to make space for one white passenger to occupy their entire row of four seats, Claudette refused to move.

"Rebellion was on my mind that day," Claudette said. She had been studying Black history and the Constitution in school. In that

Black Montgomerians walking to work during the bus boycott

moment, she decided to take a stand, by sitting. Claudette held her ground when confronted by a police officer. She was arrested.

Claudette's story resonated with Black Montgomerians. Several other people tried similar protest tactics around the same time, but individuals lashing out against the system wasn't enough to create systemic change. Claudette joined with others to file a lawsuit protesting segregation laws. Her story motivated Black people throughout Montgomery to stand together in a collective action.

But the emerging leaders of what would soon be known as the civil rights movement feared that someone like Claudette—an impulsive, now-pregnant teen girl—did not offer the right image. They had begun to think about appearances, and NAACP leader Rosa Parks, a middle-aged seamstress, struck them as a better figurehead for their protest. On December 1, 1955, Mrs. Parks boarded a city bus and sat in the whites-only section. She was arrested, and within days, the Montgomery Bus Boycott began.

"The bus boycott was a way of expressing anger at the system at last," Claudette said. "We had to do it."

Black Montgomerians stayed off the buses for months, which took great commitment and sacrifice on the part of thousands of people. Some got up at the crack of dawn to walk several miles to their jobs. Churches organized carpools, and people with cars gave rides. Some white supporters joined in to drive as well. Whole families shopped together to help lug groceries home. The effort took a huge physical toll on the Black community, but it gave them a feeling of power and control that had been lacking for so long. Black folks took pride in rising to meet the challenge. "I'm not walking for myself," said one grandmother. "I'm walking for my children and my grandchildren."

One of the Montgomery Bus Boycott leaders was a young minister, the Rev. Dr. Martin Luther King Jr. He organized a Social and Political Action Committee in his congregation, Dexter Avenue Baptist Church, and they were instrumental in pulling the citywide boycott together. Dr. King made sure every church member was registered to vote and joined the NAACP, and the church became a central gathering place for boycott volunteers and organizers. Dr. King would soon emerge as a national spokesman for the civil rights movement, due to his powerful speeches and ability to organize and motivate people, as he proved in Montgomery.

The boycott cost the City Lines bus company $3,200 per day. The company began to struggle, laying off employees and closing routes. The city used the police force to try to discourage the carpools. They monitored the major pickup and drop-off sites and made a point of pulling over and questioning Black drivers and passengers. As backlash increased, activists wondered: *How long can Black Montgomerians keep up the struggle?*

Behind the scenes, the legal battle still raged, with Claudette Colvin as a star witness in the NAACP's lawsuit against the City of Montgomery. A federal court decided in favor of Black Montgomerians on June 19, 1956, in a case called *Browder v. Gayle*. Months later, after an appeal to the U.S. Supreme Court, the ruling was upheld. The economic pressure of the boycott combined with the legal ruling left the city with no choice: the buses would have to be integrated! On December 21, 1956, civil rights leaders rode together in the front of a bus and celebrated the success of their organizing efforts. The Montgomery Bus Boycott proved that Black people working in solidarity could change the system.

It also proved that every step of civil rights progress would be met with violent backlash. Immediately post-integration, activists received threatening phone calls and feared for their safety within the city. A few short weeks later, on January 10, 1957, white supremacists tossed bombs into four Black churches—including Claudette Colvin's church—and the homes of three prominent civil rights leaders. "Those were hard, fearsome days," Claudette said.

COLLECTIVE ACTION

Many organizations worked together to achieve civil rights progress, organizing demonstrations and taking collective actions. Here are a few of the most prominent national groups fighting for civil rights:

Student Nonviolent Coordinating Committee (SNCC, pronounced "Snick"): Founded in 1960, SNCC was a group of college students who spearheaded sit-ins, the Freedom Rides, and other strategic collective actions. Stokely Carmichael, H. Rap Brown, and John Lewis (who served in the U.S. House of Representatives from 1987 until his death in 2020) were among the early leaders of SNCC.

Southern Christian Leadership Conference (SCLC): Founded in 1957 and led by the Rev. Dr. Martin Luther King Jr. along with other southern clergy, the SCLC leveraged the massive organizing potential of religious congregations. The organization was founded with the goal of ending all forms of segregation.

Congress of Racial Equality (CORE): CORE is an organization that started in the northern states in 1942, with a mission to bring about equality via strategic organizing. Well-known civil rights leaders of CORE include James Farmer, Bayard Rustin, and Roy Innis.

National Association for the Advancement of Colored People (NAACP): The oldest of the organizations, dating back to 1909, the NAACP played an important role in training young civil rights activists in how to practice passive resistance. They also provided a powerful legal effort via the NAACP Legal Defense Fund, bringing a strategic series of cases to courts nationwide that ultimately led to landmark legal decisions overturning segregation, including *Browder v. Gayle* and *Brown v. Board of Education*.

"YOUR HOUSE IS GONNA BE BLOWED SKY HIGH!"

The ripple effects of *Brown v. Board of Education* caused great uproar among white southerners as Black students began to enroll in previously all-white schools. In one of the most public early cases of school integration, nine Black students in Little Rock, Arkansas, faced down a crowd of screaming white protestors when they tried to enter Central High School on the first day of school in 1957. The crowd grew so violent and threatening that President Dwight D. Eisenhower sent in soldiers from the 101st Airborne Division of the U.S. Army to protect the nine Black teens.

The focus of this narrative—and rightly so—is usually placed upon the nine brave teenagers who showed up at school each day, risking their lives for their education. But there is a deeper significance of the 101st Airborne patrolling Central High that often gets overlooked: this deployment was a U.S. government–sanctioned example of using the threat of force to repel racist violence. It was a bold and controversial choice on Eisenhower's part, a clear indication that the president of the United States understood that the real threat posed by integration efforts was coming from white Americans.

When the 101st withdrew after a month, the Little Rock Nine continued to attend school, though without the armed protection, they endured bullying that left them with permanent emotional and physical scars. These fierce young activists acted with extreme courage in the face of hatred, violence, and fear. The Little Rock Nine were among the first in a long series of teenagers and young adults who would put their lives on the line to fight for civil rights, not just in schools but in all public spaces nationwide.

PASSIVE RESISTANCE TRAINING

The Little Rock Nine followed NAACP guidance by engaging in what was often called "passive resistance." However, there was nothing passive about this

SNCC activists training for passive resistance actions ▶

practice. It simply meant that if you were going to be a civil rights activist, you had to commit to remaining nonviolent and nonreactive at all times. You had to *appear* passive in the face of active threats. No matter what happened, no matter what racial slurs were tossed at you, no matter what violence was being done to you, even if your life was being threatened, you could not react or retaliate. Ever.

Nonviolent resistance became the hallmark of the civil rights movement. The NAACP began leading nonviolent resistance training programs in 1947 and continued to lead them throughout the 1950s and 1960s. The month-long training series included education and role-playing of simulated racist encounters for practice. Trainers would pull the trainees' hair, throw things at them, shout racist epithets, and so on, to help prepare them to sit still through the onslaught that would come in real life. The goal was to create a strong network of activists

who could do this very physical work as a team, and to provide them with the emotional and psychological support necessary to survive the experience.

A key piece of the training was to make clear to young Black activists that engaging in passive resistance did not mean "not fighting back." It meant fighting back smarter, fighting back stronger, and never mirroring the simplistic physical lashing out that racist white people relied upon. The goal was to draw attention to the injustice of segregation laws by remaining "innocent" of anything except breaking those unjust laws.

CIVIL DISOBEDIENCE

Young Black activists practiced nonviolent passive resistance in protests all over the South. They placed their bodies in the places they were not supposed to be, like whites-only lunch counters, whites-only bus seats, and whites-only theaters, knowing that they were likely to be harassed and ultimately arrested for their behavior. This was called civil disobedience—the act of deliberately breaking a law they believed to be unjust. The students' arrests opened up opportunities for lawsuits and court cases, while their actions disrupted the economic success of segregated businesses.

Four Black teens in Greensboro, North Carolina, made headlines on February 1, 1960, when they slid onto stools at an F. W. Woolworth's whites-only lunch counter and staged a sit-in. Teams of Black teens returned to visit that lunch counter every day. The staff behind the counter—even the Black workers—refused to serve them. They weren't allowed to. Sometimes protestors were arrested. White customers frequently taunted them, sometimes cursing or shoving or dumping bottles of condiments on their heads. The Black teens held fast—they had been trained in passive resistance.

Taking matters into their own hands was powerful. The protest gave Ezell Blair, one of the original four, "a feeling of liberation, restored manhood."

Every day the protest grew and grew, as more young people turned up to support the sitters. The daily protests lasted about six months, until Woolworth's integrated its lunch counters on July 25, 1960. Just as the Montgomery Bus Boycott had caused the City Lines bus company to struggle financially, the lunch counter sit-ins caused Woolworth's to lose money over all the lunches they were not selling.

This quiet, peaceful form of rebellion infuriated white southerners who favored segregation. As ever, some chose to respond with extreme violence. When interstate transportation was integrated via legal rulings, some southern states ignored the national mandate and continued sending Black people to the back of buses and trains. In the spring and summer of 1961, Black and white college students, known as Freedom Riders, boarded integrated buses in northern cities and rode south, intending to protest this practice by refusing to leave their seats. A bus that left Washington, D.C., on May 4 pulled into the Trailways bus station in Anniston, Alabama, on May 14, landing straight into an angry mob of white protestors. The mob slashed the bus's tires and pounded on its windows and sides. The driver tried to pull the bus out of the station, but it only made it a

A Freedom Riders' bus burning after an ambush by an angry white mob. Following this attack, President Kennedy sent National Guard troops to escort and protect the next wave of Freedom Riders.

short way on the damaged tires. Then someone threw a firebomb on board. The Freedom Riders stumbled out the door, choking on smoke and gasping for fresh air. The mob proceeded to beat them with pipes and bats.

The Freedom Riders weren't even guilty of civil disobedience—the buses had been legally integrated. But not nearly enough was happening to change people's hearts, minds, and behavior in the oppressive white South. Black Americans remained firm in the commitment to nonviolence even through this violent backlash and continued to hold sit-ins, boycotts, marches, and demonstrations, struggling to convince lawmakers to create and enforce equal rights.

RACISM, RINSE, REPEAT

It took a lot of courage for Black youth to show up at any given demonstration, knowing that protesting could cost them their lives. Young civil rights demonstrators marching peacefully through the streets of Birmingham, Alabama, on May 3, 1963, were met with another wave of violent attacks. Police dogs turned loose on the crowd chased and attacked the protestors. The police turned full-force fire hoses on the crowd, shooting jets of water so hard it took people's skin off. Over two thousand young people were arrested and dragged off to jail.

Journalists captured these events in photographs and video that would soon be seen around the world. People who witnessed these upsetting events saw firsthand how racism could turn ugly. They saw that Black people were not a threat to white people—more often it was the other way around.

Police officers arresting
Black children for
protesting peacefully
in Birmingham

A handful of white allies helped Black protestors along the way—there were people of all races willing to fight to make equality a value in American laws. But there was still a large and active group of white people who believed white people were superior to Black people. Plenty of powerful community members, police officers, lawmakers, and others abused their power to punish Black people for rising up. And the vast majority of white people stood by and did nothing, regardless of whether they agreed with Black activists, white supremacists, or neither. Their silence made the angry, openly racist white people believe they had more supporters than they actually did. Their violence escalated as the civil rights movement continued, despite the Black protestors' refusal to fight back.

Police ordered fire
hoses to be turned
on youth protestors
in Birmingham.

BREAKING VERSUS ENFORCING THE LAW

Some people argued that civil rights movement protestors were asking for trouble by participating in demonstrations that broke the law. Perhaps they deserved to be arrested, some suggested. In fact, that was part of the intent of the demonstrations—to show that segregation laws were unfairly punishing Black people for infractions as simple as sitting in the wrong seat. The actions of white supremacists frequently broke the law, too. It is not legal to beat someone with a pipe or throw a bomb into their home, after all. But the way various laws were being enforced was disproportionate to the point of being inhumane. Did anyone deserve to have attack dogs sicced on them, simply for walking down the street—particularly in a nation that prided itself on each citizen's right to speak freely in a public forum without fear of reprisal?

INTO THE CAPITAL

The March on Washington for Jobs and Freedom, which took place on August 28, 1963, was the culmination of nearly a decade of organized protests, not to mention the previous centuries of struggle. More than 250,000 people gathered on the Washington Mall around the Reflecting Pool, facing the Lincoln Memorial. Standing in the shadow of Abraham Lincoln, the Rev. Dr. Martin Luther King Jr. delivered powerful remarks emphasizing that a hundred years post-emancipation, Black people in America were still not truly free.

The aftermath of the Sixteenth Street Baptist Church bombing

The march represented huge progress for Black Americans: this unprecedented opportunity to gather openly and express their grievances in the nation's capital meant the world to them. The size of the crowd shocked the powers that be in Washington. Lawmakers realized this growing movement could not be ignored. Dr. King and other leaders were invited to the White House to discuss the future. What would be next?

White southerners had a familiar answer, too: anti-Black violence. Just a few short weeks after the demonstrators returned to their homes, a fireball lit up the Birmingham sky. Four Ku Klux Klan members planted a bomb in the Sixteenth Street Baptist Church, located in a Black neighborhood. It blew up on a Sunday morning, killing four young girls. Twenty-some others were injured in the attack, in addition to a great deal of damage done to the church building.

When the four little girls burned in that church, people around the country sat up and took notice of what was happening throughout the South. Demonstrators protesting in the streets knew the risks they were taking, but girls going to church? Many people—especially white people, who hadn't previously understood the extent of racial hatred in America—recognized more than ever how it put even the youngest, most innocent members of society at risk. The March on Washington may have seemed like a moment of victory, the culmination of decades of struggle. But back at home, for Black people, not enough had changed.

LOST IN THE STRUGGLE

A granite monument in Montgomery, Alabama, features the names of forty-one people who died in the course of the civil rights movement. Designed by Maya Lin and dedicated in 1989, the Civil Rights Memorial stands outside the Southern Poverty Law Center, a civil rights organization. Here are a few of the people honored on the monument:

Medgar Evers was a civil rights leader in Jackson, Mississippi. On June 12, 1963, a white man named Byron De La Beckwith hid across the street from Medgar's home with a rifle and shot him in his driveway as he returned from an NAACP meeting. Medgar's wife rushed him to the local hospital, where the staff initially refused to treat him because of his race. Beckwith was arrested a few weeks after the shooting. All-white juries acquitted him twice in 1964, but Medgar's family fought for justice for decades, and Beckwith was finally convicted of the murder in 1994, in part because he had bragged about the killing to fellow Klan members over the years.

Viola Liuzzo was a volunteer with SCLC, registering voters in Alabama. She was killed on March 25, 1965, on the road between Selma and Montgomery, when a car full of Klan members noticed her, a white woman, driving in a car with a Black man next to her, a fellow volunteer. They shot at her, running her car off the road. Viola died from gunshot wounds, and the young Black man riding with her, Leroy Moton, survived by playing dead when the assailants came to check the car.

Jimmie Lee Jackson died defending his mother and grandfather from violence at the hands of state troopers at a civil rights demonstration in Selma, Alabama. He was beaten with clubs and shot twice in the stomach. Jimmie Lee's death inspired a famous civil rights march held a few weeks later, in which voting rights activists attempting to march from Selma to the state capitol in Montgomery were met with violence from local police as they crossed the Edmund Pettus Bridge in Selma.

James Chaney, Andrew Goodman, and Michael Schwerner were volunteers with CORE who were registering voters in Mississippi. On the night of June 21, 1964, Ku Klux Klan members ambushed them on the road outside of Philadelphia, Mississippi, dragged the three men from their car, and took them to a remote location, then shot them at close range and buried them. The three activists were missing for forty-four days before their bodies were found.

Addie Mae Collins, Denise McNair, Carole Robertson, and Cynthia Wesley were the four young girls killed in the Sixteenth Street Baptist Church bombing. White supremacists planted dynamite beneath the steps of the church on a Sunday morning, and the girls were in a basement restroom that received the brunt of the blast. The FBI soon identified four suspects, but justice was again delayed for decades.

...UNTIL JUSTICE ROLLS DOWN LIKE WATERS AND RIGHTEOUSNESS LIKE A MIGHTY STREAM

MARTIN LUTHER KING JR

Civil Rights Memorial

SHALL WE OVERCOME? **53**

THE AGGRESSIVE ALTERNATIVE

A Winchester rifle should have a place of honor in every black home, and it should be used for that protection which the law refuses to give.

—IDA B. WELLS

In a vacuum, it is easy to default to saying, "Violence is never the answer." But when it comes to Black history, we mustn't forget that violence is also the question—real and ever-present violence, against people trying to vote. Or go to school. Or ride the bus. Or walk down the street. At every turn, Black Americans' pleas for equality and justice have been met with cruel, dehumanizing violence.

When the earthquake hits, and the world is shaking, it is easy to forget the eons of shifting plates.

◀ A police officer in Nashville threatening a Black protestor with a baton

Overturning segregation, a problem largely centered in the American South, was merely one challenge that civil rights activists faced. Deep-seated racial problems also existed in parts of the country where segregation was already illegal. In the northern and western states, most Black Americans lived in large cities, like New York, Chicago, Los Angeles, San Francisco, Cleveland, Philadelphia, and Detroit. Even though segregation was not the law in these places, Black people still tended to live in separate communities, and these areas were often very poor. People struggled to find jobs that paid enough to keep their homes and feed their families. Police brutality was an especially big problem. Police officers—nearly all of whom were white—would often frighten, harass, beat up, and sometimes even kill Black people whom they suspected of committing crimes. Often the Black citizens hadn't even done anything wrong.

A young Black man might be "getting his head banged in every weekend by the police," as one resident put it. Or he might end up "going to jail, just snatched out of his car for a traffic ticket, just because he was Black." Police officers could

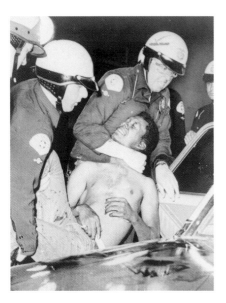

Los Angeles police restraining and choking a Black man

beat a Black man by the side of the road, accusing him of being in the process of stealing a car, when he was simply trying to retrieve the keys he had locked in his own vehicle. Black people were rarely given the benefit of the doubt and routinely presumed to be doing wrong. Police initiated violent and confrontational incidents all the time, often with no clear provocation beyond the skin color of their target. Rarely were officers disciplined for using such excessive force to arrest Black people, and many officers abused the power of their position.

The law didn't need to be changed—it needed to be enforced. Black and white people were legally equal, but police officers, who were responsible for *upholding* the law, were often the ones who broke it. The success of civil disobedience in the South was based in part on shining a light on the injustice of segregation. What about a Black man traveling alone on the city streets at night? Didn't he have the same civil rights as a Black woman sitting on a well-lit public bus, surrounded by witnesses?

On July 2, President Lyndon Johnson signed the Civil Rights Act of 1964. This new law made it illegal to discriminate against anyone based on race, color, sex, religion, or nationality, but this assertion on paper did little to change the way communities were policed or the well-established injustice of poverty.

REBELLION IN HARLEM

Black people confronted over and over again with racist violence needed an outlet for their pain and anger. Their fury and frustration, after being suppressed for many years, sometimes manifested in spontaneous protests.

Two short weeks after the Civil Rights Act became law, a fifteen-year-old Black teen, James Powell, was shot and killed by an off-duty police officer in Harlem, New York. Lieutenant Thomas Gilligan was an experienced police officer and had served in the military. He claimed Powell had threatened him with a knife, but witnesses told the story differently. Many people believed Officer Gilligan should have been able to subdue the young suspect without resorting to firing his weapon.

This incident itself was not so far out of the ordinary—what was unusual was the community reaction. On July 18, community members began a peaceful protest march to the police station. They hoped to raise awareness of the shooting and compel the police to respond by disciplining or firing the responsible officer. The crowd was met by police officers standing guard around the building. Protestors began throwing bricks and stones and yelling at the police, who responded by beating them with their nightsticks. The rebellion lasted six days, spreading through Harlem and into the Brooklyn neighborhood of Bedford-Stuyvesant. At least one person was killed, dozens were wounded, and hundreds arrested, and a million dollars of damage was done to local property.

These few days of uprising became emblematic of something deeper. Similar protests erupted in cities across the country in the months to follow. Activists called 1964 "the long, hot summer," in which Black citizens in southern and northern cities alike stood up for themselves in divergent ways.

MALCOLM X'S MINISTRY

In Harlem at the time, a young preacher named Malcolm X had become a vocal advocate for the specific needs of Black people in the northern United States. Malcolm X was a minister with the Nation of Islam, an organization of Black Muslims in the United States. The Nation of Islam encouraged Black nationalism, in the tradition of Marcus Garvey's "Back to Africa" movement of the 1920s. They argued that Black people would never gain full equality within a white-led society. Instead, they needed their own land, free of white rule, where they could self-govern, self-police, and self-rule. Unlike Garvey, the Nation of Islam did not think that land needed to be on the African continent—it could be right in the United States, in existing Black communities.

The Nation of Islam platform emphasized separatism and self-determination instead of integration. Civil rights movement leaders had been fighting for integration and full inclusion in American society, but that change was so slow to come that Malcolm X believed it would never come. Separatism differed from segregation because living in an independent Black nation would be a choice Black people made for themselves, rather than something that was forced on them, as segregation had been. Self-determination simply meant full power and control over their lives, which Black people had been denied for centuries.

The emerging Black nationalists regarded Black Americans as an internal

Malcolm X speaking ▶

colony of the United States because they were subject to whites, much as the original American colonies had been subject to British rule before the Revolutionary War. Urban Black people lived in dirty slums, working long hours for low wages that barely kept families fed—how far had they really come in the century since slavery was outlawed?

Malcolm X especially understood what young Black Americans were going through. As a young man in the 1940s, he roamed the streets of Boston's Roxbury and New York City's Harlem neighborhoods. He spoke from experience when he encouraged Black people to stand up for themselves in new ways:

> It would be almost impossible to find anywhere in America a black man who has lived further down in the mud of human society than I have; or a black man who has been any more ignorant than I have been; or a black man who has suffered more anguish during his life than I have. But it is only after the deepest darkness that the greatest joy can come; it is only after slavery and prison that the sweetest appreciation of freedom can come.

Like Dr. King, Malcolm X became known for his fiery speeches that could excite crowds of people and inspire them to action. But Malcolm X did not preach about civil disobedience and turning the other cheek—he talked about the need for Black Americans to rise up and claim their freedom "by any means necessary," up to and including armed resistance. He spoke not about civil rights, as in rights granted under the law, but about human rights, as in God-given rights that all people are entitled to, regardless of race or nationality. Black people, he argued, deserved to rise above what the American government was willing to offer them.

Malcolm X's inspiring vision, his powerful rhetoric, and his leadership skills made him a significant threat to the white establishment, to the civil rights movement, and even to the Nation of Islam itself, as he broke out on his own and began drawing followers. He began receiving threats against his life, and Malcolm X was assassinated in Harlem on February 21, 1965. He was thirty-nine years old.

Malcolm X's words and his legacy would live on, carried by his followers and by the many young people who began to defect from the civil disobedience tactics of the civil rights movement. His death struck a deep chord with urban Black teenagers in particular. It pushed them closer to the edge, knowing that someone so prominent and so powerfully able to express their fears and desires had been shot down.

A CITY EXPLODING

On the night of August 11, 1965, a young man named Marquette Frye was driving toward his home in Watts, California. Watts was a suburb of Los Angeles, and the neighborhood was populated by many poor and struggling Black families. Marquette's car was pulled over by a California Highway Patrolman on a motor-cycle. The officer, Lee Minikus, had received a report of a reckless driver in the area, and he suspected Marquette might be driving under the influence of alcohol. He pulled Marquette from the car, along with his brother Ronald, who was riding in the passenger seat. Officer Minikus tested Marquette to see if he'd been drinking and, according to the officer, Marquette did not pass the test. Minikus placed him under arrest and called for a police car as well as a tow truck for Frye's car.

It was a very hot night in Watts, and a lot of people from the neighbor-hood were outside, sitting on porch stoops and walking along the sidewalks. Marquette's brother Ronald asked the police officer if he could just drive the car home himself instead of having it towed. The officer refused to release the car, and the discussion turned into an argument.

Soon additional police officers appeared on the scene. At the same time, more and more people from the neighborhood wandered over to see what the commotion was all about. The Frye brothers continued arguing with the police, and someone went to get their mother, Rena Price, who lived nearby. She came outside and attempted to talk to the police officers, but they would not let her leave with the car or with either of her sons. She began screaming at the police officers, and they yelled at her right back.

Everyone was angry: the Fryes, their mother, the police officers, the crowd. What began as a simple roadside arrest—and perhaps even a lawful one, if Marquette was really driving drunk—quickly morphed into something much more sinister. The argument turned physical, resulting in the police officers beating Ronald with their batons, hauling Marquette to the police car by his neck, and even arresting and physically battling with their middle-aged mother.

The officers violently wrestled all three into police cars and drove away. Even though the incident appeared to be over, the scene had so enraged the crowd that the situation was only just beginning. The furious onlookers, whose numbers had grown from dozens to hundreds to over a thousand during the course of the forty-minute altercation, began to rise up in the streets. They were unspeakably angry. People began throwing rocks and bottles into storefronts, beating on parked cars, breaking windows, and setting things on fire. The streets teemed with people releasing frustration and rage, taking it out on the buildings, cars, and people in their own community.

The police department sent officers to try to stop the looting and destruction, but the uprising continued through the night and into the next day. And the day after that. It didn't show signs of stopping—in fact, things seemed to be getting worse. Finally, troops from the California National Guard were called in to help quell the violence. The Watts rebellion lasted six days and resulted in over three thousand arrests, one thousand people injured, and thirty-four deaths, in addition to multimillion-dollar damages to the Watts community.

In the months afterward, California governor Pat Brown commissioned a team of researchers to study what had happened in Watts. He wanted to understand why so many people had responded with such extreme behavior and why the uprising had gone on for so long. He wanted to understand what kind of emotions could make people destroy their own community, literally attacking it and burning it to the ground. The research team determined that the residents of Watts were so angry about their circumstances—the poverty, lack of jobs, substandard housing, and insufficient education that characterized the community—that they had erupted uncontrollably. They had been upset and angry for a very long time. The beating of Marquette and Ronald Frye by the police was merely the straw that broke the camel's back.

Watts buildings on fire during the uprising

After Malcolm X's death, and in light of the never-ending violence against Black people, some frustrated factions of the civil rights struggle picked up the mantle of Black nationalism. The Student Nonviolent Coordinating Committee (SNCC), led by Stokely Carmichael, began calling for Black citizens to defend themselves against racist violence. Stokely had followed Dr. King through rural Alabama during the civil rights march from Selma to Montgomery in the spring of 1965, when white police and guardsmen attacked marchers at the Edmund Pettus Bridge. The brutal beatings caused the day to become known as Bloody Sunday. Witnessing the violence that erupted, Stokely and other members of SNCC grew more and more frustrated with the slow progress of change. The community uprisings in Harlem, Watts, and elsewhere made sense to him. "What's happening is rebellions, not riots," Stokely said. The people needed to be heard, and they had no other way to speak.

About a year later, a Black man named James Meredith set out on a solo march through the South, believing he could show the world that the South had become safer for Black people. On the first day of his march, a white man ran up to him and shot him. Meredith survived the attack but couldn't finish the march, so hundreds of Black and white supporters joined together to finish the journey he had started.

During this March Against Fear, on June 19, 1966, police in Mississippi arrested Stokely Carmichael along with several other demonstrators. When he emerged from the jail, Stokely announced that he had been arrested twenty-seven times during civil rights protests, and he was tired of it. "We must think politically and get power," Stokely said upon his release. "We have got to get us some Black Power."

Stokely had begun working in Lowndes County, Alabama. Locals referred to the area as "Bloody Lowndes," because so many instances of Klan violence took

Stokely Carmichael popularized the slogan "Black Power."

place there. Stokely had passed through the area on the Selma–Montgomery march, and he and other SNCC members returned to help organize a movement for Black political power there. The population of Lowndes was 80% Black; if enough people came together, Black citizens could make a serious impact on local politics. Stokely believed it was essential that Black people begin forming a political power base.

Stokely and the other SNCC members started by encouraging Black citizens to register to vote. Even though constitutional amendments granted Black people

Stokely conferring with an elder voter in Lowndes County, Alabama

the legal right to vote, no Black person had successfully registered to vote in the county before. When SNCC volunteers knocked on Unita Blackwell's door, she said, "That's the first time in my life that I ever come in contact with anybody that tells me that I had the right to register to vote."

Lowndes County officials did everything they could think of to stop Black people from voting. They demanded a so-called "reading test" for voters—but the extremely challenging test was designed to be unpassable. Only Black voters were given this "reading test," even though many white voters were also unable to read. (In fact, each ballot already contained a picture or logo alongside each party's candidate so that voters did not have to read the candidates' names or even the party names in order to participate.)

Ku Klux Klan activity in the area became even worse as the SNCC workers tried to help Black people register. The court forced Black registrants to wait in long lines, and while they waited, Klan members drove past the registration lines with shotguns, shouting threats. Landowners threatened to kick tenants and sharecroppers off their land, and employers threatened to fire workers who registered. Several volunteers were shot and killed by angry whites. It became dangerous for volunteers to travel on the roads at night, so they created a local headquarters known as Freedom House.

Sixteen-year-old John Jackson's family owned the property where the SNCC workers stayed. "My father was concerned about the civil rights workers. . . . They were afraid: they were being shot at, they were being run off plantations, they were being run out of Lowndes County."

SNCC members tried to convince Black residents in Lowndes of what the white supremacists clearly already knew—that Black people organizing to gain political power would be a significant threat to white domination and control. This was true everywhere, not just in Lowndes. Civil rights groups held voter registration drives all over the country, and white supremacists responded with threats and violence in each and every place.

It was what happened next that made Lowndes County stand out. SNCC developed a political party called the Lowndes County Freedom Organization (LCFO). They encour-

The panther symbolism resonated with Black people and soon spread beyond Lowndes County. Here, a protestor in Jackson, Mississippi, holds up a sign with the Black Panther Party logo and slogan.

aged residents to carry guns to offer themselves protection, and they used a black panther image as their ballot logo, claiming it as a meaningful symbol of self-defense. The black panther hides in the shadows and does not bother passersby, but if it is attacked it will not back down—instead, it lashes out.

"When we chose that symbol, many of the peoples in our county started

LOWNDES COUNTY FREEDOM ORGANIZATION

Mass Meeting, May 3, 1966, to nominate candidat
for the November 8, 1966 general election.

LOWNDES COUNTY

SHERIFF –– put (x) before one name

– –––––MR. JESSE 'NOTE' FAVORS
X–––––MR. SIDNEY LOGAN, JR.
–– –OTHER (write in name)

saying we were a violent group who is going to start killing white folks," said Lowndes resident John Hulett. "But it wasn't that. It was a political symbol that we was here to stay and we were going to do whatever needed to be done to survive."

Hulett continued: "Those of us who carried guns carried them for our own protection, in case we were attacked by other peoples. . . . White peoples carried guns in this county, and the law didn't do anything to tell them about it, so we started carrying our guns too. I think they felt that we was ready for war, but we wasn't violent."

Feeling protected and supported by SNCC and the LCFO, more and more Black voters began to register. The two organizations formed a neighborhood called Tent City, where Black people could come live if they were evicted after registering to vote. They educated people about voting rights, helped people find jobs, and defended the community against racist attacks. Threats by the Klan increased, but the LCFO persisted. They nominated Black candidates for local offices (like sheriff) and got them on the primary ballot, under the party's panther logo.

ONE MAN - ONE VOTE

"Vote for the Panther and then go home" was the rallying cry that inspired hundreds of Lowndes County's Black residents to go to the polls for the first time. This initial Panther image was later simplified, redrawn, and refined by two women artists in SNCC, Dorothy Zellner and Ruth Howard, resulting in the familiar, iconic logo.

Nine hundred Black voters turned out to vote in the primary on May 3, 1966. About five hundred white people stood ready to meet them and stop them from entering the courthouse, but the LCFO spread the word that the voters would be armed and willing to fight for their right to vote. The white supremacists backed down, and the Black people came together and voted for the first time in each of their lives. The LCFO's candidate would not go on to win the general election against the Democrat and Republican candidates, but by standing up for their rights in spite of the risks—and especially by being willing to fight back against white violence—these Black voters had made a statement that inspired Black people around the country.

The Lowndes County Freedom Organization was one example of a shifting tide among Black communities. They had tamped down their anger, their frustration for so long, in service to the grand idea of nonviolent protest that Dr. King and others had advocated for a decade or more. How much longer were they going to have to wait? How much longer could they *stand to* wait?

BLAZE

1966–1982

Within these flames, there is freedom.

PICKING UP
THE GUN

It is criminal to teach a man not to defend himself when he is the constant victim of brutal attacks. It is legal and lawful to own a shotgun or a rifle. We believe in obeying the law.

—MALCOLM X

While Stokely Carmichael and SNCC were registering Black voters in Alabama, two college students, Huey Newton and Bobby Seale, were living in Oakland, California, near San Francisco.

"We had seen Watts rise up," Huey said. "We had seen how the police attacked the Watts community after causing the trouble in the first place. We had seen Martin Luther King come to Watts in an effort to calm the people, and we had seen his philosophy of nonviolence rejected. Black people had been taught nonviolence; it was deep in us. What good, however, was nonviolence when the police were determined to rule by force?"

Huey and Bobby knew that what happened in Watts and Harlem could easily happen in Oakland. They didn't need a governor's research study to understand what was going through people's minds in Watts during the uprising. They already understood that kind of anger and frustration. They were living it.

This iconic photo of Huey Newton holding a gun in one hand and an African spear in the other became a powerful emblem of the movement. A copy of the image hung somewhere on the wall in nearly every Panther office.

Previous spread: Kathleen Cleaver (*left*) and Tarika Lewis (*far right*) with other Panther women

HUEY NEWTON was born in Louisiana, and his family moved to California when he was young. Huey was arrested several times as a teenager and was on probation during the Panthers' founding months. As a student at Merritt College, he led organizing efforts and was already known as an intellectual powerhouse among his peers.

High school graduation photo, 1959

"We had seen the Oakland Police and the California Highway Patrol begin to carry their shotguns in full view as another way of striking fear into the community," Huey said. "We had seen all this and we recognized that the rising consciousness of Black people was almost at the point of explosion."

Huey and Bobby had met doing student activism at Merritt College. But now they both wanted to do something beyond the campus, out in the community. They understood that people in their neighborhood longed to lash out against police brutality and racism. If the kind of rebellious fury that had boiled over in Watts could be harnessed, organized, and pointed in the right direction, Black Americans might have a chance at a meaningful revolution.

"Everything we had seen convinced us that our time had come," Huey said. But it was hard to convince their fellow students to step beyond the so-called "ivory towers of the college." Huey and Bobby could riff for hours on the problems facing cities like Oakland and Watts—police brutality, poverty, poor education, inadequate housing, not enough food—but all these problems needed real-world solutions. Most of their fellow Black student activists preferred to sit around and talk about ideas, but Bobby and Huey knew it was time to move beyond talk and start getting things done.

Bobby went to work with the North Oakland Neighborhood Anti-Poverty Center, where he interacted with lots of teenagers from the community. It was important to him to connect with them and listen to their views as part of his teaching. Young people embraced Bobby's leadership because he actively worked to counteract the disrespect they had encountered from teachers and other authority figures in the past. "I never wanted to use the authoritarian-type old school tactics which I had rejected and I knew these young brothers rejected," Bobby said. Instead, he tried to meet them where they were and offer a different kind of leadership, inspiring them "to think in ways related to black people in the community surviving and black people in the black community unifying."

Bobby taught Black American history and worked with Huey on political advocacy for Oakland residents. Pursuing systemic political change was essential, they knew. "We got five thousand signatures . . . to get the city council to try to set up a police review board to deal with complaints of police brutality," Bobby said. "Well, the city council ignored us."

BOBBY SEALE was born in the South and moved to California as a child. He served in the air force, where he was discharged after a conflict with a supervising officer. He went on to college in his late twenties.

Bobby was already married with children while studying at Merritt. He co-founded the Panthers on his thirtieth birthday, and he remained one of the eldest in the organization thereafter.

Bobby with his wife and son

The thing was, Huey realized, from the perspective of the average Oakland resident, "the police . . . were really the government. We had more contact with the police than we did the city council." So responding directly to the police seemed more relevant than long-term political activism, which was aimed at changing laws from a top-down perspective. Having equality in law was important, but how those laws were being enforced mattered even more, at least to regular citizens walking the streets.

This realization came to full clarity the day Bobby was asked to bring some kids from the Anti-Poverty Center down to the police department because the police said they wanted to build better relationships with the community. A small group went, feeling somewhat reluctant and somewhat curious to interact with the police. When they arrived, they were greeted by a room full of officers with notepads, who proceeded to ask them to name other youth in the community who might be in gangs or should be investigated. Bobby quickly intervened, calling out, "Don't anybody say nothing! . . . You're not going to turn us into no operation where the police department makes us inform on ourselves." It turned out that the police department's idea of "building better relationships" meant building a base of teen informants.

After a bit more pressure from the officers, Bobby managed to end the questioning and even turn the tables on them. He invited several officers down to the community center the next day. Now that the teens were in their own space, outside the high-pressure environment of the police station, Bobby asked the young people to share stories of police brutality that they had witnessed and to express their concerns about the way police officers operated in Oakland. "Man, those kids tore into the cops," Bobby said. "They really talked about the brutality that half of them had actually witnessed. Then they talked about stories they'd heard."

One girl described seeing three police officers beat an unarmed Black woman with a billy club outside a dance hall. "Now, do you think it's right for a big six-foot cop to throw a five-foot woman down to the ground, and hit her on the head with a billy club?" she said angrily. "I don't think no cop got no right to be beatin' on no woman."

Red-faced and shaking, the officers told the teens those stories were exaggerated. They even argued that citizens have no right to self-defense, even "if a policeman unjustly, criminally attacks and brutalizes them." The officers refuted the teens' stories at every turn, but the teens did not back down from sharing the truth they knew.

"I have never witnessed anything so beautiful," Bobby said. "Those kids knew cases." But that feeling of beauty was merely the silver lining of a very significant cloud. Bobby Seale left that day knowing that he had become an enemy of the Oakland Police Department, and they would be targeting him.

FOUNDING THE PARTY

In October 1966, Huey and Bobby made a decision. There was a lot of work to be done in Black communities, but no one was doing it very effectively. "We had to start a new organization," Bobby said.

They had studied Black history and current events in depth. They studied the words of the Rev. Dr. Martin Luther King Jr. and Malcolm X, the platform of the Nation of Islam, SNCC's organizing work, and Black nationalist ideas from all around the world. Their ideology was especially inspired by Malcolm X's teachings. "I was determined to make a Malcolm X out of my own self," Bobby said.

They gathered all their ideas, organized them, and wrote them down. They called it their Ten-Point Platform and Program. They felt it was important to clearly state the needs and demands of their community, so that people would understand what they wanted to do. The Ten-Point Platform articulated "What we want; what we believe."

Their new organization's core goals matched the goals of the civil rights movements that had gone before them, especially mirroring Malcolm X's nine-point list written in 1963 detailing "What Muslims Want." They also echoed the promises made to all citizens in the U.S. Constitution. A lot of ideas in the nation's founding documents resonated with Huey and Bobby—the sense of a people oppressed by government that did not have their interests at heart, and the conviction that standing up in the face of tyranny was the only way to secure one's own freedom. "I found the Declaration of Independence of the United States of America. I started reading it aloud to myself and paraphrasing the first two paragraphs," Bobby said. "When we finished, I typed it up."

Meanwhile, "Huey went upstairs to the legal aid office and found the California Supreme Court ruling that said all citizens have a right to stand and observe a police officer carrying out his duty." This information resonated, too. Police brutality was a key concern, and knowing their rights was vital. If they were going to encourage Black people to take responsibility for self-defense, and the defense of their homes and communities, they needed to do it in legal and responsible ways.

Bobby Seale and Huey
Newton in front of
the Panther office

The first six Panthers: (*standing, left to right*) Elbert "Big Man" Howard, Huey Newton, Sherman Forte, Bobby Seale; (*crouching, left to right*) Reginald Forte, Lil' Bobby Hutton

"We flipped a coin to see who would be chairman," Bobby said. "I won chairman." So Huey took the title Minister of Defense. All they needed now was a strong name. Just like their Ten-Point Platform, the name of their new organization drew on symbolism and inspiration from the ongoing civil rights struggle. They knew SNCC was using a panther logo for the Lowndes County Freedom Organization, in part because it was a creature that would defend itself if cornered. The strong, sleek image of the black panther matched the spirit of Black Power and represented values they desired, such as courage, stealth, grace, and a positive image of blackness. "The Black Panther Party" had a nice political ring to it, they thought.

Finally, they added the phrase "for Self-Defense." A group of armed, trained Black people confronting the police was going to cause a stir. It needed to be clear that their main purpose was to defend the Black community against violence, not to instigate violence against white people.

On October 22, 1966, the Black Panther Party for Self-Defense was born and ready to take to the streets.

The Black Panther Party for Self-Defense planned to arm Black people with guns and teach them how to use them. This plan was extremely radical and very frightening to a lot of people, Black and white alike, because they thought it meant the Panthers wanted to cause violence. They didn't. In fact, Americans' biased views of Black people contributed to this fear, especially among white people. Even though white police officers armed with guns regularly committed acts of brutality, people assumed that they were in the community to do good, yet they just as readily assumed that Black people carrying legal guns in the community were there to cause trouble, even when they had not done anything wrong. The very *idea* of Black people with guns upset many Americans, regardless of what they had done with them or what they planned to do with them.

So, what *did* the Panthers want to do with their guns? Well, to Huey and Bobby, one thing was very clear: nonviolent protests had not succeeded in stopping the violence against Black people. They wondered if racist white people had started using Black people's passive resistance as an *excuse* to be violent toward them. They wondered what would happen if Black people let would-be perpetrators of violence know that they were *capable* of fighting back, but would prefer not to fight at all. Could that change the situation? Police officers might think twice about harassing people or making unlawful arrests. The community might be able to take back some of the power that had been systematically stripped from them.

Huey and Bobby also knew that arming themselves would make them susceptible to close scrutiny by the police. They did not want to advocate breaking the law. According to California law at the time, citizens could legally carry unconcealed weapons. So the Panthers purchased legal weapons and set about their business.

Lil' Bobby Hutton, the first member of the Black Panther Party for Self-Defense ▶

(Photo: Ron Riesterer/PhotoShelter)

The Party started very small. The first person to join was one of the teenagers Bobby worked with at the community center, fifteen-year-old Bobby Hutton. (Since the two had the same first name, the Panthers called the teenager Lil' Bobby.) In the first two weeks, there were only six members, but those six members got right to work.

First and foremost, the Panthers wanted to stop police brutality, so they developed a program they called "Policing the Police." Huey got himself a copy of all the California state laws and carried it with him. The newly formed Panthers would ride together in a car. Everyone in the car had a gun, legally obtained. They drove around until they found a police cruiser patrolling their neighborhood; then they followed it. If the police stopped to talk to any Black people or attempted to arrest anyone, the Panthers would stop their own car and everyone would get out, with their guns, and go to watch what happened next. This way, they created witnesses to any police interactions on the street and formed a presence that intimidated police officers into following the letter of the law.

"We park and everybody gets out of the car," Bobby said, describing one night of policing. "Some of us are carrying long guns, and others have handguns in the holster." The Panthers lined up along the curb, near where an officer had pulled a Black man over in an apparent traffic stop.

"You have no right to observe me!" the officer protested.

Huey started reciting language from the California state law. "Every citizen has a right to stand and observe a police officer carrying out their duty, as long as they stand a reasonable distance away." A reasonable distance was legally determined to be at least eight to ten feet, and Huey was about twenty feet from the officer.

Seventh Street was busy that night, and people along the street paused to watch the Panthers in action. Some stepped out of stores and businesses to see what was going on.

"Is that gun loaded?" the officer asked, attempting to approach Huey and seize the weapon.

"You cannot remove my property from me without due process," Huey responded, naming the relevant court ruling. He did not let the officer take his gun.

The officer became angry, but Huey had asserted his rights, and the officer knew he was correct. He finished the traffic stop, quickly arresting the man and driving off.

Huey and Bobby addressed the crowd that had gathered, letting them know exactly what had just happened. They passed out flyers containing the Ten-Point Platform and Program and told everyone to check out the Panther meetings. The next night, twenty-one new people showed up to find out more.

The Panthers' message of self-defense resonated with the sisters and brothers on the block—the most systemically impoverished and disenfranchised young people in the community—because they, too, were fed up with having no power.

"You don't have to carry a gun. It's not about that," Bobby Seale said to them, first thing. "We're here to organize political, electoral, community unity. . . . We're going to have real change in our community."

Night after night, the Panthers policed the police. The Oakland Police Department was not happy. They felt threatened by the Panthers with guns. But anytime the police officers threatened to arrest Huey, he read aloud from the California law book to show that everything he was doing was legal. This angered the police even more. Huey argued that if the police couldn't do their jobs the same way with a group of concerned citizens watching, what did that say about the way they had done their jobs before?

Policing the police helped balance the power between police officers and ordinary Black folks. The Panthers did not try to stop the police from making lawful arrests, nor did they try to interfere or encourage anyone to resist arrest. They simply wanted to observe.

"I actually think that the bright red pickup truck with a bunch of black brothers in it was on the Oakland PD blotter with the words 'avoid confrontation,'" said founding Panther member Elbert "Big Man" Howard. "As a result, there was no loss of life in the community. That is not to say there were not ambushes, harassment and false arrests."

In one fell swoop, the Panthers changed the rules of the civil rights movement, by encouraging Black people to take a defensive stance against race violence. And they didn't stop there. The need for self-defense extended beyond the physical. It extended to defending the community against all threats and inequalities, like the lack of access to health care, the failing neighborhood schools, the many hungry families, and the flawed criminal justice system that regularly put innocent Black people behind bars.

The final point on their Ten-Point Platform succinctly summed up their demands: "We want land, bread, housing, education, clothing, justice and peace."

Guns in hand, the Panthers set out to change everything.

WHAT WE WANT, WHAT WE BELIEVE

THE OCTOBER 1966 BLACK PANTHER PARTY PLATFORM AND PROGRAM

1. We want freedom. We want power to determine the destiny of our Black Community.

We believe that black people will not be free until we are able to determine our destiny.

2. We want full employment for our people.

We believe that the federal government is responsible and obligated to give every man employment or a guaranteed income. We believe that if the white American businessmen will not give full employment, then the means of production should be taken from the businessmen and placed in the community so that the people of the community can organize and employ all of its people and give a high standard of living.

3. We want an end to the robbery by the white man of our Black Community.

We believe that this racist government has robbed us and now we are demanding the overdue debt of forty acres and two mules. Forty acres and two mules was promised 100 years ago as restitution for slave labor and mass murder of black people. We will accept the payment in currency which will be distributed to our many communities. The Germans are now aiding the Jews in Israel for the genocide of the Jewish people. The Germans murdered six million Jews. The American racist has taken part in the slaughter of over fifty million black people; therefore we feel that this is a modest demand we make.

Bobby Seale's handwritten initial draft of the Ten-Point Platform

WHAT WE BELIEVE

(1.) WE BELIEVE THAT BLACK PEOPLE WILL NOT BE FREE UNTIL WE ARE ABLE TO DETERMINE OUR DESTINY.

(2.) ~~WE WANT FULL EMPLOYMENT FOR BLACK PEOPLE NOW~~

(2.) WE BELIEVE THAT THE FEDERAL GOVERNMENT IS RESPONSIBLE AND OBLIGATED TO GIVE ~~MENT~~ OR A ~~____~~

4. We want decent housing, fit for shelter of human beings.

We believe that if the white landlords will not give decent housing to our black community, then the housing and the land should be made into cooperatives so that our community, with government aid, can build and make decent housing for its people.

5. We want education for our people that exposes the true nature of this decadent American society. We want education that teaches us our true history and our role in the present-day society.

We believe in an educational system that will give to our people a knowledge of self. If a man does not have knowledge of himself and his position in society and the world, then he has little chance to relate to anything else.

6. We want all black men to be exempt from military service.

We believe that black people should not be forced to fight in the military service to defend a racist government that does not protect us. We will not fight and kill other people of color in the world who, like black people, are being victimized by the white racist government of America. We will protect ourselves from the force and violence of the racist police and the racist military, by whatever means necessary.

7. We want an immediate end to POLICE BRUTALITY and MURDER of black people.

We believe we can end police brutality in our black community by organizing black self-defense groups that are dedicated to defending our black community from racist police oppression and brutality. The Second Amendment to the Constitution of the United States gives a right to bear arms. We therefore believe that all black people should arm themselves for self-defense.

8. We want freedom for all black men held in federal, state, county and city prisons and jails.

We believe that all black people should be released from the many jails and prisons because they have not received a fair and impartial trial.

9. We want all black people when brought to trial to be tried in court by a jury of their peer group or people from their black communities, as defined by the Constitution of the United States.

We believe that the courts should follow the United States Constitution so that black people will receive fair trials. The Fourteenth Amendment of the U.S. Constitution gives a man a right to be tried by his peer group. A peer is a person from a similar economic, social, religious, geographical, environmental, historical, and racial background. To do this the court will be forced to select a jury from the black community from which the black defendant came. We have been and are being tried by all-white juries that have no understanding of the "average reasoning man" of the black community.

10. We want land, bread, housing, education, clothing, justice and peace. [And as our major political objective, a United Nations–supervised plebiscite to be held throughout the black colony in which only black colonial subjects will be allowed to participate, for the purpose of determining the will of black people as to their national destiny.][1]

When, in the course of human events, it becomes necessary for one people to dissolve the political bands which have connected them with another, and to assume, among the powers of the earth, the separate and equal station to which the laws of nature and nature's God entitle them, a decent respect to the opinions of mankind requires that they should declare the causes which impel them to the separation.

We hold these truths to be self-evident, that all men are created equal; that they are endowed by their Creator with certain unalienable rights; that among these are life, liberty, and the pursuit of happiness. *That, to secure these rights, governments are instituted among men, deriving their just powers from the consent of the governed; that, whenever any form of government becomes destructive of these ends, it is the right of the people to alter or to abolish it, and to institute a new government, laying its foundation on such principles, and organizing its powers in such form, as to them shall seem most likely to effect their safety and happiness.* Prudence, indeed, will dictate that governments long established should not be changed for light and transient causes; and, accordingly, all experience hath shown, that mankind are more disposed to suffer, while evils are sufferable, than to right themselves by abolishing the forms to which they are accustomed. *But, when a long train of abuses and usurpations, pursuing invariably the same object, evinces a design to reduce them under absolute despotism, it is their right, it is their duty, to throw off such government, and to provide new guards for their future security.*

---

1 The plebiscite language (in brackets) was actually added later, in 1967. A plebiscite would be a vote by the entire population of Black people in America to decide their own future. The Panthers hoped the United Nations would agree to serve as an impartial facilitator of the vote because they knew such a vote would never happen in America without outside supervision. Plebiscites in other nations during and after political turmoil had helped give regular people a voice in determining their future government.

"THE RACIST DOG POLICEMEN MUST WITHDRAW IMMEDIATELY FROM OUR COMMUNITIES, CEASE THEIR WANTON MURDER AND BRUTALITY AND TORTURE OF BLACK PEOPLE, OR FACE THE WRATH OF THE ARMED PEOPLE."

HUEY P. NEWTON, Minister of Defense

BLACK PANTHER PARTY
P.O. Box 8641, Emeryville, Calif.

A COLD RECEPTION

I'm one of the 22 million Black people who are the victims of Americanism. I see America through the eyes of the victim. I don't see any American dream. I see an American nightmare.

—MALCOLM X

"We're not a self-defense group in the limited fashion that you usually think of self-defense groups," Huey P. Newton said. "The primary job of the party is to provide leadership to the people."

The Panthers believed that if Black communities were ever going to see justice, the United States of America needed to experience a complete social, political, and economic upheaval. In short: they wanted to inspire a revolution. Just as the colonists took up arms against the British during the American Revolution, the Black Panthers believed that eventually Black Americans would need to rise up and use force to claim the right to govern themselves.

The decades-long struggle over civil rights had already proved that the nation would be slow to change on its own. To see new progress, Black communities

This iconic photo of Huey and Bobby is often used to represent the Party. Here, it appears in a poster version with a Huey quote underneath.

would have to be strategic and think outside the box of the existing structures of American society. Those structures, after all, were designed to keep Black people hungry, jobless, uneducated, and corralled into substandard housing. Education about these systemic issues was key for the Panthers.

"It is . . . the people that will cause the change in the country," Huey wrote. "The Black Panther Party is simply the vanguard of the revolution. And we plan to teach the people the strategy and the necessary tools to liberate themselves."

A VISION OF SOCIALISM

Most of the Panthers' solutions are based on socialism, a political ideology that emphasizes shared resources being controlled by the government and distributed equally among people. The Panthers' interest in socialism made them unpopular in the United States. The American system is based on capitalism, a political ideology that emphasizes individualism, private property ownership, and a free market in which goods and services are privately controlled. It is a system in which some people can become very, very rich while others remain very, very poor.

The Panthers believed that capitalism promoted an "every man for himself" system of values that left too many people out in the cold. They preferred socialism because it meant people were taken care of, through equal sharing of vital resources like food, shelter, and jobs. American capitalists preferred the "every man for himself" system because they believed it inspired people to work harder. They believed socialism offered a free ride for people who didn't want to work.

But under the American system, too many people who wanted to work didn't have jobs, and too many people who were working hard in low-wage jobs still couldn't afford to feed and house their families. The Panthers believed that a system of shared resources would be good for the Black community because it would help promote equality and justice.

COLD WAR POLITICS

The late 1960s was a particularly difficult time for two young Black leaders to be so vocally critical of capitalism and the economic structures of the United States. The ongoing Cold War between the United States and the Union of Soviet Socialist Republics (USSR) made the Panthers' politics a touchy subject. These two superpower nations, who were close allies during World War II, now stood at ideological odds with each other: the United States thought capitalism was the best economic system and democracy the best form of government, while the USSR believed in communism, a form of socialism that was enforced using a dictatorship. Since the end of the war, international politics had been dominated by the competition between American democracy and Soviet communism.

This conflict was further strained by the fact that smaller nations around the world began to revolt against European colonial rule, in a way that paralleled the uprisings happening in the American civil rights movement. Following World War II, at the same moment in time when Black American servicemen were returning from the battlefields to find themselves treated as second-class citizens, people of color worldwide also realized that it was time to take a stand against injustice.

This great global war had ostensibly been about freedom and democracy. It had been about the world rising up to defeat the

The American paradox of claiming to fight for freedom for "all" while keeping some people as second-class citizens preoccupied the Panthers.

Nazis' oppressive, fascist rule over Germany and their attempt to take control of other nations. Yet the world was populated by European colonies. If Germany didn't have the right to march into France and take over its land and its people, what right did other European powers have to keep control of lands they had invaded in a similar fashion, just because it had happened decades or even centuries ago? The war spurred colonized people all over the world to renew the fight to govern themselves.

Colonized nations in Africa and Asia took up arms against their oppressors. Algerians rose up against French colonial rule using guerrilla warfare tactics. Other African nations followed suit. Mozambique and Angola overthrew the Portuguese, and Kenya fought against the British. Cubans waged revolution against a dictator. In India, a decades-long struggle finally ended in independence from Great Britain.

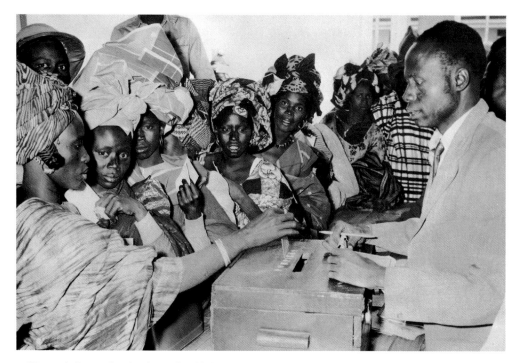

Women in Senegal voting for national independence, 1956

One by one, nations fighting for freedom claimed victory. European colonial powers withdrew, leaving the newly independent nations to start from scratch. Many wanted to follow the American model of capitalist democracy, with a constitution modeled after that of the United States. But other nations preferred socialist ideals and favored a communist government like the Soviet Union's. Because of the Cold War tensions that existed between the United States and the USSR, each of these powers wanted to prevent smaller countries from aligning themselves with the other. The American and Soviet governments quietly and not-so-quietly intervened in liberation struggles worldwide, providing arms and support to revolutionary movements that might one day be in power in the hopes of gaining new allies.

THE WAR IN VIETNAM

Cold War anxieties and interests led the United States to get involved in a complex military action in the Asian nation of Vietnam. Communist forces from North Vietnam were trying to take over democratic South Vietnam, and U.S. forces hoped to ward off the rise of communism there. Beginning in 1955, the American government sent small groups of soldiers to help repel the North Vietnamese—and the number of soldiers kept increasing. By the time the Panthers became active in the spring of 1967, nearly 500,000 American troops were on the ground in Vietnam.

The U.S. military recruited young men to serve in this controversial conflict through the Selective Service System, known as "the draft." The draft involved a lottery that called men ages eighteen to thirty-five to serve based on their birth date. Thousands of young Americans were drafted into military service. Some enlisted willingly, others against their will, and plenty found ways around it. Some went to prison in protest or chose illegal options, like going into hiding

Black soldiers in South Vietnam. Melvin Morris (left) ultimately received a Medal of Honor for heroism, which was initially denied to him because he was Black.

or fleeing the country. Anti-war protestors often tore up their draft cards as a symbolic gesture that they refused to join the military.

Many Black Americans refused to serve because they recalled how Black soldiers had fought in defense of democracy in World War II and returned home to a half-measure of freedom under segregation. They believed that before Black Americans should be required to go to war on behalf of their country, they needed to be full citizens. The Panthers believed that they were already soldiers in a war to protect democracy, right in the streets at home.

The most immediate and obvious way the Panthers chose to enact that fight was by policing the police. They continued to acquire legal weapons and follow the police around the community, quoting California state law and defending their rights. Unfortunately, no matter how careful the Panthers' actions were, the police rarely responded to them as law-abiding citizens. Therefore, people have often perceived them as lawbreakers instead. "What has been amputated from our history is that law book," said David Hilliard, a student and longshoreman who joined the Black Panthers in the early days.

Like the 101st Airborne who protected the Little Rock Nine when they integrated Central High School or the troops escorting the Freedom Riders, the Panthers were using a legal show of force to protect innocent Black citizens. Like the soldiers who defended against racial violence in those cases, the Black Panthers had guns and uniforms. They, too, acted out of a moral obligation to help better America. But rather than being treated as a group of people trying to uphold the law, they were treated as outlaws. In responding to the Panthers, the police and the government repeatedly proved the Panthers' own point—the United States of America as it currently existed could not and would not allow Black people to enjoy full citizenship. It would not allow them to be truly free.

David and Patricia Hilliard with their three children. David and Huey were childhood friends, and he joined the Panthers early on.

FILLING THE RANKS

No political party can possibly lead a great revolutionary movement to victory unless it possesses revolutionary theory and knowledge of history and has a profound grasp of the practical movement.

—MAO TSE-TUNG

Policing the police was the first, most visible Panther activity, but it was not their only project. Each point on the Panthers' Ten-Point Platform and Program articulated something that needed to be done in the community.

Some points in the platform demanded broader social change within the American system that was out of the Panthers' control, such as release of prisoners, military exemptions, and availability of new jobs and housing, but there was plenty that they could do to push their ideas to the forefront, and Huey and Bobby set about recruiting people to join these efforts.

The Panthers started by teaching people about the history of Black people's struggle in America. Black people were living in rough conditions, but most had not been taught about politics, economics, or history, so they did not fully understand the context of their situation. After decades of poor education and being

Panther members standing in formation

Political education and discourse were vital components of the Panther platform. Learning how the system worked was the first step toward creating change.

denied opportunities, an educated and organized Black population would be the key to turning the struggle around.

THE LITTLE RED BOOK

One of the Panthers' first educational programs involved a slim little red book called *Quotations from Chairman Mao*, by Mao Tse-tung. Most people referred to it simply as the Little Red Book. The color red symbolized socialism, and the book contained quotations and speech excerpts from Mao, who was a Chinese revolutionary leader and socialist. He spoke about gathering power for the people and about strategies for creating a system of shared wealth and resources. The Panthers sold Red Books at Merritt (Huey and Bobby's alma mater) and other college campuses in the Bay Area, such as Stanford and Berkeley. It was an opportunity to educate people about socialism, and the Panthers also made money off the sales, which helped them buy weapons and, eventually, acquire an office space.

Huey and Bobby moved the Panthers to their own headquarters in January 1967. From there, they began trying to recruit other members. The office was located on Grove Street, in the heart of North Oakland.[1] "That was important,"

---

[1] Grove Street has since been renamed Martin Luther King Jr. Way.

Bobby said. "The establishment of an office meant that something was functional. The people in the black community could relate to it."

"We had to transform what we learned into principles and methods acceptable to the brothers on the block," Huey said. The sisters and brothers "on the block" were the poorest of the poor, the most disenfranchised Black people, most of whom readily accepted the Panthers' message, ideology, and tactics.[2] These folks responded to the siren call of self-defense and the Panthers' "we'll do whatever it takes to get what we need" attitude.

"We painted a sign in the window . . . and a lot of people came by in those first days that we opened that office," Bobby said. The brazen way they confronted police officers made community residents sit up and take notice. Panthers were considered the biggest, baddest, boldest brothers and sisters around.

RECRUITMENT

The Panther uniform quickly became recognizable around Oakland. Black leather jackets, powder-blue shirts, and black pants were staples of the outfit. They wore berets "because they were used by just about every struggler in the third world. They're sort of an international hat for the revolutionary," Huey said. The big, prominent weapons they carried also attracted plenty of attention—and drew in new recruits.

The Panthers' main gatherings were political education meetings. The most important tools for liberation and revolution were intellectual engagement and mental freedom, not the carrying of weapons. They helped people learn to read and developed a recommended reading list for Panther recruits who were beyond the Little Red Book. Some of their favorite titles were *The Wretched of the Earth* by Frantz Fanon, a West Indian psychologist who wrote about the challenges

[2] The Panthers frequently referred to "brothers on the block." In this book, I have chosen to expand the language to include "sisters," since women were equally drawn to the Party's platform and program and ultimately formed the majority of the party's membership. Women's participation is often underrepresented in historic accounts, and I want to draw attention to their presence rather than perpetuate the practice of erasure, especially since the Panthers' own use of this male-centric language diminished over time.

PANTHER FASHION

The Panthers' typical uniform of black pants, a powder-blue work shirt, a black leather jacket, and a black beret made individual members stand out as Panthers. When they demonstrated en masse, rows of Panthers in uniform readily communicated an organized, military-style presence and a willingness to confront authority.

The Panthers arrived at this "black and blue" color scheme deliberately. Bobby saw Huey wearing a similar outfit one day, early in the life of the Party, and in a flash he realized, "That's it."

It reminded them of an old Louis Armstrong jazz song, "Black and Blue," which laments the conditions of life for Black Americans. According to Bobby, the song equates the despair of Blackness with being "beat-up black-and-blue from over two hundred years of racist discrimination." They went out and bought some berets—as a nod to the legacy of revolutionaries worldwide, from the World War II French Resistance to Che Guevara in Cuba—and a uniform was born.

of throwing off the colonial mindset, and *Guerrilla Warfare* by one of the leaders of the Cuban revolution, Che Guevara.

The sisters and brothers on the block flocked to the Panther political education classes. For many, it was the first time that education had felt relevant and exciting. Many came just to listen and learn. Those who had been initially attracted by the promise of guns discovered other, better reasons to stay involved in the movement. But only the most committed and passionate became official members of the Black Panther Party.[3]

The first Panther member, Lil' Bobby Hutton, was promoted to treasurer, even though the Party coffers were quite modest in those early days. Funds were used to keep up the office headquarters and to provide bail and legal aid to Panthers who got arrested in the line of duty.

The Panthers' self-defense platform drew interest from people of all genders.

Tarika Lewis became the first woman to join the Party, in the spring of 1967. She was a sophomore in high school, attracted to the Panthers because she could tell they were going to do a lot of good in the community. Following the Panthers' lead at Merritt College, Tarika helped organize for a Black Studies program at her high school. Tarika's determination to join the movement convinced the founders that it wasn't just men who would be interested in fighting for their community.

In one instance early in the life of the Party, Tarika recalled, there was an intersection in a Black neighborhood where accidents frequently occurred. The

---

[3] What it meant to be an official member of the Black Panther Party evolved over time, but many people participated in the movement without taking the step of pledging their lives to the Party.

This is what the Black Panther Party reading list looked like around 1967–1968. The list was published every week in the *Black Panther* newspaper to remind people that the Panthers' priority was advancing political education for communities through their social justice curriculum.

Black Panther Party BOOK LIST

MALCOLM X	The Autobiography of Malcolm X
FANON, FRANTZ	Wretched of the Earth
NKRUMAH, KWAME	I Speak of Freedom
DAVIDSON, BASIL	The Lost Cities of Africa
APTHEKER, HERBERT	The Nat Turner Slave Revolt
Aptheker, Herbert	American Negro Slave : evolts
	A Documentary History of the Negro People in the U.S.
Bennett, Lerone Jr.	Before the Mayflower
Bontemps, Arna W.	American Negro Poetry--Story of the Negro
Cronin, E.D.	Black Moses (The story of Garvey and the UNIA)
DuBois, W.E.B.	Black Reconstruction in America--Souls of Black Folk
	The World and Africa
Davidson, Basil	Black Mother, the Years of the African Slave Trade
Fanon, Frantz	Studies in a Dying Colonialism
Franklin, John Hope	From Slavery to Freedom--Negro in the United States
Frazier, C.F.	Black Bourgeoisie
Harrington, Michael	The Other America
Garvey, Marcus	Garvey & Garveyism--The Philosophy & Opinions of Garveyism
Herskovitts, Melville J.	The Myth of the Negro Past
James, C.L.R.	A History of Negro Revolts
Janheinz, John	MUNTU: The New African Culture
Jones, LeRoi	Blues People
Lincoln, C.E.	Black Muslims in America
Malcolm X	Malcolm X Speaks
Mwmmi, Albert	The Colonizer and the Colonized
Nkrumah, Kwame	Ghana
Patterson, William L.	We Charge Genocide
Rogers, J.A.	Africa's Gift to America
	World's Great Men of Color; 3,000 B.C. to 1946 A.D.
Wesley, Charles H. &	The Negro in Our History
Woodson, Carter G	
Woodward, C. Van	The Strange Career of Jim Crow
Wright, Richard	Native Son

city council had repeatedly failed to respond to petitions asking for a traffic light, so armed Black Panther members took matters into their own hands and stepped into the middle of the street to direct traffic. When the police saw what the Panthers were doing, they moved the Panthers out and took over the job themselves. In a matter of weeks, a new traffic signal was installed.

Every small act that Panthers performed in the community made an impact. Dozens of young people noticed these powerful changes and showed up, wanting to help out.

THE WIDOW SHABAZZ

In another of their first significant acts of protection, the Panthers provided an armed escort for Malcolm X's widow, Betty Shabazz, when she visited San Francisco in February 1967 to speak at a conference. Mrs. Shabazz remained a high-profile Black leader, continuing the work she had done alongside her husband, and the conference organizers did not want her to be harassed by police or media during her visit, so they asked the Panthers to guard her.

A group of about ten Panthers showed up at the San Francisco International Airport, where Mrs. Shabazz's plane was to land. Airport security tried to turn them back, on account of their large firearms, but the Panthers cited the law and pushed through to the tarmac to greet the plane. (This occurred long before the installation of extensive Transportation Security Administration checkpoints.) As soon as the airplane's staircase came down, the Panthers surrounded Mrs. Shabazz, shielding her from the police and media who had gathered to witness the spectacle.

Working in the crowd that day was a Black reporter named Eldridge Cleaver, who was impressed by the Black Panthers' organization and intensity. His experience as a journalist and writer made him an ideal person to help with one of the Panthers' most compelling new education projects: the *Black Panther* newspaper.

Black people in Oakland were well aware of the Black Panther Party for Self-Defense because they could see the group in action firsthand—but what about people outside of Oakland? Local media outlets tended to frame the Panther movement as dangerous and scary. (A headline in the *San Francisco Chronicle* the day after the Panthers protected Mrs. Betty Shabazz called them a "Frightening 'Army.'") If the Panthers could start their own newspaper, they'd be able to provide community education and revolutionary news from their own perspective. Eldridge Cleaver became Minister of Information for the Black Panthers. His job would be to oversee their public communications, and he set to work organizing the Panthers' message to the public.

The newspaper was called the *Black Panther.* In each issue, they printed the Ten-Point Platform and Program, the Panther reading list, as well as articles, photographs, and art by Panther members. Tarika Lewis contributed artwork to several early issues of the paper. The paper also included a "Pocket Lawyer of Legal First Aid," which community members were encouraged to cut out and carry around with them. The "Legal First Aid" clipping explained what to do if you were arrested and reminded people of some of their basic rights, like the right to remain silent, the right to an attorney, and the right to a phone call. The Panther office phone numbers were listed in the article so that arrested people would know whom to call for help. The earliest issues of the newspaper sold for fifteen cents, but within a few months the price was raised to twenty-five cents.

The first issue of the *Black Panther*, published in April 1967, ran with the headline "Why Was Denzil Dowell Killed?" The article was about a young Black man who was shot to death by a deputy county sheriff in Richmond, California.

Denzil's story was all too familiar. Just before four a.m. on the night of April 1, 1967, ten gunshots were fired in North Richmond. In the aftermath, Denzil Dowell's body was lying in the street; he had been shot in the back and head.

Officers from the county sheriff's department were on the scene, but no ambulance had been called. The officers claimed Denzil had been running away from the scene of a robbery and resisting arrest, but there were a number of facts that did not align with this account. To start with, Denzil had a bad leg and would have been unable to run. The liquor store showed no evidence of a robbery. The coroner's report indicated that he had been shot with his hands raised, but the county refused to allow additional scrutiny of the body or the evidence. Denzil's family recognized the police officer who shot Denzil because he had threatened to kill Denzil in the past. Finally, Denzil's body appeared to have been moved to a different place on the street sometime after he was shot. Based on all of this evidence, his family suspected a cover-up. They believed Denzil had been murdered.

Denzil's family sought help from the Panthers, and Bobby and Huey went to meet

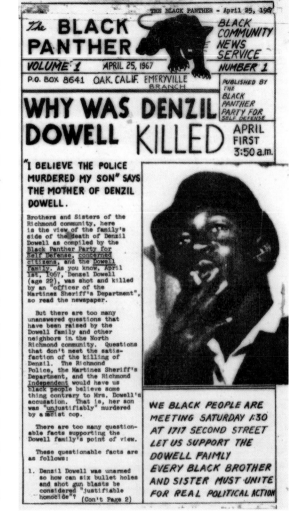

The front page of the first issue of the *Black Panther*, published April 25, 1967

with them. "I was really impressed," said George Dowell, Denzil's brother. "They made me feel like they were really interested in the people, and they knew what they were doing." And they were. The Panthers were genuinely interested in what had happened. They investigated, talked to people in the community, and committed to seeking justice for Denzil.

THE POCKET LAWYER OF LEGAL FIRST AID

This pocket lawyer is provided as a means of keeping Black people up to date on their rights. We are always the first to be arrested and the racist police forces are constantly trying to pretend that rights are extended equally to all people. Cut this out, brothers and sisters, and carry it with you. Until we arm ourselves to righteously take care of our own, the pocket lawyer is what's happening.

1. If you are stopped and/or arrested by the police, you may remain silent; you do not have to answer questions about alleged crimes; you should provide your name and address only if requested (although it is not absolutely clear that you must do so). But then do so, and at all times remember the Fifth Amendment.

2. If a police officer is not in uniform, ask him to show his identification. He has no authority over you unless he properly identifies himself. Beware of persons posing as police officers. Always get his badge number and his name.

3. Police have no right to search your car or your home unless they have a search warrant, probable cause or your consent. They may conduct no exploratory search, that is, one for evidence of crime generally or for evidence of a crime unconnected with the one you are being questioned about. (Thus, a stop for an auto violation does not give the right to search the auto.) You are not required to consent to a search; therefore, you should not consent and should state clearly and unequivocally that you do not consent, in front of witnesses if possible. If you do not consent, the police will have the burden in court of showing probable cause. Arrest may be corrected later.

4. You may not resist forcibly or by going limp, even if you are innocent. To do so is a separate crime of which you can be convicted even if you are acquitted of the original charge. Do not resist arrest under any circumstances.

5. If you are stopped and/or arrested, the police may search you by patting you on the outside of your clothing. You can be stripped

of your personal possessions. Do not carry anything that includes the name of your employer or friends.

6. Do not engage in "friendly" conversation with officers on the way to or at the police station. Once you are arrested, there is little likelihood that anything you say will get you released.

7. As soon as you have been booked, you have the right to complete at least two phone calls—one to a relative, friend or attorney, the other to a bail bondsman. If you can, call the Black Panther Party, [office phone numbers listed], and the Party will post bail if possible.

8. You must be allowed to hire and see an attorney immediately.

9. You do not have to give any statement to the police, nor do you have to sign any statement you might give them, and therefore you should not sign anything. Take the Fifth and Fourteenth Amendments, because you cannot be forced to testify against yourself.

10. You must be allowed to post bail in most cases, but you must be able to pay the bail bondsmen's fee. If you cannot pay the fee, you may ask the judge to release you from custody without bail or to lower your bail, but he does not have to do so.

11. The police must bring you into court or release you within 48 hours after your arrest (unless the time ends on a weekend or a holiday, and they must bring you before a judge the first day court is in session).

12. If you do not have the money to hire an attorney, immediately ask the police to get you an attorney without charge.

13. If you have the money to hire a private attorney, but do not know of one, call the National Lawyers' Guild or the Alameda County Bar Association (or the Bar Association of your county) and ask them to furnish you with the name of an attorney who practices criminal law.

The Panthers were a well-known local entity by the spring of 1967, and they wanted to go bigger. Black nationalist groups were organizing all over the country, motivated by the clarion call of "Black Power!" One of the biggest groups was SNCC, which had a very large and active membership concentrated in the South and East.

The Panthers hoped to partner with SNCC to become a larger national organization. Stokely Carmichael and other SNCC leaders like Kathleen Neal, James Forman, and H. Rap Brown met with the Panthers to plan their work going forward. Huey, Bobby, and Eldridge talked and negotiated with them over a period of many months. All of these young people wanted the same things for Black people—freedom, education, opportunity, and a political voice.

Kathleen Neal, a SNCC leader from New York, organized a SNCC conference in Nashville, Tennessee, in March 1967. The Panthers sent Eldridge Cleaver as a representative to speak there and to build bridges with SNCC. "The Panthers were the first group in the country to organize on the basis of Black Power. The very first. Stokely Carmichael was so thrilled, so impressed with that," Kathleen said. But despite their mutual respect, the Panthers and SNCC could not quite see eye to eye. Both groups thought Black Power was part of the answer, but they did not agree on how to go about getting it.

One sticking point was the fact that the Panthers wanted to partner with groups of different races, and SNCC leaders thought there was no room in "Black Power" for white people. As long as white people had been in control of American society, Black people had been pushed down. The Panthers agreed, but they also thought it was the *society* that was oppressive, not all white people. Some white people agreed with the need for Black Power, and the Panthers hoped to use their support and resources to advance the movement.

"We were essentially in compatible, parallel organizational modes, but not in the same place," Kathleen said. However, Kathleen and Eldridge became close during their time in Nashville. She recognized the potential in what Eldridge had to say on behalf of the Party. Within a few months, Kathleen left SNCC and joined Eldridge at the Black Panther Party headquarters in California. A few months after that, they would marry.

Meanwhile, SNCC and the Panthers continued to debate about how they might join forces. On June 29, 1967, Huey issued Executive Mandate #2, drafting Stokely Carmichael into the Black Panther Party, as Field Marshal. The Panthers hoped this proactive announcement would solidify their position as the true leaders of the movement. Despite the mandate, Stokely didn't join the Panthers at that time, but the leaders of both groups continued to look for ways to work together.

Kathleen Neal Cleaver was born in Memphis, Texas. She attended Oberlin College and Barnard College and became active as a leader in SNCC before joining the Panthers. Eldridge Cleaver served time in prison before focusing on a career in journalism. While in prison, he wrote a collection of essays that would later be published in his best-selling book *Soul on Ice*. Kathleen and Eldridge married in December 1967.

Another group the Panthers sought to collaborate with was the Los Angeles–based United Slaves (US) Organization, led by Ron Karenga. But with US, too, there were conflicts. The Panthers took a more militant, politically oriented stance than the US Organization. US members were cultural nationalists, which meant they especially valued a return to African culture and values. They enjoyed wearing African clothing, eating African food, and studying African music and culture. They believed that Black Power stemmed from embracing their roots. The Panthers wanted more focus on education about Black life and history in America, and to engage Black people in social and political action at home.

As the Panthers continued to become more prominent on the Black Power scene, tensions mounted with these groups and others, including the Nation of Islam, which was active in the Midwest and Northeast, and less prominent groups like the Revolutionary Action Movement (RAM). As they grew, the Panthers sought to define themselves as unique and powerful within the movement.

SNCC and US Organization members holding a press conference, with Ron Karenga and H. Rap Brown (*seated behind the microphones*) speaking

GUNS IN THE LEGISLATURE

Standing out, for the Panthers, ultimately happened organically. Everything changed on May 2, 1967, the day they marched into the California state legislature to protest the Mulford Act. The proposed gun-control law would prevent citizens from carrying firearms in public, and it had come about largely as a way of limiting the scope of the Panthers' legal options for armed resistance against the police. The congressman who proposed the legislation, Don Mulford, had made it clear through his statements to the press that he was going to do something to stop the Panthers from policing the police.

The Panthers received national news coverage for this dramatic act. Reporters had captured video of the Panthers, with their guns, coming in and out of the legislature. Those images were broadcast nationally. They instantly tapped into the deepest fears of white Americans and the most powerful fantasies of Black Americans.

Twenty-four Panthers were arrested after the walk-in. They could not be charged for their weapons, so they were charged with misdemeanors for disrupting the legislature because they had walked through the wrong door. As the leader of the demonstration, Bobby Seale served a six-month prison sentence.

National law enforcement agencies cataloged the Black Panthers as a growing threat. But among their core support base of poor urban Black people, the Panthers' star was on the rise.

The Panthers in a Sacramento Municipal Court building for a hearing on their march into the state capitol

The Panthers plunged onto the national scene at a moment when young Black people were ready to receive them. Uprisings in Watts, Harlem, Detroit, and elsewhere had shown the direction of the movement shifting away from nonviolence. Stokely Carmichael and fellow SNCC leader H. Rap Brown toured the country, energizing crowds of young people with fiery speeches proclaiming Black Power. They, like the Panthers, hoped to tap into the sparking rage of Black youth and direct it toward creating positive social change.

Aaron Dixon, a high school senior in Seattle, heard one of those speeches, which inspired him to join the Black Power movement. Aaron and his younger brother Elmer grew up in Chicago, but their father was frightened by the street gang activity there, so before his sons reached high school, he moved his family to Seattle, where he felt his sons would be less susceptible to violence and peer pressure. In Seattle "racism was not out in the open, staring you in the face, thrusting you into confrontations or forcing you to question your own integrity," Aaron said. "Nevertheless, it was there."

Aaron and Elmer sat front-row center to hear Stokely's speech. "We had gone out and bought some black Ray-Ban Wayfarer sunglasses, just like the ones Stokely was so often seen in," Aaron said. They were thrilled to hear him in person, and Stokely did not disappoint. "I walked out of the auditorium transformed," Aaron said. "From that day forward, I looked at the world and everyone around me with anger and rage. . . . The anger I had held at bay for so long had now surfaced."

POWERFUL
LEADERS
EMERGE

H. Rap Brown   **Aaron Dixon**

Fred Hampton, also eighteen, knew firsthand how rough-and-tumble the Chicago street scene could be. Despite the gangs all around him, Fred pointed himself in a positive direction and became the leader of the local youth chapter of the NAACP. An avid reader, he had already studied many of the books the Black Panthers recommended to their members. Fred believed that organizing and political action would be more effective than revolution in the streets, but after everything he had witnessed in Chicago's Black neighborhoods, he also understood the value of self-defense.

Nearer to Oakland, in Los Angeles, Elaine Brown participated in Black Student Alliance organizing and became one of the first women to represent the group in the Black Congress, a coalition of Black activist organizations in the area. She admired fellow activist Angela Davis, an accomplished student and political theoretician, for her ability to spar intellectually with the men who led the group. When Panther representatives came to the Black Congress, Elaine was intrigued by their presence and platform.

Also in Los Angeles, Alprentice "Bunchy" Carter was inspired by the Panthers. Bunchy met Eldridge Cleaver when they were both in prison, and as a former street gang member, Bunchy knew firsthand how difficult life could be for the sisters and brothers on the block. Bunchy had gained political awareness in prison, and he wanted to do something more positive with his life once he got out. Bunchy came to visit the Panthers in Oakland, hoping to figure out how he could do some of the same things in his hometown of Los Angeles.

Soon, each of these young people would find a place in the Black Panther Party.

Fred Hampton

Elaine Brown

Angela Davis

Bunchy Carter

OFF THE PIGS!

If violence is wrong in America, violence is wrong abroad. If it is wrong to be violent defending Black women and Black children and Black babies and Black men, then it is wrong for America to draft us and make us violent abroad in defense of her. And if it is right for America to draft us, and teach us how to be violent in defense of her, then it is right for you and me to do whatever is necessary to defend our own people right here in this country.

—MALCOLM X

Stokely's fierce call for Black Power rang out loud and proud, and the Panthers' response remained militant, strong, and bold. The radical demands of the Ten-Point Platform gave them grounding, and they constantly looked for new ways to express the feelings, the frustrations, and the needs of the Black community.

Their rhetoric—the specific language they used to talk about issues—developed a unique tone and a vocabulary all its own. They did not shy away from using big words or expressing complicated ideas. They felt it would be a disservice to the people not to be honest and clear and challenging.

◀ The Panthers' main vehicle for sharing their vision and rhetoric was the *Black Panther* newspaper, which members sold to earn money for the Party and for themselves.

The Panthers' rhetoric had several specific effects. First, it allowed them to discuss the systemic problems in American society, rather than talking only about individual actions. When they talked about oppression, they talked about a "racist power structure" and "avaricious politicians" who stole from the people, literally and metaphorically. In speeches, political education classes, and articles in the *Black Panther*, they laid out their views for people. "All power comes from the people, and all power must ultimately be vested in them," Huey wrote. "Anything else is theft."

Second, their rhetoric expressed a vision for a different power balance in the United States. Calls for Black Power excited people, but the Panthers took time to break down what that really meant. What would it look like if Black people did have power? What if the tables were turned on those who most benefited from racism?

As part of this effort to upend the power structure using language, the Panthers referred to police officers as "pigs." The purpose of the label was to undercut the authority of police and to dehumanize them in the same way white people had been dehumanizing Black people for centuries. They used many variations of this theme, like "capitalist pigs" and "racist swine" when referring to wealthy businesspeople and politicians, too. A common phrase uttered among Panthers was "Off the pigs!" which meant "kill the police." The language seemed harsh to people outside the Black community, but to those who had suffered police brutality for decades, it seemed right on. Finally, someone was speaking the deepest desires and frustrations from the heart of the Black community.

The Panthers' rhetoric energized Black people and frightened white people. Making people uncomfortable was part of their intent. They hoped to challenge all Americans to think differently about the structures of society, and that meant seeing things from a different angle. As white people grappled with their

RHETORIC ON A ROLL!

Panthers became known for their rhetoric, Huey explained, because "we recognize the significance of words in the struggle for liberation." The Panthers hurled their words like weapons, and they often hit their mark. Some important terms for the Panthers included the following:

Avaricious: Greedy; craving wealth and power at all cost; insatiable in the quest to own and control as much as possible. The Panthers used this term to drive home the extreme nature of capitalistic greed. *(Example: avaricious politicians.)*

Pig: Police or government agents. A recurring item in the *Black Panther* defined the term further: "What is a pig? A low natured beast that has no regard for law, justice, or the rights of the people; a creature that bites the hand that feeds it; a foul depraved traducer who's usually found masquerading as a victim of an unprovoked attack." *(Variations: swine, racist pig, racist swine, capitalist pig, capitalist swine, pig department.)*

Racist: This word was not always as familiar as it is today. Its first known use occurred in 1902. Even during the civil rights era, people tended to speak in terms of "prejudice" and "discrimination," and it was not until around 1970 that the word *racist* became part of popular parlance. The way the Panthers used this language during the height of their influence (1966–1972) likely helped alter the way American society as a whole views and uses the word. *(Examples: white racist, racist pig, racist power structure.)*

Vanguard: A group of people leading the way. The Panthers referred to themselves as the vanguard party, which underscored their goal of creating a broad revolution and gaining many followers. It also reminded people of their connection to socialism, as the term is used in Marxist-Leninist theory.

The Panthers' rhetoric was visual as well as verbal. This political cartoon by Emory Douglas, featuring pigs, critiques state violence in all its forms.

discomfort over the threat of Black violence against white people, it illuminated the comfort they'd apparently always felt with white violence against Black people. Not everyone awoke to this recognition on a conscious level, but part of the purpose of rhetoric is to tap into people's deepest biases and emotions.

"Words could be used not only to make Blacks more proud," Huey said, "but to make whites question and even reject concepts that they had always unthinkingly accepted."

The Panthers' attitude of speaking unvarnished truth to power helped build their reputation as revolutionaries. They did not want to be polite or to apologize for their opinions. They did not look down on people who didn't know as much or who disagreed with them. Instead they tried to educate them and raise their level of consciousness. "We must recognize the difference between what people *can* do and what they *will* do," Huey said. "When we raise their consciousness they will understand even more fully what they in fact can do, and they will move on the situation in a courageous manner."

In the process, slogans like "Off the pigs!" frightened a lot of people. For Black and white folks alike, there was uncertainty about where the line between rhetoric and action actually fell. The Panthers did not intend to go out and start shooting police officers, but many people assumed that was exactly what they meant to do.

The police, for their part, seemed unwilling to allow Black people to even speak about self-defense. The violent rhetoric did not deter police aggressions; rather it spurred them on, as if violent rhetoric against the police was a form of violence in itself. It didn't seem to matter that the Panthers' actual actions—such as policing the police—were legal, nonviolent, and rooted in self-defense. Conflicts seemed inevitable.

REVOLUTION IN OUR LIFETIME

The Panthers desperately wanted to inspire a revolution. Party members would often call out "Revolution in our lifetime!" as a rallying cry for their movement. But what did that really mean? The strange thing is that no one actually knew. The idea of revolution was hypothetical, meaning that the Panthers were constantly trying to guess and imagine what it might look like.

They had historical examples to compare themselves to, like the American colonies' war for independence against the British and other anti-colonial struggles going on worldwide. But the situation of Black people in the United States was different because they were not the majority. In most places in the world, where European colonists were in the minority, collective actions and even armed revolution succeeded because the people had the strength of numbers.

For some Panthers, armed revolution against the government was the ideal long-term goal. They envisioned forming a true army and going after the police and storming the halls of government, not just to make a political statement but to actually take over.

To others, such violence wasn't the ideal but simply seemed inevitable, given the consistently violent actions of police and government and the Panthers' commitment to self-defense.

But many—perhaps most—Panthers believed it was possible to achieve social change without bloodshed. "We were taught that the revolution could not be fought or won without the people," Jamal Joseph said, "and that if the masses were organized and unified enough that armed struggle might not even be necessary."

Panthers discussed and debated the meaning of revolution constantly in the course of their work. They agreed on one thing: if all Black people could stand together, great things could be possible.

Emory Douglas art from the *Black Panther* newspaper

SHOOTOUT

In October 1967, a few short months after the Panthers' march on Sacramento, Huey and his friend Gene McKinney were driving to get some soul food when red flashing lights appeared in the rearview mirror. It was about four a.m., and Huey assumed it would be a routine traffic stop. Officer John Frey, who pulled Huey over, radioed that he might need backup because he was stopping a known Panther vehicle. Officer Frey then came forward and asked for Huey's identification, even though he already knew who he had pulled over—Oakland police knew Huey Newton's face as well as anyone's.

Officer Frey ordered Huey and Gene to get out of the car. A second officer, Herbert Heanes, arrived on the scene. Huey obeyed and got out, bringing his law book, which he began quoting from, as he was used to doing in front of the police.

"Am I under arrest?" he asked.

"No," the officers told him. So Huey quoted a bit more from the California state laws.

In a matter of minutes, bullets were flying. No one is certain exactly how the shootout happened, but when the bullets stopped, Officer Frey lay dead, and Officer Heanes and Huey were both wounded.

Huey had been shot in the abdomen. Gene McKinney flagged down a passing car and helped Huey get to the emergency room. Shortly thereafter, a swarm of police officers arrived at the hospital to arrest Huey for shooting Officer Frey. They handcuffed Huey to a gurney and beat him up, even though he was already wounded. As soon as it was clear he would survive his injuries, Huey was charged with the first-degree murder of Officer Frey, attempted murder of Officer Heanes, and kidnapping of the man driving the car that brought him to the hospital.

The legal case against Huey turned out to be very circumstantial. The evidence was limited. The police never tested his hands to see if he had fired a gun. They said Huey used his own gun in the shooting, but all the recovered bullets

Huey in jail, with his attorney, Charles Garry

had come from the police officers' guns. A supposed eyewitness said that he had seen Huey shoot Frey, but his description of Huey didn't match, and it was later shown that he was a mile away from the incident at the time. Even the surviving officer, Herbert Heanes, later testified that he had never seen Huey holding a gun. Charles Garry, an experienced trial lawyer, represented Huey and tried numerous legal tactics to get the case thrown out. But the Alameda County District Attorney insisted on going ahead with the charges against Huey. They sent him to prison to await trial.

FREE HUEY!

The Panthers organized rallies to call attention to Huey's case, and they raised up a public outcry for his release. It would be an uphill battle, they knew, because the justice system was not built to give Black people a fair shake. It would have been an uphill battle even if the full facts of the case had been clear. But they weren't.

Since the truth of what happened that morning was uncertain, several competing narratives emerged to explain the events. Most Panthers believed Huey had been set up by the Oakland Police Department. Officer Frey had such a significant history of incidents with Black citizens that he was scheduled to be transferred to work in a different community. Could it really be a coincidence that an officer with such a history pulled over Huey P. Newton on the very night Huey's probation for a previous issue had expired?

Some people believed Huey had shot Officer Frey in self-defense, and they held him up as a shining example of the Panthers' revolutionary platform. Sisters and brothers on the block lit up over the idea that Huey P. Newton wasn't just talk—he had put himself on the line for his movement. That scenario brought hope and excitement into the community in a time of discouragement—the Mulford Act had passed and would soon take effect, limiting the Panthers' ability to legally police the police. Could this be a promise that the Panthers' protection of the neighborhood would continue?

Others wondered if it was possible the officers had accidentally shot each other while both attempting to shoot Huey. Officer Heanes testified that Officer Frey and Huey had scuffled, and that Heanes had fired his own weapon at them, attempting to intervene. Or, given that Seventh Avenue was a busy street, even at that hour—could there have been an additional shooter that no one noticed?

The truth was a mystery, and in the meantime, Huey was behind bars, about to be tried for capital murder. If convicted, he could get the death penalty, but Huey tried to stay strong—after all, death was always a risk for those who dreamed of sparking revolution.

The Panthers chose to see Huey's imprisonment as not just a tragedy but an opportunity. The whole world would be watching Huey's trial. Perhaps the Panthers could leverage Huey's imprisonment to advance the movement. The facts of the specific case weren't the most important thing because there was a deeper truth to tell, about the ways the American system of government worked to hurt Black citizens like Huey.

"I wanted to use the trial as a political forum to prove that having to fight for my life was the logical and inevitable outcome of our efforts to lift the oppressor's burden," Huey said. "The Black Panthers' activities and programs, the patrolling of the police, and the resistance to their brutality had disturbed the power structure; now it was gathering its forces to crush our revolution forever."

It made sense to the Panther leadership to prioritize "the ideological and political significance" of Huey's moment in the spotlight. This meant taking a big risk for Huey. "I needed to know the legal ramifications of any move," Huey said, although "the goal of the trial was not primarily to save my life, but to organize the people and advance their struggle."

Kathleen and Eldridge Cleaver, the Panthers' Information Ministry team, organized the message to the masses: Huey Newton must be set free as a symbol of the revolution, as a sign that there is hope for a better future for all oppressed people. At protests on the steps of the Alameda County courthouse, hundreds and sometimes thousands of people gathered, chanting and holding banners that cried, "Free Huey, or the sky's the limit!"

Panthers at a Free Huey rally, standing on the steps of the Alameda County Courthouse

REVOLUTIONARY ART

Press coverage of the Free Huey movement catapulted the Panthers to a position of significance among human rights and liberation struggles worldwide. In the midst of it all, the Panthers worked hard to keep the rest of their message and their demands front and center, too.

The Panthers hoped to increase the reach of the *Black Panther* newspaper, which was their main method of speaking directly to the people. Art, poetry, and music became very important ways of connecting culture and politics. *Black Panther* articles gave voice to the Party, and the pictures that decorated its pages were worth a thousand words.

"A lot of grassroots people won't read a sea of type," Bobby Seale said. An image-heavy focus especially helped the Panthers communicate with those who could not read well, and for everyone who picked up the *Black Panther*, these images lent strength to the message.

Emory Douglas had joined the Party early on in 1967 and almost immediately became the resident artist for the Panther movement. He took the title Minister of Culture. While Kathleen and Eldridge spearheaded the national message and wrote articles, Emory designed and laid out the paper each week. The layout "was basically done by hand, mostly by cutting and pasting the articles in place on the layout sheets," Emory said. "We couldn't afford a computer."

The *Black Panther* regularly featured Emory's drawings. He penned striking and sometimes gruesome political cartoons dramatizing police brutality and political corruption, bringing the image of racist police and corrupt government officials as "pigs" vividly to life. "I did my art and whatever needed to be done," he said. Over the next decade, Emory would design the vast majority of the visual art displayed in the Panthers' literature.

"Emory's images . . . helped the average protestor and grassroots organizer define the phenomena of who and what our oppressors were," Bobby Seale said.

"Images of the people fighting back, defending themselves, and the deaths of some of those who wrongfully attacked our people" inspired Panther members.

"The Black Panther newspapers . . . were irresistible to me," said Colette Gaiter, a high school student in D.C. at the time. "With their huge typographical headlines, use of color, and strikingly rendered drawings of black people . . . I was attracted to Douglas's images because they showed both anger and hope."

The *Black Panther* also frequently ran visual art, poems, and song lyrics created by other members. These pieces helped express the creativity and the desires of the Black community and gave regular people a chance to contribute to the Panther message. The newspaper always had a section of ads selling Panther posters, buttons, books, and records, which began to feature volumes of poetry and albums of political music produced by Panther members.

"The Black Panther Black Community News Service is not an ordinary

Emory Douglas, Minister of Culture, with a sister identified as Barbara E. at a Free Huey rally

Emory Douglas's "All Power to the People" poster

newspaper," wrote one of the early Panther members, Landon Williams. "It is the flesh and blood, sweat and tears of our people. It is a continuation of the story of the middle passage, of Denmark Vesey, of Nat Turner, of Harriet Tubman, of Malcolm X, and countless other oppressed people who put freedom and dignity beyond personal gain. The Black Panther Black Community News Service, is truly a mirror of the spirit of the people."

As such, the newspaper became another target for police repression. When the Panthers first sought to increase distribution, they did it by printing extra copies of the paper in Oakland and shipping them by air freight to other major cities. Copies were printed in Oakland on Thursdays and brought to the airport on Fridays to be delivered around the country, ready for distribution on Saturday morning. When the Federal Bureau of Investigation (FBI) discovered this plan, they showed up at the airports to intervene. They sprayed water all over the bundled newspapers, soaking them and destroying them. These actions showed that law enforcement agencies beyond Oakland had begun taking an interest in the Panthers, hoping to squash the Party's growth and stop them from spreading their message.

The Panthers regrouped and contacted local presses in Chicago, Detroit, New

York, and Philadelphia. The papers could be printed locally elsewhere and avoid the airport step entirely. Soon the *Black Panther* newspaper was being distributed beyond Oakland, even overseas, and in the coming years, circulation rose to as many as 400,000 copies per week. The Panthers' message and rhetoric was alive and well . . . and growing.

MIDNIGHT RAIDS

Portraying the police as cruel, dirty pigs did nothing to help the Panthers' image in the eyes of law enforcement. Police remained suspicious of and hostile toward the Panthers. They continued the habit of stopping Panther vehicles and writing them tickets. They arrested Panthers for selling papers and for carrying weapons— even legally—and did what they could to intimidate potential members.

Once the Mulford Act went into effect, the Panthers could no longer patrol the streets while armed, but they could keep weapons in their homes and in the Panther office. Police began storming into Panther spaces, arresting people, seizing weapons, destroying files and paperwork, and generally trashing the places.

In order to legally search a Panther home or office, police were required to get a search warrant approved by a court of law. Specific protections in the U.S. Constitution prevent law enforcement officers from searching people's homes or offices without a good reason. Some police officers believed that the Panthers' explosive rhetoric was reason enough to come after them, but the law did not support that conclusion. Free speech and freedom of the press are constitutional rights granted to all U.S. citizens. Thus, police often had a hard time getting warrants to search Panther properties.

The Black Panthers worked hard to study the law and follow it in every way. They did not engage in intentional civil disobedience like their forerunners in the civil rights era—they did not seek to be deliberately arrested, and they were advised never to resist arrest. Paradoxically, it was the police who repeatedly broke the law in the effort to prove the Panthers were doing something wrong.

On January 16, 1968, at about three thirty in the morning, armed police officers with no warrant illegally broke down the door of Eldridge Cleaver's home. They claimed they had received a tip that two Black men driving a car similar to Eldridge's had committed a robbery, and they tore the place apart, looking for illegal weapons or other contraband. They didn't find anything.

A month later, a similar thing happened to Bobby Seale. Acting on an anonymous tip that "someone" was planning a murder, the police arrested a handful of Panthers leaving Bobby's home after a meeting. Then the police came to the door, on the pretense of asking about a disturbance in the area. When Bobby tried to turn them away, they entered the house with guns drawn and arrested Bobby and his wife, creating a legal case that took over a year to resolve. The arrests were ultimately deemed illegal. The Panthers believed this strategy was deliberate on the part of police, a way to complicate their lives and drain Party resources.

Big Man Howard, whose truck was on a list of known Panther vehicles, was frequently stopped for minor traffic violations. "Whenever I got arrested, it was a good opportunity to catch up on some sleep if the cellblock was quiet," Big Man said. "I caught up on my sleep because I didn't have to stay awake watching out for the cops or FBI raiding our homes or offices."

The Panthers raised a lot of money to pay bail for their members who were arrested. Being arrested for a minor violation might get a Panther caught up behind bars for just a few days, but plenty of Panthers spent much longer in prison. Huey, for example, spent ten months in prison just waiting for his trial to begin because he was denied bail entirely.

Frequent arrests rapidly became a hallmark of Panther membership. But the Panthers knew it was what they had to endure for the sake of the movement. "If you go to jail, so what?" Malcolm X once said. "If you're black, you were born in jail."

BAIL

To get someone out of jail after they are arrested, friends or family have to pay a set amount of money, which is known as bail. The court decides on the amount of money: usually it is a small amount for a minor crime and a larger amount for a serious offense. The bail money acts like a credit. You get it back if you show up for your court date, which is sometimes weeks or months later. If you do not show up and "skip bail" instead, you lose the money, and a warrant would probably be issued for your arrest.

Courts have a great deal of power to decide people's fate—including choosing their bail amounts. For someone the judge perceives as very likely to skip bail, the court would either set the bail so high that the person could not afford it or deny them the chance for bail at all. In Huey's case, the court denied him the chance to pay bail, which meant he had to stay in jail until his trial.

RHETORIC IN ACTION

On March 1, 1968, Huey and Bobby delivered Executive Mandate #3, which called for all Panthers to arm themselves and prepare to defend their homes by force. "We draw the line at the threshold of our doors," they said.

> Our organization has received serious threats from certain racist elements of White America, including the Oakland, Berkeley, and San Francisco Pig Departments. Threats to take our lives, to exterminate us. . . . Therefore, those who approach our doors in the manner of outlaws; who seek to enter our homes illegally, unlawfully and in a rowdy fashion; those who kick our doors down with no authority and seek to ransack our homes in violation of our HUMAN RIGHTS will henceforth be treated as outlaws, as gangsters, as evil-doers.

The mandate appeared in the *Black Panther*, alongside an image of Kathleen in a doorway, wearing a black jacket and tall leather boots, pointing a shotgun toward the camera. As rhetoric goes, the photo screamed loud and clear: to cross a Panther threshold uninvited was to place yourself in peril. Self-defense was not just an idea but a practice.

The use of this image foreshadowed another important truth about the Black Panther Party. While the founders and most prominent Panthers to date were predominantly men, the Party would soon be led, staffed, strengthened, and kept alive by women. As long as violent repression continued, Panthers of all genders would be ready to respond.

Kathleen Cleaver stands in the doorway, prepared to defend her home. This picture accompanied Executive Mandate #3 in the *Black Panther*.

DEATH OF THE KING

When he died, I think something died in all of us. Something died in America.

—REPRESENTATIVE JOHN LEWIS

On April 4, 1968, the Rev. Dr. Martin Luther King Jr. walked out onto the balcony of his second-floor room at the Lorraine Motel in Memphis, Tennessee. He was in Memphis to lend support to the local sanitation workers' strike. It was about six in the evening. Moments after Dr. King stepped into view, a gunshot rang out from across the street. The bullet pierced Dr. King's cheek and neck, and he fell onto the balcony. His friends surrounded him, shouting for help and trying to stop the bleeding. They rushed him to the hospital, but it was no use. Dr. King died an hour later.

Dr. King's violent death marked a watershed moment for activists at all points on the civil rights spectrum. Though the civil rights struggle would continue, it would never be the same. It was perhaps the most shattering loss to date for Black Americans; it rose above the many tragic losses that had come in the years

Dr. King (*center*) with his colleagues Jesse Jackson (*left*) and Ralph Abernathy on the balcony of the Lorraine Motel, where he would be shot and killed the following day

before. Dr. King himself had become such a strong symbol of his message—that nonviolent passive resistance would ultimately lead to the radical social change necessary to secure civil rights for Black Americans. His death quickly became the single most compelling argument in favor of the new Black militancy that the Panthers practiced. Dr. King never raised a hand against a white person. His death drove home a difficult truth: violence may beget violence, but if you are Black in America, nonviolence also begets violence.

NONVIOLENT NO MORE

Throughout the evening, people around the country learned of King's death. Radio and television news broadcasts carried the terrible story. People who didn't hear an official report right away heard the news from family members, friends, and neighbors as the night wore on.

A Black teen named BJ reported walking with a friend down Seventh Avenue in Harlem, New York. He heard a woman scream, "an *eerie* scream, one that sent chills through you." Down the street, he saw "an old brother . . . he was shaking and crying and about this time you could hear footsteps, people coming out of the buildings hollering and screaming, 'they killed him, they killed him!'"

BJ didn't yet know what the screaming was all about, but people poured into the streets around him, crying and shouting. The "old brother" managed to tell him that King was dead. Suddenly everyone—including BJ—was smashing windows and releasing their rage all over the white-owned businesses of Harlem. "All hell broke loose," BJ said.

Also in Harlem that night, Jamal Joseph saw "protestors and rioters swarm the streets, clashing with cops, overturning cars, setting trash can fires, and hurling bricks at white-owned businesses." Jamal found himself fleeing from cops who wanted to arrest him, even though he did not directly participate in the protest. Hundreds of arrests occurred, not just in Harlem, but all over the country as people in over one hundred cities took to the streets in sorrow and anger.

Jeff Haas, a young white lawyer in Chicago, went down to the jail to offer legal counsel to Black teens who got caught up in the frenzy. He said, "Almost all were arrested for being in the street, rather than any specific unlawful act. . . . [Yet the] judge set bonds requiring more than the defendant's family could make." And to make matters worse, Mayor Richard Daley ordered Chicago police to "shoot to kill" any arsonists and looters. Nine Black men died, shot by police in the chaos; several of them were not involved at all, but merely innocent bystanders who got caught in the crossfire.

The frustration and anger people had been holding in—largely because Dr. King asked them to—had broken loose. Even before his death, the tides were shifting, but now people feared that his movement would lose direction entirely. With the assassin's bullet, the era of nonviolent protest for civil rights fell into a sharp sunset. The dawning era of Black Power had reached full light.

Stuck in jail in Seattle after a nonviolent protest, Aaron Dixon heard the news of Dr. King's assassination from a television broadcast. As he watched the footage of cities catching fire, "I kicked and banged the steel table, throwing whatever I could throw, wishing I were out there on the streets." The emotional devastation was immense:

> Anger filled me that night. There would be no more tears and no more dialogue. The war began that night all across America. I vowed to myself that Martin's death would not go unavenged. . . . For me, the picket sign would be replaced, and in its place would be the gun.

Aaron Dixon

The repeated uprisings occurring in Black communities across the nation puzzled and intrigued white lawmakers. What was causing so many people to lash out and take to the streets? From their point of view, the uprisings seemed reckless and irrational.

In 1967, President Lyndon B. Johnson appointed the National Advisory Commission on Civil Disorders to study the forces that led to Black uprisings. The group became known as the Kerner Commission, after its chair, Governor Otto Kerner Jr. of Illinois. The commission's eleven members enlisted over a hundred experts—social scientists and investigators—to look into the causes and dynamics of urban uprisings, like those that happened in Watts in 1965, Detroit in 1967, and numerous cities in the wake of Dr. King's assassination in 1968.

These researchers came back with a detailed analysis, concluding that racism was so pervasive in the institutions of society that many Black Americans "feel it is legitimate and necessary to use violence against the social order. A truly revolutionary spirit has begun to take hold . . . an unwillingness to compromise or wait any longer, to risk death rather than have their people continue in a subordinate status."

The researchers who drew this conclusion about systemic racism were fired, and their analysis was removed from the Kerner Commission's report. The finished report downplayed their initial recommendations to invest heavily in education and economic opportunities for poor Black communities and instead emphasized the need for additional policing to keep order. The government's willful disregard of powerful (and repeated) feedback about the true problems in Black America helped establish and perpetuate the dynamics between police and communities that still exist today.

Thousands of young people took the loss as new motivation. If even Dr. King, the most peaceful man imaginable, could get shot down, then it was time for a different kind of action. Phones at the Panther office rang and rang. People wanted to know how they could join.

AMBUSH!

The Panthers, too, mourned the loss of Dr. King. They might not have agreed with his methods, but they respected him as a leader. The night of his death, Panthers patrolled the streets of Oakland to help calm people down, successfully preventing the type of widespread uprising that was happening elsewhere. They urged people to channel their frustration into a more organized form of resistance, like what the Panthers could offer to people who joined their ranks.

At the time of Dr. King's death, the Panthers were in the midst of preparations for another Free Huey event in the community—people were passing out flyers, cooking, and organizing to get ready. But seeing the tumultuous footage from around the country had convinced a few Panthers that the assassination had been the last straw for Black people everywhere. They figured an armed revolution against the police and the government was going to break out at any moment, and they wanted to be on the front lines.

On April 5, the day after Dr. King's murder, Lil' Bobby Hutton visited Big Man Howard and asked to borrow a rifle. When Big Man asked why he needed it, Lil' Bobby told him it was for going on patrol. But later Lil' Bobby invited another friend to come along, saying they were going to "do something" to local police the next night.

On April 6, the evening before the Free Huey rally, a group of nine Panthers, including Lil' Bobby and Eldridge, loaded guns and supplies into cars. They started driving and had just pulled over to the curb when several police officers arrived. Eldridge claimed that he had ducked behind a car to relieve himself

Burning buildings on Chicago's
West Side, April 5, 1968

when police cars rolled up and shone a flashlight on him. The Panthers ended up in a forty-five-minute shootout with police in and around the neighboring houses.

It remains unclear how the shooting actually got started. The police may have started it, upon seeing the Panthers with guns, or the Panthers may have started shooting when the police appeared, believing that they were under attack. In one version of the story, a Panther shotgun went off accidentally, and the police returned fire in earnest. In another version, the shootout occurred because both sides were prepared for a fight: the Panthers had heard a rumor that a police raid would happen that night, and they were arming themselves to respond when the police arrived early.

Fleeing the gunfire, Eldridge and Lil' Bobby holed up in the basement of a house on the street. Police shot at the building and tossed tear gas canisters inside. One hit Eldridge and nearly set him on fire. He stripped off his shirt. Eventually the house caught fire. Eldridge and Lil' Bobby shouted to the police that they would surrender. Eldridge took off the rest of his clothes,

Eldridge and Lil' Bobby took refuge in this house during the April 6 shootout with police. Lil' Bobby was killed just outside.

hoping to prove to police that he was unarmed. Lil' Bobby stripped down, too, but was too shy to take off his shorts.

When they came out of the house, hands raised, the police officers nudged Lil' Bobby forward until he fell down. Then they shot him six times, right where he lay. Later they would claim he had been running, trying to escape, when he was shot and killed.

The Panthers were devastated at losing one of their own in the shootout, especially someone so young and so beloved, and especially when he had been in Oakland police custody, trying to surrender. Even one of the police officers at the scene testified that sixteen-year-old Lil' Bobby had been unarmed, lying on the ground in surrender at the time he was shot. But this officer's statement was never presented to the jury who heard the officers' case. The court determined it was a "justifiable homicide," and Lil' Bobby became yet another statistic in the legal system's injustice toward Black citizens.

In the wake of this tragedy, the Panthers couldn't help but reflect on how they had ended up in the shootout with police in the first place. Nothing could excuse the shooting of an unarmed Black teen mid-surrender, of course, but the whole situation haunted them. The Panthers publicly described the event as an unprovoked attack by police, but internally they agonized over a number of things that had gone wrong on their side of the equation. There remained the question of what exactly the group of Panthers had intended to do with their weapons that night, and how they found themselves so vulnerable to assault. "There was no discipline," Bobby Seale said. "You had a lot of people coming to the party and they didn't understand guns and weapons. They think it's just some power, baby, and acting the fool." Bobby had been in the U.S. Air Force in the 1950s, and with the help of other ex-military Panthers, he instituted new weapons training protocols for the growing organization. The way the police were gunning for the Panthers, they could not afford to make tactical mistakes.

Lil' Bobby's tragic death struck a chord with people around the country. It further drove home the fact that young Black men were at great risk in their own communities. These tragedies, compounded by the nation's sorrow over the loss of Dr. King, caused more and more Black people to punch their fists toward the sky and call out, "Black Power!"

Aaron and Elmer Dixon traveled from Seattle to San Francisco and attended Lil' Bobby's funeral at St. Augustine Church in Oakland. They wore Panther berets for the first time and folded themselves in among the crowd of over twenty-five hundred. The sounds of people crying filled the room. Even though they hadn't known him personally, Aaron said, "Looking into the casket of Little Bobby Hutton had been almost like looking into the future and glimpsing what the movement might hold. It was not the glory and the victory we romanticized." But the threat of death did not dissuade them. After the funeral, Aaron listened to Bobby Seale speak, and by the end of the night, he told Bobby that he wanted to start a Panther chapter in Seattle.

The Panthers wanted this expansion, but it was a difficult moment. "The sudden arrests and Lil' Bobby's death threw our party into chaos," said Kathleen Neal Cleaver. "Those of us living in the Bay Area were under siege—pulled into a deadly vortex of anger, violence and love."

Soon Bobby Seale brought a small group of Panthers to visit Aaron Dixon in Seattle. They talked about the Panther platform, rules, political education, and requirements for opening and operating a new chapter. Bobby invited Aaron to come back to Oakland for leadership training. Everything sounded scary to Aaron but also exciting.

That spring more new Panther leaders emerged, fueled by sadness, rage, and the determination to change the system. Ericka Huggins's life had changed that day at St. Augustine Church, too. She and her husband, John, had started out just like Huey and Bobby—as student activists who wanted to do work beyond their campus. After attending Lil' Bobby's funeral, Ericka and John committed their lives to the movement and became leaders in the Party. They joined with Bunchy Carter, Eldridge's friend, to build a Los Angeles chapter.

Later that month, Ericka was working in the L.A. office when twenty-five-year-old student activist Elaine Brown walked in. Elaine had recently attended a Free Huey rally in Los Angeles and been intrigued. Afterward she'd listened to Eldridge speak about the new Southern

Ericka Huggins grew up on the East Coast. She joined student activist efforts at Lincoln University before heading west with her husband, John, to join the Panther movement.

California chapter of the Black Panther Party. Now Elaine was ready to serve.

"Nonviolence was dead," Elaine said. "National Guardsmen all over the United States were still trying to put down the wrath of black people over King's assassination when . . . Bobby Hutton was killed." And there seemed no end in sight. Waiting no longer felt tenable.

Over the next year, the Panthers opened chapters in other cities around the country: Panther offices soon existed in New York, Dallas, Boston, Detroit, Philadelphia, and Washington, D.C., as well as smaller cities, like Kansas City, St. Louis, Baltimore, Indianapolis, Cleveland, and New Haven, Connecticut. "The murder of King changed the whole dynamic of the country," Kathleen said. "The Panthers were all of a sudden thrust into the forefront of being the alternative, and maybe they weren't quite anticipating as much attention as they got."

GOING
NATIONAL

There is a world of difference between thirty million unarmed submissive Black people and thirty million Black people armed with freedom, guns, and the strategic methods of liberation.

—HUEY P. NEWTON

Growth happened fast—perhaps too fast. Within the space of two years, the Party went from being a local cadre of half a dozen sisters and brothers policing the police to a national organization with thousands of members nationwide.

It became hard for Oakland leadership to keep up with what was happening around the country. Groups calling themselves the Black Panther Party popped up all over the place, with no firm connection to the Oakland Panthers. On the upside, growth meant it would no longer be so easy for the police and the legal system to seek and destroy the small band of activists. On the downside, keeping control of the movement was going to be difficult.

◀ As the organization grew, it diversified. At its peak, more than half of Panthers were women and members' median age was nineteen.

Bobby Seale and fellow leader David Hilliard traveled all over the country to meet with these newly formed groups. They trained those who were willing to truly join the Party and asked that the others change their name to avoid confusion. In this delicate moment of expansion, they felt cohesion and control were important, in order to ensure people were practicing what Huey referred to as the "correct strategic methods" for revolution.

Much of the Panthers' attention during this time of expansion was focused on the ongoing Free Huey movement. Huey's murder trial began on July 15, 1968. A crowd of about five thousand people showed up to support the Panthers outside the Alameda County Courthouse when the trial began, and many returned daily throughout the trial to stand in solidarity. Soon the Panthers would know if the protests had shifted the course of the trial at all.

Certainly the Free Huey movement was succeeding in other areas, including the ability to draw such a crowd, which included many non–Black faces. The Panthers' alliances with other political groups, and especially with white activists—such as Hollywood personalities like Donald Sutherland and Jane Fonda—helped them stay in the spotlight and raise money, some of which went to providing the best possible legal defense teams for Huey and other Panthers facing criminal charges. Inside the courtroom, Charles Garry mounted a passionate defense of Huey that brought the concerns and perspective of the Black Panther Party to light.

Huey's trial would last over a month, and a lot would happen elsewhere in the meantime.

ALLIANCES AND CONFLICTS

Many civil rights groups were more receptive to the Panthers' self-defense platform after King's death, and with the war continuing to build in Vietnam, the anti-war movement among white liberal college students had really taken off.

Anti-war protestors facing off with National Guard outside the Democratic National Convention in Chicago

(Black activists had been among the first to denounce the U.S. involvement in Vietnam, but the movement gained significant traction once white people picked up the mantle.) Both of these populations were finding common cause with the Panthers.

"By framing the practice of armed self-defense as part of a global anti-imperialist struggle, the Panthers were able to draw broad support both from other black political organizations and from non-blacks," explained one historian.

Still, these groups did not always see eye to eye, as the Panthers continued to be more interested in political education and organizing, while the US Organization placed higher value on cultural celebrations of Blackness. And while the Panthers and SNCC did join forces for a time, it was a predictably short-lived partnership, as SNCC shied away from the more militant aspects of the Panther platform.

As for the white protest groups, their goals aligned with the Panthers' only to a certain extent. In August, Bobby Seale went to Chicago to support anti-war demonstrations led by Students for a Democratic Society (SDS), a group composed of white college students. He spoke at their rally outside the Democratic National Convention, attempting to inspire white radicals to join with the Panthers' socialist message. SDS had publicly endorsed the Black Panther Party, but still, the white protestors were not very receptive. Most of them came from more privileged backgrounds and couldn't really identify with the struggles of poor Black people. While several SDS leaders had participated in civil rights demonstrations in the South, like Freedom Rides and voter registration, many white protestors had joined the anti-war movement out of self-interest—they weren't invested in creating a socialist revolution, but simply did not want to fight in the Vietnam War.

The entire nation watched on television as white anti-war demonstrators raged in the streets, physically confronting the police. Mayor Daley's police force was known for its brutal practices. This was the same city in which the mayor had called a shoot-to-kill order on Black citizens who rose up in the days after Dr. King's murder, just a few months before. Outside the Democratic National Convention, police assaulted the protestors with tear gas, clubbed them with batons, and dragged hundreds to jail. But no one got shot. No one was killed. The Panthers couldn't help but wonder: If those hundreds of angry protestors had been Black, how many would have died in the streets of Chicago?

VERDICT

On September 8, a jury of eleven white people and one Black man convicted Huey of manslaughter in the death of Officer Frey. Manslaughter was a lesser charge than murder; it meant the jury believed that the shooting was not planned in advance. Huey was also found not guilty of attempted murder. (The kidnapping charge had been dismissed during the trial.)

It was a mixed outcome. At least Huey would not be executed by the state, but he was still sentenced to serve two to fifteen years in prison. Attorney Charles Garry planned to appeal Huey's case, but for the time being, the Panthers' leader and figurehead would remain behind bars.

Two Oakland police officers expressed their displeasure with the fact that Huey had not been convicted of murder by firing a dozen rounds through the

Bullet holes in the front window of the Panther headquarters after two off-duty police officers fired into the building

front windows of Panther National Headquarters. There is no way to know for sure what the two officers were thinking—they may have been shooting at posters of Huey in the window, or they may have been trying to initiate a firefight with Panthers. Luckily, the office was empty at the time, but it was a reckless act, regardless, as the building also housed apartments. One stray bullet entered a café next door.

"These dudes are breaking the law, but they keep saying *we* are the law-breakers," Bobby said. "It's a felony to shoot inside of any building where people are living."

Even the chief of police recognized the public relations disaster on his hands. The officers were suspended and ultimately fired from the police force, and the police chief publicly appealed to the rest of the force, asking them not to "do anything else" in response to the Huey Newton verdict.

"All that stuff exposed those pigs," Bobby said. "The people saw it for what it was. . . . Every time we turned around those pigs would be blasting people away, arresting dudes, railroading them, and attacking cats."[1]

In court, however, the two officers in question received probation rather than jail time for their felonious actions. Once again, the system proved that the rules were different for white people with guns versus Black people with guns.

---

[1] *Cats* was slang for people, similar to *guys* or *dudes*.

Eldridge Cleaver was still in serious legal trouble over the shootout with police on the night Lil' Bobby Hutton was killed. After he was arrested that night, he had been held in jail for two months, but a judge had released him in June, on the grounds that he was being held solely for political reasons.

A campaign poster for Eldridge's presidential bid

Later that summer, the Panthers collaborated with the Peace and Freedom Party, a liberal political party, to run Eldridge Cleaver for president of the United States. The Peace and Freedom Party took a strong anti-war and anti-racist stance, in contrast to the Democratic Party, which they perceived to be pro-war and ignoring civil rights efforts. Eldridge was an unusual candidate, as a formerly incarcerated Black man with additional charges pending, but the whole point of the movement was to reframe how Americans think about the law and about power. The Panthers knew Eldridge was unlikely to be elected in 1968, but they wanted to advance the national conversation about who can hold power in society, and who deserves to make and benefit from the law.

Over the fall, Eldridge spoke to thousands of students at college campuses across California, bringing them around to the Panthers' platform and the Peace and Freedom Party's message of liberation for all people, until a higher court reconsidered Eldridge's release from prison and ordered him to return. But when police arrived at his home to escort him back to prison on November 27, 1968, Eldridge had disappeared.

Eldridge knew that if he went back to prison, he might never get out, so he chose to go into exile by leaving the country. He traveled first to Cuba, then around Europe, and ultimately settled in Algeria, a nation that had successfully thrown off its colonial oppressors a decade earlier. From there, Eldridge planned to build an international arm of the Black Panther Party and work to unite revolutionary forces worldwide.

ORGANIZATION

Keeping order among the Panthers proved to be very challenging as the organization expanded from a tight local unit in Oakland to a sprawling national movement. It took a great deal of wrangling to get everybody working on the same page.

The Party organized itself in a military style, with a strict hierarchy of power. Each member had specific responsibilities according to their rank and title. The leadership structure was collaborative, with most major decisions routing through a Central Committee made up of senior Panthers and the most experienced organizers, including Huey, Bobby, Kathleen, Eldridge, Emory Douglas, David Hilliard, Ericka and John Huggins (from L.A.), and Masai Hewitt (also from L.A.). For a while, Stokely Carmichael held the title of Field Marshal.

Bobby's role as Chairman kept him busy shaping the Panthers' political voice and supervising the Party's general operations. He helped structure community service programs, organized political rallies and voter registration drives, and often spoke to the press on behalf of the Party.

As Minister of Defense, Huey's stated responsibilities were planning and organizing the Panthers' defense activities. He wrote up policies and procedures for the Panthers' use of weapons and organized the original police patrols in

Oakland. Once in prison, he naturally took a much more limited role, but continued to write and communicate with the rest of the Central Committee. He remained a voice of the Party and a potent symbol of what the Panthers stood for.

As Minister of Information, Eldridge managed the newspaper content, produced Panther flyers and brochures, and released official statements to the press. (Though once he went into exile, his day-to-day responsibilities shifted.) Kathleen worked alongside him as Communications Secretary, tasked with keeping the Central Committee in touch with all the local chapters nationwide. When the Central Committee made decisions, she made sure everyone in the Party knew about them. Emory Douglas worked closely with them as Minister of Culture. He coordinated the newspaper production and created revolutionary art to fill its pages.

Each state chapter had positions that echoed the Central Committee. There would be a Deputy Minister of Defense for the state of Illinois, for example, who would direct weapons training and strategy for all the Panther offices in the state. In addition, local chapter leaders had an entire network of lieutenants, captains, and rank-and-file members reporting to them. Field marshals screened new recruits to be sure they were committed to the Panther movement.

LOCAL LEADERS EMERGE

The major challenge of the Panthers' organizing was to keep everyone pointed in the same direction. In order to make change happen, they needed lots of people to come together and create problems for the white establishment.

The Panthers tapped nineteen-year-old Fred Hampton to lead the Chicago Party. From the time he was sixteen, Fred had organized an NAACP youth chapter on Chicago's West Side. Under his leadership, the group had grown from a few dozen members to a couple hundred. Fred used his organizing skills to build the Panther ranks, too.

Fred Hampton led NAACP youth programs as a high schooler in Chicago. His exceptional leadership and coalition-building skills made him a clear choice for chapter leader when the Panthers came to town. Fred's dynamic public speaking abilities moved people to action and brought national attention to his work. People often compared him to Dr. King and Malcolm X.

Aaron Dixon, already in place in Seattle, faced a similar challenge of how to organize. "We had many recruits," he said, but not a clear idea or "model of exactly what we were supposed to be doing on a daily basis and also in the long term." One thing they did was organize a Speakers Bureau, through which members would go to people's homes, churches, or community meetings to talk about the Panther Ten-Point Platform and educate people about what the Panthers hoped to do. Students, veterans, activists, young parents, and many more from the community turned up to support the Panthers.

Former SNCC activist Joudon Ford stepped forward to lead the New York chapter, along with Chairman David Brothers. New York Black communities were ripe for the movement to take hold. Joudon found himself needing the whole auditorium at a Brooklyn university to hold their monthly political meetings. Many leaders of the city's small economic and political activism groups brought their constituencies over to the Panthers, due to an "emerging consensus that the Panthers epitomized Black Power."

DISTRIBUTION OF POWER

While the Oakland Panthers viewed themselves as the absolute leaders of the entire Party and sought to enforce a strict hierarchy, in reality the story of the Black Panther Party began to shift and change. The Panthers' rallying cry was "All Power to the People," and thanks to effective political education, the people understood. The power was theirs now. It was right and good for Black people to claim control over their home communities and to start creating change. This was, after all, what the Ten-Point Platform boldly demanded.

With Huey in prison, Eldridge in exile, Kathleen soon to join him, and David Hilliard and Bobby scrambling to pick up the slack, new leadership was ripe to emerge.

The Party took on a life of its own in New York, Chicago, Seattle, and everywhere else the Panther flag flew. From 1969 forward, the Party was really defined and sustained by its members on the ground.

Young people offering the Black Power salute outside a Panther office

WITH FISTS RAISED

The symbol of a raised tight fist stood for Black Power. Panthers and other Black nationalist groups used it as a greeting when they met one another and as a way of emphasizing a point. Speeches and meetings typically began and ended with a raised fist and a call for "Black Power!" The Panthers cried "Black Power," too, but their signature chant became "All Power to the People!" The simplicity and the strength of the fist spoke volumes.

Olympic athletes Tommie Smith and John Carlos showed just how powerful such a symbol could be. They won gold and bronze medals in the 200-meter race at the 1968 Summer Olympics in Mexico City. On the podium, as the national anthem played loud and strong, both men bowed their heads and raised their fists, in a show of solidarity with the Black Power movement. The International Olympic Committee subsequently expelled the two athletes from the Games, saying that political acts were against the Olympics' goal of international cooperation. Back home many Americans, too, saw it as a sign of disrespect for the flag and for the country. But the athletes didn't intend to be disrespectful.

They just wanted to call attention to the Black Power movement and the struggles of Black people in their country.

The fist was one of many symbols the Panthers used to express their vision. They sold buttons and posters proclaiming: "Black Power," "All Power to the People," and "Free Huey!" Buttons featured Huey's face, Bobby's face, the silhouette of a rifle, a snarling panther, or a simple fist. An iconic poster of Huey showed him in a high arch-backed wicker chair, wearing his Panther jacket and beret, holding a shotgun in one hand and an African spear in the other. The determined, defiant expression on his face spoke to Black people's desires for power and for a connection to their roots.

LIFE IN THE PARTY

There is no single, national Panther history but rather myriad Panther histories.

—YOHURU WILLIAMS

Fifteen-year-old Jamal Joseph never forgot what he saw on television the day the Panthers stormed the state capitol in Sacramento. So when they came around to his own city, New York, and guys he knew began to join, he was intrigued. More than anything, he wanted a place to put his anger, as well as a place to belong.

Jamal grew up without his parents, raised by his grandmother. She nurtured and protected him, and she did not like the idea of him joining the Panthers. He hid his interest in the group from her, lying to her the first time he went down to a political education class to check out the Panther program.

He didn't have a clear idea of what he was getting himself into. His friends told him rumors about what it would take to become a Panther. "Man, you know you gotta kill a white dude in order to be a Panther," one friend told him.

◀ **Panthers offered loving and protective spaces for people of all ages in their communities.**

"I don't care," Jamal answered, even though the idea made him nervous.

"Naw, get it straight," said another guy. "You have to kill a white cop."

Terrified, Jamal worked to gear himself up for the challenge. He sat through the political education class, listening to the Panther at the front reading through the Ten-Point Platform. Nervous as he was, Jamal wanted so badly to prove himself that he suddenly leaped up and called out: "Choose me, brother. Arm me and send me on a mission. I'll kill whitey right now."

The Panther called Jamal forward, reached into the desk, and pulled out a stack of books. He handed them to Jamal, who said, "Excuse me, brother, I thought you were going to arm me."

The Panther answered, "Excuse me, young brother, I just did."

Jamal was not the only young wannabe Panther who learned this hard lesson on day one. Arming themselves mentally interested the Panthers more than arming themselves with guns. In early 1968, the Black Panther Party dropped "Self-Defense" from its name to de-emphasize the role of guns in the organization, but it wasn't so easy to shrug off the striking image that had put the Panthers on the map.

The Party attracted young people for many different reasons—frustration, activism, a desire to lash out—but all were soon united by the determination to bring Power to the People.

RULES FOR MEMBERSHIP

Among the strict rules for Panther Party members was the commitment to attend political education classes for a while prior to receiving weapons training.

"Guns were around, but in a drawer or a closet, and not as constant companions to Panthers on duty," Jamal said. "There was a lot of talk in Panther literature and speeches about armed revolution, but it was made clear that the duty of a Panther was to organize and teach so that the political consciousness of the broad masses of people could be raised to the point that they were ready to engage in revolution."

Many of the sisters and brothers who showed up eager to fight were confused by the Panthers' view of education and solidarity as the path to revolution. They understood revolution to mean blood in the streets, really taking it to the Man once and for all. Instead, they got a bunch of homework and talking.

"At each Wednesday-night meeting, there would be fifty to a hundred new recruits," Elaine Brown said about the L.A. chapter. "Many did not return. They were driven away by the discipline and the reading."

This strategy made for a highly structured and organized membership within each chapter. Rules were strict, including rules for how firearms were to be used and handled—never without training, never under the influence, and never pointed at anyone unnecessarily. Further rules governed how Panthers fulfilled their day-to-day responsibilities. As membership expanded, it became necessary to formalize these expectations in writing. In early 1968, the Central Committee developed a list of ten rules for Panther Party members, which they published regularly in the *Black Panther*. By early 1969, they had expanded the list to twenty-six rules and included a list of Eight Points of Attention. Every Panther was expected to memorize these rules and the Ten-Point Platform and be able to recite them verbatim—exactly as written—anytime they were asked.

"When I came out of high school, I was semi-illiterate," said Ajamu Strivers of the Sacramento chapter. The Panthers' political education meetings changed that. The class offered a different balance of structure and support than he had found in school. "They would help you with the words you couldn't read—there were a lot of them. They'd say the word with you. Then you'd interpret the meaning of that paragraph."

"It gave me more self-confidence," Ajamu said. "Nobody was snickering or laughing, because it wasn't like that." Building that kind of intellectual confidence in their membership was vital in the Panthers' view. They believed revolution would be successful only when all Black people fully understood the forces of society that were acting against them and could stand up and protest with one voice.

EIGHT POINTS OF ATTENTION

1. Speak politely.

2. Pay fairly for what you buy.

3. Return everything you borrow.

4. Pay for anything you damage.

5. Do not hit or swear at people.

6. Do not damage property or crops of the poor, oppressed masses.

7. Do not take liberties with women.

8. If we ever have to take captives do not ill-treat them.

RULES OF THE BLACK PANTHER PARTY

CENTRAL HEADQUARTERS
OAKLAND, CALIFORNIA

Every member of the BLACK PANTHER PARTY throughout the country of racist America must abide by these rules as functional members of this party. CENTRAL COMMITTEE members, CENTRAL STAFFS, and LOCAL STAFFS, including all captains subordinated to either national, state, and local leadership of the BLACK PANTHER PARTY will enforce these rules. Length of suspension or other disciplinary action necessary for violation of these rules will depend on national decisions by national, state or state area, and local committees and staffs where said rule or rules of the BLACK PANTHER PARTY WERE VIOLATED.

Every member of the party must know these verbatim and by heart. And apply them daily. Each member must report any violation of these rules to their leadership or they are counter-revolutionary and are also subjected to suspension by the BLACK PANTHER PARTY.

THE RULES ARE:

1. No party member can have narcotics or weed in his possession while doing party work.

2. Any party member found shooting narcotics will be expelled from the party.

3. No party member can be drunk while doing daily party work.

4. No party member will violate rules relating to office work, general meetings of the BLACK PANTHER PARTY, and meetings of the BLACK PANTHER PARTY ANYWHERE.

5. No party member will USE, POINT, or FIRE a weapon of any kind unnecessarily or accidentally at anyone.

6. No party member can join any other army force other than the BLACK LIBERATION ARMY.

7. No party member can have a weapon in his possession while DRUNK or loaded off narcotics or weed.

8. No party member will commit any crimes against other party members or BLACK people at all, and cannot steal or take from the people, not even a needle or a piece of thread.

9. When arrested, BLACK PANTHER MEMBERS will give only name, address and will sign nothing. Legal first aid must be understood by all Party members.

10. The Ten-Point Program and platform of the BLACK PANTHER PARTY must be known and understood by each Party member.

11. Party Communications must be National and Local.

12. The 10-10-10 program should be known by all members and also understood by all members.

13. All Finance officers will operate under the jurisdiction of the Ministry of Finance.

14. Each person will submit a report of daily work.

15. Each Sub-Section Leaders, Section Leaders and Lieutenants, Captains, must submit Daily reports of work.

16. All Panthers must learn to operate and service weapons correctly.

17. All Leadership personnel who expel a member must submit this information to the Editor of the Newspaper so that it will be published in the paper and will be known by all chapters and branches.

18. Political Education Classes are mandatory for general membership.

19. Only office personnel assigned to respective offices each day should be there.

All others are to sell papers and do Political work out in the community, including Captains, Section Leaders, etc.

20. COMMUNICATIONS—all chapters must submit weekly reports in writing to the National Headquarters.

21. All Branches must implement First Aid and/or Medical Cadres.

22. All Chapters, Branches, and components of the BLACK PANTHER PARTY must submit a monthly Financial Report to the Ministry of Finance, and also to the Central Committee.

23. Everyone in a leadership position must read no less than two hours per day to keep abreast of the changing political situation.

24. No chapter or branch shall accept grants, poverty funds, money or any other aid from any government agency without contacting the National Headquarters.

25. All chapters must adhere to the policy and the ideology laid down by the CENTRAL COMMITTEE of the BLACK PANTHER PARTY.

26. All Branches must submit weekly reports in writing to their respective chapters.

Originally printed in the *Black Panther,* January 4, 1969

PANTHERS IN THE MAKING

Panther recruits eventually received weapons training, learning how to aim and fire different guns, how to put them together, and how to handle them safely. Jamal and other recruits even had to learn how to put a gun together blindfolded, so that they would be skilled enough to do so in the dark if they ever needed to. Panthers applied for legal firearms permits to own weapons, and if a criminal background prevented them from being able to get one, they learned to use guns that belonged to other members. The goal was for everyone in the Party to be proficient at using them—but also for the guns to be legally owned and registered.

Panthers gathered for physical education, too, learning hand-to-hand combat and keeping themselves in good physical condition with jogging, calisthenics, and group drills. Panthers lined up on the streets or in city parks in rank-and-file order like a military unit, chanting and jumping and keeping themselves physically and mentally energized for the work ahead of them.

They had to write down "what happened from the time you came into the office to the time you went off duty at the end of the day," New York Panther Safiya Bukhari said, and turn it in to the supervisor. If a Panther broke a rule or was late, they would be "brought up on charges" and disciplined. The discipline usually involved either physical activity, like running around the block; political education, like having to read a book and write a paper about it; or simply an extra duty, like cleaning up around the Panther office. The Panthers thought discipline should be productive for the member and the Party.

DAY-TO-DAY BUSINESS

Day-to-day work in the Party was exhausting and often grueling. Panthers routinely worked eighteen-hour days, doing whatever needed to be done at the moment. "Your role was to do what people taught you to do, and do it well," said Phyllis Jackson, who served the Party at National Headquarters in Oakland.

Aaron Dixon (*right*) speaking with Vanetta Molson in the Seattle office. Vanetta ran the free breakfast and health clinic programs for that chapter.

"People observed you and saw what your skills were. You didn't apply for a position. You were selected and assigned based on what you had done previously."

Tasks around the office ranged from making phone calls and writing letters to organizing food drives or clothing drives. "The easiest way to say it is just to imagine worker bees," said Claudia Chesson-Williams, of the Corona, Queens, branch in New York City. The chapters varied widely in the total number of members—perhaps ranging from around a dozen to nearly a hundred—but at any given time you might find anywhere from a half dozen to several dozen members on duty.

Many Panther members lived on the proceeds from newspaper sales because they didn't have another job. Safiya Bukhari sold the *Black Panther* in Harlem. For each paper she sold at twenty-five cents, she turned in fifteen cents to the Panther office and got to keep ten cents for herself. Selling the paper was risky because police constantly targeted Panther members.

"I was told to get off the corner," Safiya said. "I was down on Forty-second Street selling papers, and I was told to move on by the police. . . . A uniformed officer got out his gun and his nightstick and I moved." Safiya felt lucky not to be arrested that day for selling the papers. "Police arresting people was a daily thing. . . . We had to go in pairs, so that if one person got arrested, the other one could call the office to tell people."

Panther members constantly risked arrest when they went out on Party business. If they got in trouble, their first phone call would be to the Panther office, so someone always had to be at the other end of the line.

On the flip side, when the Panthers had news they wanted to share with the community, they implemented their 10-10-10 Rule: When there was a meeting or action, everyone was responsible for contacting ten people to tell them about it. Those ten people would then each tell ten more people, and word would spread quickly through the neighborhood, even for those without telephones. The same was true of Panther recruits on a broader level—each person the Panthers trained was expected to turn around and share their knowledge by seeking to educate and empower ten others.

Back in Oakland, Big Man Howard took care of basic office tasks. He spent a lot of time answering phones and opening mail. He came in and opened the office at nine a.m. every day, so that the office would have regular hours that people could count on. He would intercept people who came in wanting to join, telling them about what was required of members.

Sitting behind a desk, surrounded by piles of Panther books, posters, and newspapers, Big Man accepted donations, sold newspapers, and sorted the good mail from the bad. A typical mail delivery might contain some news clippings that a supporter sent in, a few donations by cash or check, a letter of thanks from someone the Panthers had helped, an invitation for Huey or Bobby to come speak somewhere, and often a few pieces of hate mail or death threats.

External threats and concerns were ever present in the Party, but Panthers took it all in stride, one day at a time.

Jamal Joseph rose quickly through the Panther ranks and became a section leader at the age of sixteen. Once he'd received his own training, he began leading political education classes himself and teaching others gun-handling skills and weapons safety. The New York Panthers placed him in charge of their youth cadre, a group of about twenty high-school-aged Panthers.

Section leaders were assigned an area of about five or six city blocks to manage. They would get very familiar with everyone living or working in their section—tenants, business owners, landlords, schools, churches, and so on. Talking to people was the rule. If you were selling the paper, you talked to people. If you were working in the office, you talked to anyone who came in. "It all started by going door-to-door," said Billy X Jennings, a leader in the East Oakland office. "How else were you going to know who was in your section?"

Getting to know people helped build trust within the community. Section leaders paid attention to community concerns in their area—complaints about housing code violations, an infiltration of rats in the neighborhood, or an incident of police brutality. The section leader's job was to catalog these complaints and help organize actions in response. Panthers gathered signatures on petitions, coordinated boycotts, and educated people about their legal rights so they would not be taken advantage of by ruthless landlords and local politicians who seemed not to care about people's suffering.

Because of their constant presence, people in the communities learned that they could turn to the Panthers for help with any problem, small or large. "The Panther office became the emergency center for damn near everything," said New York Panther Thomas McCreary. Whenever "people had emergencies, they would come to us." If there were roaches on the block, people came. If there were police bothering somebody down the street, people came. If the heat was off and the landlord wasn't fixing it, people came. If a young mother needed someone

to watch her children, she brought them down to the office, and the Panthers would get somebody to watch them while she took care of whatever business she needed to.

"We had a grievance board," said Billy X Jennings. "Instead of calling the police . . . you could call the Panther office. We'd come out there and try to settle the argument." The Panthers made it a point to really be there for people, and Black communities grew to love them. And above all, the Black Panthers loved the people right back.

FOR LOVE OF THE PEOPLE

For rank-and-file Panthers who showed up to serve the community day after day, their motivation came from their deep and abiding love for Black people. Regardless of how they came to the Party in the first place, they stayed because they discovered "this idea of love, this undying love for the people," according to Jamal Joseph.

"It's love that would make you work in the welfare centers and the housing takeovers, and organizing the schools and then do those community patrols and then sell newspapers and try to raise money for political prisoners," Jamal said. "It's love that would make you, when you . . . saw the cops had somebody against the wall with their guns drawn, that would make you [go] stand between those cops and those drawn guns for someone that you hadn't met but that you understood was your brother or sister."

The Panthers loved the people enough to put themselves on the line day in and day out, in hopes of making a better community and a better world for their fellow citizens. They loved enough to give up their lives for the people. And they showed up to work each day knowing that death was a genuine risk.

Their individual sacrifice would be worth it, they felt, if it moved the community forward. "I knew I was fighting for my rights," said Cyril Innis Jr., known as Brother Bullwhip, from the Corona, Queens, branch. "I was fighting for something that I truly believed in my heart."

Serving barbecue to the crowd at a Free Huey rally. Panthers took care of people's basic survival needs, so food and fellowship were a big part of most Panther gatherings.

The Panthers took care of one another as well as the community. "When you joined the party, and you were there for a while . . . [t]he party became your family," said Madalynn "Carol" Rucker, a San Francisco Panther. "We were in that very vulnerable situation together, not unlike soldiers. You just trusted that people would have your back, and you had to be willing to have theirs."

Full-time Panthers typically lived together in houses and small apartments, known as "Panther pads." They shared food, clothes, and resources. Many were so committed to the Panther mission that they gave up regular jobs so they could devote themselves fully to the movement.

The median age of Panther members was nineteen, so people's personal circumstances varied widely. There were members in high school or college; there were young twenty-somethings entering the workforce; there were parents with small children. Plenty of Panthers, especially younger teenagers, still lived at home with parents, grandparents, or other elders.

For everyone, the Panther office itself became a second home, full of food, affection, and camaraderie. After political education class, "you would eat dinner," Jamal Joseph said. "There'd be a big pot of food," and everyone would gather round to eat and socialize.

"I set up cooking crews," Bobby Seale said. "We had sixty to seventy-five people working out of the national headquarters. . . . Some of the other chapters and branches may have had ten or twenty. But they cooked their own meals."

Kathleen Cleaver observed Bobby being the one who made sure everyone had something to eat. "He was a parent," she said. "He had a little boy. He had a wife, a sister, a family," and he folded the Panthers as a whole into his fatherly care.

Like Bobby, a lot of Panthers became parents, raising families of their own in the midst of the movement. The community took special care of these Panther cubs. Gloria Abernethy, who worked on the *Black Panther* in Oakland when her daughter was young, said the work was so demanding that "there were times where I had to withdraw from her and let her just be the party's baby." Such was her commitment to the organization, and such was the organization's commitment to supporting her as a woman and mother.

"In a time when the other nationalist organizations were defining women as barefoot, pregnant, and in the kitchen, women in the Black Panther Party were working right alongside men, being assigned sections to organize just like the men, and receiving the same training as the men," said Safiya Bukhari. "Further, the decisions about what a person did within the ranks of the party were determined not by gender but by ability."

Politically and intellectually, the Panthers wrote and spoke passionately about gender equity. Women readily took on leadership roles and participated in weapons training for self-defense. The bylines in an average issue of the *Black Panther* newspaper illustrated the extent to which women's words, presence, and ideas were foundational to the Party's vision and ideology.

Nevertheless, sexism did still rear its ugly head within the Party ranks. "Men and women don't stop being in the roles we were trained to play because we join an organization, right?" said Ericka Huggins. "The socialization was there before we joined the BPP."

As an organization founded by men, with an aggressive, stereotypically masculine public image, the Panthers had to work hard to counteract social conditioning. Many early recruits, young men who had never been offered power and self-determination before, were drawn to the Party because of that hypermasculine image. Even as the Panthers' mission became more grounded in stereotypically feminine pursuits—caregiving, food programs, education, community uplift— it proved difficult to overcome ingrained gender biases. The prevailing views of the Party by media and outsiders reinforced how some members viewed the gender dynamics.

"Whatever was going on in the community and society as a whole was reflected in the interaction of the members of the Party," Safiya said. The Panthers fought against all forms of oppression, and sometimes it meant fighting against themselves. Just as they struggled to educate Black people about history and politics, and to overcome the racism in society, they struggled to overcome sexism in their own ranks.

"We used criticism and self-criticism to beat back the various levels of male chauvinist activity," Bobby explained. This concept was introduced by Audrea Jones, the leader of the Massachusetts Black Panther Party. "If I made a mistake of saying something, a sister came to me and told me, 'Chairman, you shouldn't . . .'" When women raised concerns, he listened and sought to understand what they were saying so he could adjust his behavior. In so doing, he modeled a way of learning and addressing deep issues. This was the ideal, if not always perfectly replicated. "Do not take liberties with women" was included in the Eight Points of Attention to make extra sure that all members understood the importance of respect.

A Panther feeding a small child at a Free Huey rally

"In changing this society, we have to change how we deal with each other," Safiya said. "We have to acknowledge that there is something wrong with how we view each other, how we deal with each other, and how we think of each other." This idea went deep into the Panthers' beliefs about education and the potential for both individual and community transformation.

"There were too many different personalities for everybody to think we were always happy and laid back," said Margo Rose-Brunson of the Sacramento chapter. But life in the Panther ranks always came back to a radical love and desire to care for one another with compassion and justice.

A LIFETIME COMMITMENT

The love, meaning, and connection to be found within the Panther sphere was constantly juxtaposed against the challenge of moving through the world as Panthers, and by the fact that the country's law enforcement agencies were not prepared to let a Black revolutionary movement stand unopposed. For all the warmth and comfort that the Panthers sought to provide, they knew that at any moment the other shoe could drop.

"I got arrested a lot," said Richard Brown. "That was one of the tactics they used to drain our resources and undermine the Party." The Panthers hoped to draw attention to the way the so-called justice system was being used to punish the community for trying to organize. The constant arrests caused the Panthers to pay bail bonds for members on an almost daily basis. This meant the Panthers were constantly required to pay money to the government to ensure their members' freedom. "I was good business for them," Richard said.

As Ronald Freeman, from the L.A. chapter, put it, the government "worked so hard to keep things from changing that it made me become more dedicated to seeing things change. . . . I thought my efforts and the work . . . were going to really bring about social change."

**Panthers at a
Free Huey rally**

Membership in the Black Panther Party required making a lifetime commitment to advancing the struggle. They devoted their lives in their entirety to the people. "We thought about death and dying," said J. Yasmeen Sutton, from the Corona chapter. "That's not natural for young people. But we were blinded by our love and devotion. I think that's what revolution is."

"It was an honor to be a Panther," Brother Bullwhip said, "and if I were to die, to die as a Panther."

SURVIVAL
PENDING
REVOLUTION

If we suffer genocide, we won't be around to change things.

—HUEY P. NEWTON

The Panthers' work cast new light on a painful truth: Black people in the United States existed in a state of peril. The Panthers' Ten-Point Platform called for systemic change, and it would take time to build Black communities that were organized and empowered enough to wage revolution. The challenge facing the Panthers was not only how best to fight for justice, but how to survive long enough to continue the struggle.

What community has the energy to fight a revolution when half its people are starving? Who has time to think about raising their voice when they can't afford the medication to heal a simple cough? Black communities had basic needs that weren't being met—not by the government, and certainly not by the private industry that American capitalism championed. To the Panthers, this lack of

◀ **A child enjoying a meal at the Free Breakfast for School Children Program** public support for the poorest citizens was a form of genocide—a systematic attempt to destroy a particular community or race of people.

The dawn of 1969 saw three things happening simultaneously in the life of the Black Panther Party. First, membership continued expanding and the Panthers' reach into Black communities grew deeper and more sustainable. Second, the organization moved beyond political education and armed self-defense, implementing a series of visionary social service programs that was revolutionary in its own right and drew a diverse coalition of allies to their cause. Third, the police response to the Black Power movement became increasingly organized and vicious. Survival remained an open question, not only for the Panthers themselves, but for the entire Black community.

SURVIVAL PROGRAMS

A January 1969 article in the *Black Panther* proclaimed that until a full revolution was possible, "we must concentrate on the immediate needs of the people, in order to build a united political force, based on the ideology of the Black Panther Party. Survival pending Revolution is our immediate task and to do this we must meet the needs of the people."

The survival programs took up the concrete task of providing food, clothing, medicine, and other necessities for people in need, via meal services, food pantries, clothing drives, free community health clinics, and dozens of other projects implemented nationwide. The programs were staffed by support volunteers from the community, while Black Panther Party members provided guidance and leadership.

"The legacy of the Black Panther Party is the way in which we organized people," said Ericka Huggins. The Panthers understood that people would "participate in their own upliftment" if they understood the importance of stepping up, and if their basic needs were met along the way.

"Our children need a nourishing breakfast every morning so they can learn," wrote Gwen Hodges in an article for the *Black Panther* announcing the Panthers' plans to create a free breakfast program to help starving children in Black communities.

The first breakfast program was established in Oakland in January 1969. A local church, St. Augustine, hosted the program. Panthers and volunteers from the community came in early to cook the food, serve the meal, and clean up afterward. A typical breakfast meal might be eggs and bacon served with bread and fresh fruit, or pancakes with sausages and canned fruit salad. Panther chapters around the country began implementing free breakfast programs, too. By the end of 1969, more than twenty chapters had at least one breakfast site up and running.

Safiya Bukhari volunteered in a Panther breakfast program in New York. "I got up early in the morning and went over to Chambers Street Memorial Church in Manhattan and made breakfast for the children. I cooked breakfast for them and helped them with their homework and got them off to school."

The most challenging part was getting enough food to serve. Panther members went door to door, visiting local businesses and asking for support. Local community restaurants, grocery stores, and businesses donated food whenever

Panther volunteers led the children in songs over the meal. One call-and-response lyric went: "Black is beautiful!" "Free Huey!" "Set our warrior free!" "Free Huey!"

Panther volunteers arrived early to prepare breakfast for the children.

they could to help out. One place might offer several pounds of bacon per month, while another sent a few cartons of eggs every week. When the breakfast programs reached peak attendance, Panthers chapters served a total of about ten thousand breakfasts each day nationwide.

The Panthers' declaration that well-fed children would perform better in school has since been supported by numerous scientific research studies. Hunger caused more than physical suffering—it handed Black children serious disadvantages that affected every aspect of their lives, including their chances for a brighter future.

Marsha Turner joined the Panthers at age fifteen. In 1968, she became the head of the national Free Breakfast for School Children initiative.

Schoolchildren were not the only ones going hungry. Parents often showed up to the breakfast along with their children. Building on the success of the free breakfasts, the Panthers' Free Food Program established food pantries to support those who could barely afford to feed their families. Each family would receive a week's worth of groceries, including important staples like milk, bread, eggs, rice, potatoes, chicken, cereal, and canned goods.

Panthers sought donations to help secure trucks and refrigerators to store and transport the food. They rented warehouses and received deliveries from grocery stores and wholesale food distributors to fill the bags. Local stores donated the food items, as they did for the breakfasts.

The smallest local businesses, like mom-and-pop groceries and corner stores, could not always afford to give much, but many did their best to contribute. That was fine with the Panthers. If they were able to get ten stores to give just a dozen eggs each, they could feed a lot of people. Participation mattered.

The businesses that refused to donate at all tended to be larger businesses, including some regional chain grocery stores, like Safeway in Oakland. The Panthers set up a picket line in front of the store, encouraging people to spend their money elsewhere. They even provided shuttles down the street to a smaller grocery that supported the breakfast program. One of their picket signs read: SUPPORT THE STORE THAT SUPPORTS THE SURVIVAL PROGRAMS.

Boycotts encouraged communities to use their economic power to speak up for their needs. They sought to spend their limited resources at community-owned businesses, where it would do the most good for the local people.

By engaging local stores in the program, the Panthers wanted to enact point three on the Ten-Point Platform: "an end to the robbery by the white man of our Black Community." When stores charged higher rates for food and basic necessities than people in the neighborhood could afford, Black citizens were starving while the store owners (mostly white) made money. The Panther program encouraged store owners to "lower their prices in order to maintain their businesses in the community, and as a result . . . become unified with the people in the fight against economic exploitation."

The owners of Safeway began losing business because so many people were shopping elsewhere. They accused the Panthers of trying to blackmail them into donating to the food programs. In the Panthers' view, they were simply making the community members aware that they had a choice about what kind of business to support. Why should Black citizens spend their hard-earned money to line the pockets of already-wealthy white businessmen who chose to prioritize their own profits over helping to feed hungry Black children?

UNDER A MICROSCOPE

The Panthers had gained such a strong reputation for militancy that plenty of people were surprised to see them developing community programs. Some people wondered if a group like the Black Panthers could even be trusted to provide food to children or to be responsible for people's health and well-being.

"While I was working with the breakfast program, the number of children attending started dropping off," Safiya said. "What we found out was that the police were telling the parents we were poisoning the children . . . to keep us from feeding them, they were saying we were giving them poisoned food." For her, it was a moment of awakening about "how the police lie, how the system lies and hurts people."

It turned out that the police had also been telling local businesses that the food was not being used as it should be. These lies made it more difficult for the Panthers to get donations temporarily, but over time the business owners saw with their own eyes that the Panthers were doing good work to help people, and donations flowed freely again.

THE PEOPLE'S FREE MEDICAL CLINICS

Beginning in 1969, the Panthers opened the People's Free Medical Clinics in their communities, to provide people with access to doctors and medications that they could not otherwise afford. The clinics represented another form of self-defense,

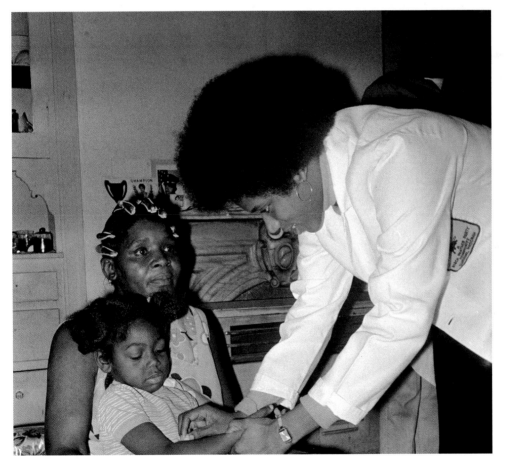

A doctor examining patients at the Panthers' free medical clinic in Los Angeles

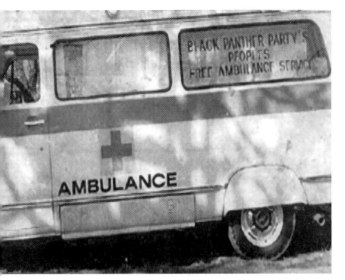

The Winston-Salem chapter's free ambulance service

a response to biomedical neglect, as Black people have consistently been a medically underserved population.

White and Black doctors alike, as well as medical and nursing students, volunteered their time to staff the clinics, and the Panthers collected donations to help provide equipment and medications. The clinics provided basic medical care and first aid to poor people of all ages and races, including treatment for illnesses, screening for common conditions, immunizations, physical exams, blood tests, and all forms of preventive medicine. When someone needed more advanced services, like a hospital or a specialist, the clinic would help them get those services.

The first health clinic opened in Oakland in 1969, and within a year the Panthers had opened (or had plans to open) clinics associated with every chapter nationwide, in cities including Chicago, Des Moines, Detroit, Kansas City, New York, Memphis, Dallas, Los Angeles, and Seattle.

In Winston-Salem, North Carolina, Black people had trouble getting the county ambulance service to serve them. When Black citizens called for help, the ambulance attendants sometimes demanded payment before they would bring a Black person to the hospital. "They were leaving a lot of people at home, and we had people who died," said chapter leader Larry Little. So a few Panthers went to the community college and took emergency medical technician training. They raised funds to purchase a brand-new ambulance and started the Joseph Waddell People's Free Ambulance Service, named for a local Panther who died in prison.

Panther Leonard Colar helping an elder with her shopping as part of the Senior Escort program ▶

A MULTITUDE OF NEEDS

The Panthers' feeding programs and health clinics responded to the communities' most urgent needs. But their help didn't stop there. In some cities, they also operated the People's Free Shoe Program and the People's Free Clothing Program, supporting other basic needs. All these services were provided completely free of charge, fueled by donations and volunteer labor.

Some communities offered prison busing, so that people could visit loved ones who were locked up. They continued a variety of legal aid services, including bailing out members who were arrested and securing volunteer attorneys.

Several cities offered a bodyguard service for senior citizens, called SAFE. Older community members often received monthly payments from Social Security, a government fund that helps take care of retired people. Many seniors did not have bank accounts, so when they would receive a check in the mail, they simply cashed it. The problem was, they then had to walk home from the bank carrying a large sum of cash, which typically was all the money they had to

cover their living expenses for that month. Clever thieves learned the pattern of when the checks would arrive, making these seniors prime targets for mugging. Through SAFE, Panther members would escort seniors to and from the bank to protect them from would-be thieves. This seemingly small act of support did a lot of systemic good by preventing seniors from going hungry or losing their homes.

Each of these programs arose in response to the vital needs expressed by a community. The Panthers paid close attention, making observations about the micro-level challenges their neighbors faced and setting out to solve them.

A VICIOUS BACKLASH

The Panther survival programs immediately came under police scrutiny. Jamal Joseph was serving at a breakfast program in New York City when police stormed in, declaring that they were there to search for illegal weapons. That day, the police left after only exchanging a few harsh words with the volunteers, but there were many instances where police would enter a breakfast site and tear the place up, frightening the children and staff.

In one particularly upsetting incident, the police raided a breakfast program site in Chicago, acting on a warrant to search for illegal weapons. The found no such weapons. Then, in what appeared to be an act of frustration or retaliation, they piled the Panthers' entire food supply in the middle of the kitchen floor and set fire to it. Panther health clinics were similarly raided and emptied, with medicine and supplies confiscated or destroyed by police.

The aggressive and violent police response to even the most humane Panther programs lent credence to the Panthers' accusation of genocide. If Black people couldn't be allowed to feed themselves or take care of their bodies without being directly challenged and obstructed by the political systems of the country, that certainly suggested a coordinated effort to destroy Black lives.

The survival programs quickly became the central piece of the Black Panther Party's mission. People who wanted to participate in the Black Power movement but didn't want to carry guns and wage war against police officers came forward to help, and community involvement in Panther programs surged.

"We say that the survival program of the Black Panther Party is like the survival kit of a sailor stranded on a raft," said Huey P. Newton. "It helps him to sustain himself until he can get completely out of that situation."

Even as the Panthers' programs evolved further and further from armed self-defense, their rhetoric about race and the economy continued to challenge the power dynamic. The survival programs were not in themselves a cure for the chronic disease of oppression, but a temporary fix for some of its worst symptoms.

"We did everything we did so that people would feel empowered to make changes in the world they live in and then go beyond that smaller circle to the larger one and develop a global understanding," said Ericka Huggins. "I saw this with my own eyes. It was brilliant."

"When consciousness and understanding is raised to a high level then the community will seize the time and deliver themselves from the boot of their oppressor," Huey said. In the meantime, "if they have a need we will serve their needs and attempt to get them to understand the true reasons why they are in need in such an incredibly rich land."

ALL POWER TO THE PEOPLE

A chicken just doesn't have it within its system to produce a duck egg. It can't do it. It can only produce according to what that particular system was constructed to produce. The system in this country cannot produce freedom for an Afro-American. It is impossible for this system, this economic system, this political system, this system, period. It's impossible for this system, as it stands, to produce freedom right now for the black man in this country.

And if ever a chicken did produce a duck egg, I'm quite sure you would say it was certainly a revolutionary chicken!

—MALCOLM X

The Panthers' survival programs frightened the U.S. government as much as the threat of violence against police. As they reached out to help people in need, the Panthers began talking less about the divide between Black and white, and more about the divide between rich and poor. They no longer talked only about civil

◁ The Panthers' survival programs drew people to the movement, which led to broad-scale community empowerment and engagement.

rights for Black people, but human rights for all. Their shifting rhetoric concerned the U.S. government because it brought human rights and socialism to the forefront. The Cold War was still going on, and anyone talking about socialism was considered an enemy of the state.

MARXIST-LENINIST THEORY

The Black Panthers' beliefs built upon the ideas of political thinkers who came before them. Karl Marx and Friedrich Engels wrote *The Communist Manifesto* in 1848, and the theories they wrote about became known as Marxism. At the time, the Industrial Revolution was spreading across the world, and new inventions and technology were making it easier for people to do things like harvest crops, do metalworking and woodworking, and make clothes.

These technologies transformed the way people produced goods to sell, and as they developed, people became more and more reliant on machines, equipment, and other tools to help them do their work. The people who owned and controlled these tools and technology had great power in society. This is why plantation owners in the South during Reconstruction had so much power over the sharecroppers—they owned the land and the tools used to farm it. As Black people migrated north, the people in power were factory owners and landlords. Regular workers who did not own land or tools could not participate in the economy unless the owners allowed them to.

Marxist theory criticizes capitalism, saying that it is unfair to the workers, who make up the majority of the population. A few wealthy people own all of the factories, farms, and businesses, which Marxists refer to as the "means of production." Workers sell their labor to these owners in exchange for wages, but those wages represent only a small portion of the profits that their work earned. For example, the owner of a factory with one hundred employees that brings in profits of $100,000 per month might pay each worker just $200 per month, allowing him to keep $80,000 for himself, even though he did none of the physical labor. Marxists ask: Did the owner really work for what he earned? Is it fair for the workers to toil and then have the products of their labor essentially stolen?

This structure results in a social class system in which wealthy owners (also called the bourgeoisie) form the upper class while poor workers (also called the proletariat) form the lower classes.

The Marxist solution to this problem is to take control of the means of production away from the factory owner and give it to the workers. In other words, if that same factory were owned by the workers, each employee would receive $1,000 a month for their effort, in addition to having a say in any major decisions about the company.

In the 1920s, a Russian leader named Vladimir Lenin offered his own spin on Marxism, which became known as Leninism. Lenin talked about the political challenges of overcoming a social class system. He suggested that a vanguard party needed to act first, showing the people how to change their system. (*Vanguard* means going first or leading the way.) Revolution would follow, Lenin said.

The Panthers called themselves Marxist-Leninist because they agreed with the points of view Marx and Lenin expressed. They considered themselves the vanguard party, and their slogan "All Power to the People" reflected that belief. Under American capitalism, a few people at the top (mostly white men) held all the political, economic, and social power. The Panthers criticized these "capitalist pigs" who owned all the property, ran all the businesses, and controlled the government. These wealthy white individuals controlled how many jobs were available, and they deliberately kept wages low, knowing that people would have no choice but to work in order to survive. The Panthers wanted that power distributed among a broader base, so that all people could participate in the system, not just as workers but as stakeholders.

Following Marxist-Leninist theory should ultimately lead to a proletarian revolt, but the Panthers faced numerous barriers to the massive armed revolution they wanted. In the first place, there was social stratification even among Black people. The Panthers' base, the sisters and brothers on the block, were marginally employed or jobless, often even homeless. They would fight because they had little or nothing to lose. (In Marxism, they are known as the "lumpen proletariat," the most economically powerless people.)

The majority of the Black communities, though, were working-class people, with families. Sure, they wanted better wages, better housing, and more opportunities for their children, but they also didn't want to lose what little they already had. They saw how the police responded to the Panthers and knew they'd be risking everything if they joined in.

And if joining in meant taking up arms, plenty of Black Americans didn't want to do it at all. The principle of responding with nonviolence still resonated

with many people, especially older Black folks. That is why people became most excited when the Panthers offered new ways to fight—community service programs and organized activism, like petition signing and workplace strikes. These actions allowed people to use their power to try to change the system without promoting violence.

On top of everything, Black people in the United States were outnumbered. Part of what made armed revolutions successful in Algeria, Ghana, Kenya, Mozambique, and elsewhere was the sheer volume of people available to fight. Black people in African nations had won liberation through guerrilla warfare because the white rulers had been in the minority. If Black Americans were going to succeed in their fight, they needed more people to join their cause. As the Panthers became increasingly socialist and anti-capitalist, they began reaching across lines of race, gender, nationality, and culture to unite the poor and oppressed communities.

RAINBOW COALITION

Although the Panthers had struggled to cooperate with other Black activist groups, like US or SNCC, they managed to reach across racial lines to connect with other ethnic radical groups such as the Red Guards (Chinese American organizers) and the American Indian Movement.

Fred Hampton, the young leader of the Chicago Panthers, proved to be a particularly exceptional organizer. He established what he called a "Rainbow Coalition" of multi-ethnic groups active in Chicago, including the Young Lords (a group of Puerto Rican activists), the Young Patriots (an organization of working-class white people), and Students for a Democratic Society (SDS) (white anti-war protestors).

Fred reached out to Chicago's Black street gangs, as well. The Blackstone Rangers were the largest and most feared group operating on Chicago's South

Panthers discussing politics and
ideology during a Free Huey rally

Side, and Fred met with their leader, Jeff Fort, a number of times, trying to reach an agreement or partnership. For almost a year, Jeff rebuffed Fred's advances. He did not want to give up any power or any territory to the Panthers. What Fred wanted, though, was to bring the Blackstone Ranger members under the Panther banner. By working together, they would have a huge base of people to run Panther community programs and to protect the streets in poor Black neighborhoods, instead of terrorizing them like the Rangers were known for. The Rangers ultimately renamed themselves the Black P. Stone Nation—the *P* stood for *peace*, but the timing also implies a nod to the possible collaboration with the Panthers—and they set about community organizing.

Rainbow Coalition organizations worked together on local Chicago projects, and they also sent representatives to national and international gatherings to show support and unity. The scope of the Panthers' work grew larger and larger.

THE INTERNATIONAL BPP

Eldridge Cleaver, in exile in Algeria, hoped to take the Panthers' efforts global. He arrived in Algiers, the capital of Algeria, in May 1969. There, he established the International Headquarters of the BPP. The Algerian government—made up of people who had come to power through a revolution of their own—backed the Panthers, giving them financial support and military training. Eldridge continued to publicize the Panthers' work as he always had, now on a larger scale.

The Panther movement interested other international governments, too, especially those with socialist or communist leanings. Panther representatives visited North Korea, China, North Vietnam, Cuba, the Dominican Republic, and various nations of Europe. Citizens of Japan, Germany, the Netherlands, and other nations donated funds to help the Panthers.

The Panthers still hoped to gain support from the United Nations, to host their plebiscite among Black Americans. The U.N. had intervened on behalf of colonized people elsewhere in the world, helping to create a safe and fair environment in which to begin the process of restructuring power dynamics. If the U.N. decided to help, they could support Black leaders in their negotiations with the U.S. government, design and implement a process of popular consultation to determine what Black citizens wanted and needed, and intervene to protect Black voters from intimidation or violence by the state. Eldridge lobbied the United Nations from abroad, arguing the Panthers' case. Numerous Panthers who feared arrest in the United States traveled to Algeria to seek asylum and to support the growing international liberation movement.

Front page of the *Black Panther*, August 9, 1969

Living in a place like Algeria, where the people had successfully overthrown the government in a violent revolution, made Eldridge more and more convinced that Black people needed to rise up and claim power with weapons. "Revolution in our lifetime" had been the Panthers' call to arms, after all. Plus, U.N.-supervised plebiscites had typically come about after a period of violence, as a means to restoring peace and ensuring justice. Eldridge hoped to learn from the Algerians about how to wage physical revolution, even while on the home front in the United States, the conversation was shifting toward dialogue, coalitions, and organizing.

THE WOMEN'S MOVEMENT

In reaching across lines of race, culture, geography, and nationality, the Panthers managed a perhaps unprecedented feat of cross-identity organizing. But there was one group already within the Panther ranks whose participation the Party seemed to be taking for granted: women. With all the talk of coalitions and strength in numbers, it became more and more important for the Panthers to address gender discrimination and misogyny (ingrained prejudice against women), especially in Black communities.[1]

While Black people were organizing to gain civil rights, a similar movement was taking place among white women, seeking equal opportunities in education and employment. Several white women's groups allied with the Panthers politically, although these groups did not often take Black women's specific experiences into consideration in their advocacy.

"Our struggle was not a struggle to be liberated so we could move into the workplace, but a struggle to be recognized as human beings," said Safiya Bukhari. Black women had been working for centuries, in and outside the home, but the women's movement painted the whole issue of sexism with a broad white brush. Black women were left to contend with a particular intersection of invisibility, with the white woman at one extreme and the Black man at the other.

"Black women are oppressed because they are black and then on top of that, black women are oppressed by black men," said Panther Roberta Alexander at a conference in 1969. "That has got to go."

Within the Party, women had been fighting this battle all along. Many women

---

[1] The ingrained prejudice against Black women has been termed misogynoir.

Elaine Brown speaking at a fundraising gathering. The free breakfast program and health clinics drew interest from wealthy white donors, many of them women.

were already Black Panther Party leaders, and most Panthers were proud of the fact that men and women alike cooked and served breakfast, and men and women alike took up arms—yet some men in the Party felt domestic tasks should be handled exclusively by women. Some even suggested that Panther women had a responsibility to have sex with Panther men, in order to make and raise a new generation of Black revolutionaries to advance the movement.

Many women criticized Eldridge Cleaver for expressing deeply misogynist views in his book *Soul on Ice*, published in 1968. As a Panther leader, his words carried extra weight. Black women pressed for the Panthers to talk about gender equality right alongside racial equality, and pointed out ways that women in the ranks could receive more recognition and equal treatment.

It was unusual at that time for a Black Power organization (or any organization) to take a formal stance in favor of women's rights. But the Panthers did. In the summer of 1969, Eldridge apologized for his misogynistic writing, saying, "The liberation of women is one of the most important issues. . . . [I]f we go around and call ourselves a vanguard organization, then we've got to be the vanguard in all our behavior, and also [set an example] in the area of women's liberation."

Huey addressed the (white) women's movement by saying that the Panthers should see women's rights activists as allies. As fellow oppressed people, he said, women of all races should join the fight for freedom and self-determination.

Did these words solve all gender issues within the Party? Certainly not. "But the enemy of our people will not wait for us to resolve the questions of gender and sexism," Safiya wrote. "Those of us who are truly about the work of making revolution and creating a revolutionary culture must be willing to die the death of a thousand cuts." And, frankly, Black women were already long accustomed to suffering the ills of the world. The Panther movement, however imperfect, gave them the opportunity to create new mechanisms and new language to confront all aspects of that suffering, and to work to overturn it.

And work they did. By 1970, women made up a significant majority of Black Panther Party members and volunteers.

"Women *were* the party," said Ericka Huggins, and yet the mainstream view of the organization continued to be the stock image of Black men with guns. Even with the onset of the survival programs, which responded to stereotypically feminine concerns of community caregiving, the Panthers' image could not be de-masculinized. National media regularly covered police raids on Panther spaces, but said little about the social programs going on in those establishments.

The cultural tendency to prioritize the experiences, words, and images of men contributed—and continues to contribute—to an erasure of women's presence as the bedrock of the Panther movement.

STRENGTH IN NUMBERS

The Panthers needed women in their ranks. They needed white allies. They needed people young and old, rich and poor, to stand up alongside them. They needed everyone they could get—especially since so many of their leaders were being imprisoned, killed, harassed, or forced into exile.

The most effective avenue to change was economic pressure applied by large numbers of people. In fact, it was the only thing that had ever been effective. In the civil rights era, Woolworth's had integrated its lunch counters because the

Panthers and community members marching in a picket line during a boycott while members of the Panthers' singing group, the Lumpen, perform at the center ▶

store lost money every day that Black students sat in. Same with the Montgomery Bus Boycott. Those outcomes had been celebrated, despite the fact that the manner of victory revealed a lot about how flawed and how racist the system was: white-owned businesses were not motivated to change out of a desire for actual justice or a moral recognition that all races should be treated equally; they were solely motivated by a desire to mitigate damage and loss of profits.

The Panthers applied this concept in their work. Panther section leaders organized rent strikes to protest poor living conditions and boycotts of local businesses to force higher wages for employees or lower prices for customers. Using the strength of numbers and their collective economic power proved effective. Black people saw the Panthers succeeding at these small-scale efforts, and they became energized.

"We worked closely with teacher unions in the city of Oakland, and when the teachers were going to go out on strike we aligned with them," said Billy X Jennings. The Panthers helped organize worker strikes at a General Motors plant in California and sent volunteers to demonstrate alongside Cesar Chavez and the United Farm Workers. "The work the party did with unions is rarely covered," said Billy X, but it was a powerfully effective example of the organizing the Panthers hoped to see across all aspects of Black community life.

"The power of the oppressor rests upon the submission of the people," Huey wrote in an article for the *Black Panther*. "When Black people really unite and rise up in all their splendid millions, they will have the strength to smash injustice."

THE WRATH OF COINTELPRO

A top secret Special Report *for the president [said]* . . . *"a recent poll indicates that approximately 25 per cent of the black population has a great respect for the BPP, including 43 per cent of blacks under 21 years of age." On the basis of such estimates of the potential of the party, the repressive apparatus of the state proceeded against it.*

—NOAM CHOMSKY

The Panthers knew they were being watched by the police and the FBI. They knew their efforts were being undermined by law enforcement, and that they lived in a nation where the powers that be would rather watch young children starve than see them given a political education and an equal chance to learn. No Panther program was exempt from scrutiny, and the Panthers learned to look over their shoulders because any moment could lead to imprisonment or death.

◀ **Jamal Joseph outside the Panther office in Harlem**

What the Panthers didn't know was how high the operation went, and how organized it had become. Behind the scenes, the FBI, working with local police departments, was running a covert counterintelligence program dedicated to destroying the Black Panther Party and other radical political groups operating in the United States.

The FBI nicknamed the program COINTELPRO, as a shorthand for "counterintelligence program." COINTELPRO originated in the 1950s, to prevent socialist movements from developing in the United States, and the program rose to new heights in the Black Power era. Even prior to Stokely Carmichael's first calls for Black Power in 1966, the FBI was organizing to undermine civil rights movement efforts. The Black organizations they labeled as "militant" included not only Stokely's SNCC but also the Rev. Dr. King's Southern Christian Leadership Conference, a group that never wavered in its dedication to nonviolent civil disobedience. Between 1963 and 1971, the FBI ran nearly three hundred separate COINTELPRO operations against Black nationalist groups, the majority of which targeted the Black Panther Party. The program's major goals were to:

1. Prevent the coalition of militant Black nationalist groups, as there would be strength in unity.

2. Prevent the rise of a "messiah" who could unify and electrify the movement, such as the Rev. Dr. King or Malcolm X.

3. Prevent violence, ideally by neutralizing movement leaders before they could become violent.

4. Prevent Black nationalist leaders from gaining respectability, ideally by discrediting them in the eyes of white people, Black people, and radicals of all races.

5. Prevent young people from joining the groups and increasing their membership base.

With these goals in mind, the FBI's counterintelligence program unleashed a series of assaults upon the Black Panther Party. This was simultaneously the most visible threat to the Panthers' survival and the most invisible one.

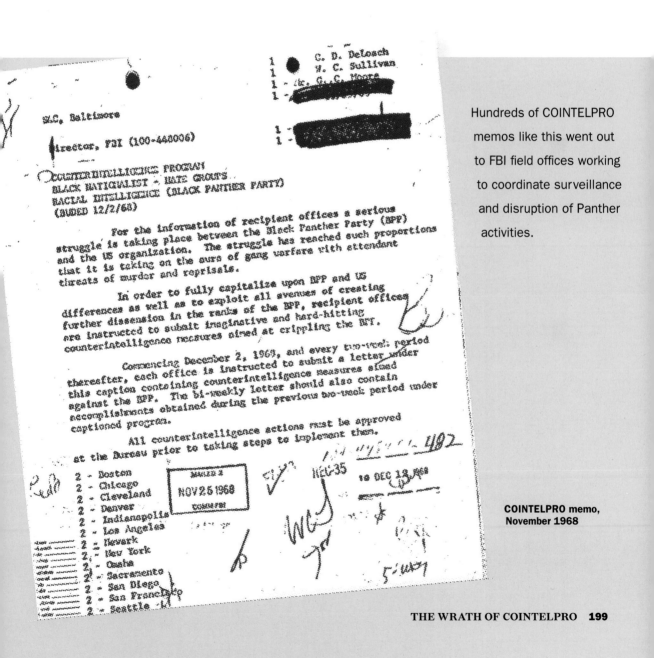

Hundreds of COINTELPRO memos like this went out to FBI field offices working to coordinate surveillance and disruption of Panther activities.

COINTELPRO memo, November 1968

COINTELPRO agents gathered as much information as they could about the Black Panthers. They wanted to learn how the organization operated, who the leaders were, and what the dynamics within the group were like. They studied the Panthers' strengths and identified areas of weakness. They tapped Panther phones, searched Panther offices (sometimes secretly, other times while pretending to be regular police), tailed Panther members, and peeked at mail that was coming in and out of Panther offices.

The FBI kept this program top secret because their agents frequently broke the law and violated the Panthers' constitutional rights while conducting this surveillance. U.S. citizens have the right to form political organizations and protest. The First Amendment protected the Panthers' right to free speech, which allowed them to publish their newspaper and make public speeches. FBI agents did not inherently have the right to monitor people's mail, to search homes and offices, or to tap phones—they would have needed warrants to legally enact that kind of surveillance, but usually they could not get such warrants, in part because the Panthers' actions were too lawful to justify them. While some Panther members occasionally broke the law, by doing so they also broke Black Panther Party rules. The Panthers' policies insisted that members follow the letter of the law, which is part of why the COINTELPRO agents had to break the law themselves in order to get to the Panthers.

FBI Director J. Edgar Hoover authorized his offices to "submit imaginative and hard-hitting counterintelligence measures aimed at crippling the BPP." This memo was written in November 1968, when Panther chapters were opening all over the country and the organization was gearing up to implement its survival programs for the first time.

This moment also coincided with a pivotal presidential election. Republican candidate Richard Nixon had campaigned on a "law and order" platform, focused on quelling crime and violence in American cities. His tough-sounding words soothed white Americans' fears about racial unrest. He used what we now call coded language (or dog whistles) as a way to express to white people that he was on their side and would work to keep Black people in their place, without ever saying so directly.

A man placing a tap in a phone, circa 1968. COINTELPRO operations may have used similar technology to surveil Panthers.

Meanwhile, Democratic candidate Hubert Humphrey struggled to unite his party, which had fractured profoundly over differing views on the Vietnam conflict. Young liberal Democrats (such as those who protested in the streets of Chicago outside the Democratic National Convention in August 1968) wanted a strong anti-war candidate. Humphrey's candidacy appealed to more moderate Democrats, causing him to win the nomination, but his pro-war position could not gain him enough support to carry the nation.

Before Nixon's election on November 5, 1968, not a single Panther office had ever been raided by police. Within a few months of his election, multiple offices were raided. Perhaps the president-elect's "law and order" campaign embold-ened law enforcement agencies, directly or indirectly empowering them to push back against Black organizing. These raids marked the beginning of a new era in COINTELPRO operations. Memos bounced back and forth between FBI national headquarters and at least forty-three separate FBI field offices nationwide, strat-egizing ways to surveil, confront, neutralize, discredit, and ultimately destroy the Black Panther Party.

Three Panthers were at work in the Indianapolis office on the morning of December 18, 1968. Suddenly, several metal canisters came flying through the windows, sending up clouds of tear gas. Police and federal agents stormed in. According to the federal marshals, they were looking for illegal, unregistered weapons, but they did not find any on the premises. Nevertheless, they tore up the office and arrested the Panthers inside. This became an extremely common strategy for entering private Panther spaces. Police would often claim to be searching for illegal weapons, despite the Panthers' many clear and public statements about following the law.

Throughout the month of December, similar raids occurred in other Panther offices, most of which had only been up and running for a few weeks or months. The Denver office was raided when everyone was away at the chapter leader's wedding reception. A team of one hundred police and FBI agents descended on the Des Moines Panther headquarters and arrested two Panthers on arson charges. Two police officers in an unmarked car tossed bombs into the Newark office, injuring four Panthers in the blast and resulting fire.

These sensational raids and arrests made headline news in the national media, which added to the Panthers' rough image. The news tended not to mention that arrested Panthers were often released without being charged with any crime.

As 1969 dawned, the Panthers knew they were under siege. Offices all over the country had been raided, but at the same time membership and community support were growing. Panthers were busy training new recruits, leading political education, selling newspapers, developing and staffing brand-new survival programs, and living communally in Panther pads. Black communities came to recognize the Panthers as a source of strength and support in times of need.

The Party's growth and the COINTELPRO backlash seemed to go hand in hand. As the commitment to survival programs deepened, so did the surveillance. The organization leaned into its resonant message "All Power to the People!" and the boot of the oppressor came down hard and harder.

STIRRING UP TROUBLE

FBI agents used the information they gathered to cause problems within the Panther ranks. Instant communication methods like cell phones and the internet did not exist yet. People could phone one another using landlines, but long-distance calls were costly, and communication often happened through letters sent in the mail. COINTELPRO agents used this to their advantage. They would illegally intercept, alter, and sometimes intentionally misdirect letters that were being sent from chapter to chapter. They wrote and sent false letters, too, with the intent of causing conflict between the Panthers.

In Chicago, they wrote false letters to the Blackstone Rangers, at the precise time Fred Hampton was trying to negotiate with Jeff Fort. One letter, signed by a fictitious, anonymous Black man ("A black brother you don't know"), warned the Ranger gang leader that Fred Hampton was planning to kill him. "I know what I'd do, if I was you," the letter continued. The FBI agents were trying to provoke

A Panther office in shambles after a police raid

the Blackstone Rangers into attacking the Black Panthers. They wanted Fred out of the picture, and him being shot by a rival group leader might take care of the problem, without anyone realizing the police were involved.

It might have seemed a logical step to send a similar letter to Fred Hampton, but the FBI decided against it. An internal memo explained why: "Consideration has been given to a similar letter to the BPP alleging a Ranger plot against the BPP leadership; however, it is not felt this would be productive, principally because the BPP . . . is not believed to be as violence prone." In other words, the FBI understood that it would be impossible to provoke the Panthers to initiate violence. Yet despite their own assessment, COINTELPRO agents and police around the country continued to attack the Panthers, treating them as if they were volatile and violent criminals.

FALSE LETTERS, BROKEN ALLIANCES

COINTELPRO failed to keep the Panthers and the Blackstone Rangers apart in Chicago, probably because Fred Hampton's exceptional organizing skills had given him a solid reputation in Chicago that was hard to undermine. But the FBI did succeed in stirring up tension within other Black nationalist organizations and between them and the Panthers. They sent false letters between SNCC leaders Stokely Carmichael and H. Rap Brown, seeking to exacerbate conflicts within the SNCC ranks and drive a wedge between SNCC and the Panthers.

Internal memos show that COINTELPRO agents also took advantage of the Los Angeles–based US Organization's frustration with the expanding success of the Black Panthers. They planted more seeds of mistrust between the groups, again using false letters and propaganda to make both sides believe the other was out to get them. Director Hoover himself drafted a memo demanding that his agents "capitalize on BPP and US differences . . . to exploit all avenues of creating further dissention in the ranks of the BPP."

BLACK STUDIES ORGANIZING

Many Black Panthers came to the movement through their role as student activists. Huey and Bobby, Ericka and John, Elaine, Kathleen, Stokely, and plenty of others got their start in campus organizing. Though their efforts quickly spread beyond their schools to the broader community, they did not let go of the goals they had for improving higher education.

One of those goals was to introduce Black Studies and Black History courses and curricula into mainstream educational institutions. At the time, few if any schools were teaching about Black lives and culture and history. The version of history being presented as the whole truth was steeped in a white viewpoint.

In 1968, with support from the Black Panther Party, San Francisco State College students submitted a proposal for a Black Studies program. They demonstrated for months, culminating in a student strike the following November, which led to widespread disruption of the college. Their efforts ultimately succeeded. In March 1969, San Francisco State announced that it would establish the United States' first Black Studies program, under the umbrella of an

Ethnic Studies Department that would also include Asian studies and Latinx studies programs.

Similar protests took place at nearly three hundred colleges across the country in 1969. In Los Angeles, the Panthers worked with the UCLA Black Student Union. "When we say Black Studies Program, we're dealing with . . . the survival of a race of people who have been brought to this country, brutalized and mis-educated," John Huggins said. If schools would begin to teach the sort of political education that the Panthers taught, they felt they would be one step closer to achieving true social revolution.

The Panthers gained support for Black Studies curricula even from some academics who didn't agree with their viewpoint. For many it was not just an issue of civil rights, but a question of academic freedom, free speech, and justice.

A Black Student Union leader at San Francisco State College speaking to demonstrators, 1968

Alprentice "Bunchy" Carter

The disagreement reached a head on January 17, 1969. Members of the US Organization and several L.A. Panthers, including chapter leaders John Huggins and Bunchy Carter, met with Black Student Union members on the UCLA campus. The student group had organized to begin a Black Studies program at their school, and the Panthers and US had different recommendations about which professor should be hired to lead the program. The students listened to the recommendations and seemed to be siding with the Panthers.

The tension stoked by COINTELPRO erupted between US and the Panthers. Amid the fray, two US members shot John and Bunchy. Both of them died from their wounds. The shooters fled the scene.

CONSPIRACY?

The day John and Bunchy were killed, Panthers gathered at the Hugginses' apartment to provide support to John's widow, Ericka, to comfort one another, and to grieve. Some had been at the student union when the shooting occurred and had come to report what they saw and recover from the trauma. Ericka had stayed home that day, caring for her three-week-old baby daughter.

John Huggins

Over one hundred police descended on the apartment. They busted through the door and arrested all the Panthers in the home, seventeen in total. The charges ranged from possession of illegal weapons to conspiracy and murder. As was the pattern with police arrests of Panthers, the charges were eventually dropped.

It struck the Panthers as odd that no members of US had been similarly arrested that day. The Panthers did not know about COINTELPRO at the time, but the events surrounding the murders of John and Bunchy seemed very suspicious. The *Black Panther* newspaper proclaimed it "A Political Assassination" and theorized that US members were working with the government. After all, US cooperated with law enforcement much more than the Panthers did, even to the point of receiving government funds and support, which the Panthers suggested made US a tool of the power structure. The Panthers felt sure that the individuals who pulled the triggers that day, whoever they really were, were part of a bigger system seeking to undermine the Panthers. Two US members ultimately served time for conspiracy to the murders, but the individuals who witnesses said actually did the shooting were not arrested.

These murders unsettled the L.A. Panther chapter, which had to regroup with new leadership in place. Elmer "Geronimo"

The FBI created inflammatory editorial cartoons to provoke tension between the US Organization and the Panthers. These cartoons depict US targeting Panther leaders for destruction.

Pratt became the chapter leader, with Elaine Brown and others also taking the lead on much of the organizing.

After "neutralizing" John and Bunchy, the FBI continued their surveillance of the L.A. Panthers. They even appeared at John's funeral, where they photographed all the guests and confiscated the sign-in book.

Ericka Huggins moved back east to be closer to family and helped found the Black Panther chapter in New Haven, Connecticut, becoming the chapter leader. She had served on the Central Committee and had years of organizing experience to apply to her new situation. New Haven was home to Yale University, which soon would be the site of numerous rallies in support of the Panthers and a place for continued coalition building.

THE CHICAGO 8

While the FBI acted behind the scenes, the so-called justice system kept on confronting the Panthers more directly. On March 20, 1969, Bobby Seale was indicted, along with seven white anti-war protestors, on charges related to the chaos that had occurred outside the Democratic National Convention the previous summer. The group became known as the Chicago 8, and they were charged with conspiracy and crossing state lines with the intent to incite a riot.

Unlike the other seven, Bobby had not actually been one of the demonstration organizers. He had been at the protest as a guest speaker. But federal authorities had likely been grasping for any viable legal charges to bring against Bobby, and this was the best they could do.

The Chicago 8 indictments made big headlines. For the white students in the anti-war movement, it was among the first and most tangible consequences for their acts of protest and rebellion against the establishment. For the Panthers, it was business as usual, as they grappled with yet another government attempt to accuse them of crimes they hadn't committed.

On April 2, 1969, in the wee hours of the morning, police pounded on the door at Jamal Joseph's grandmother's house. When he answered the door, they burst inside, pinned him against the wall, and announced that he was under arrest.

"I was a little shook up, but I was proud, too," Jamal said. "Being arrested at sixteen or any age for being a Panther was a mark of honor. It meant that you had become enough of a thorn in the system's side for them to come after you." He assumed they would lay a small-time gun charge on him because he'd started carrying a handgun.

It wasn't until he got down to the police station and heard the charges being read against him that he realized he was in much bigger trouble: conspiracy to commit murder, conspiracy to commit arson, and attempted murder. The New York District Attorney's office charged Jamal—along with twenty other New York Panther leaders—of being part of a Panther plot to bomb New York City landmarks.

Jamal went to jail that night, his bail set at a shocking $100,000. There was no way the Panthers could raise nearly $2 million overnight to bail out everyone who had been arrested, which is what the police were counting on. The New York 21, as they soon became known, had not committed any crimes—even according to authorities, they were being charged with conspiracy to commit a theoretical future crime, which made the bail demand especially extreme.

The New York District Attorney claimed the police had uncovered a Panther plot to murder police officers and place bombs at public locations around the city. There was no evidence of such a plot, aside from some police informants who had attended Panther meetings and testified that they had heard the Panther leaders talking about committing violence. The story of a bombing plot

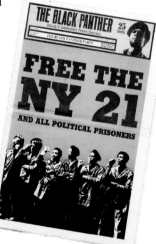

Front page of the *Black Panther* featuring the New York 21

Demonstrators protesting the imprisonment of the New York 21

was an outright attempt to frame the Panthers, but that seemed not to matter to anyone in power. The police and prosecutors seemed to believe that the barest of evidence would be enough to convict, but their machinations proved extremely transparent. From very early in the case, it was clear to many that the Panthers had not done anything wrong, except to have a political agenda that went against the powers that be. A huge public outcry went up on behalf of the twenty-one, rallying supporters across races and socioeconomic status.

SUSPICIOUS BEHAVIOR

With so many New York Panther leaders in jail awaiting trial, the New York chapter suffered. Into this leadership vacuum walked George Sams, who had been expelled from the Party in Oakland the previous year for stabbing another Panther, but was given another chance in the New York chapter.

In May 1969, George Sams took another New York Panther, Alex Rackley, with him up to New Haven, Connecticut, to the chapter headed by Ericka Huggins. Claiming he was acting on orders from Oakland, Sams told Ericka and the New Haven Panthers that Alex was a traitor who had helped set up the New York 21. Sams told them that the National Headquarters had ordered them to question Alex about his involvement with the police.

Sams ordered the New Haven Panthers to lock Alex in the basement, where Sams proceeded to torture him to get information. This was beyond the norm of Panther discipline, but Sams was aggressive and insistent. Then Sams and two New Haven Panthers, Lonnie McLucas and Warren Kimbro, took Alex to the middle of a marsh and shot him.

The day after Alex Rackley's murder, his body was discovered based on a tip to law enforcement. Police rounded up and arrested eight New Haven Panthers, including Ericka, Warren, Lonnie, plus one other man and four other women, charging them with conspiracy, kidnapping, and murder.

Suspiciously, George Sams was nowhere to be found when the FBI came raiding. He had left New Haven and traveled to other Panther offices, including those in Chicago.

On June 4, police raided the Chicago Panther office, possibly on the pretext of searching for Sams. (They did not present a warrant at the time, but Sams's fugitive status might have given the FBI a reason to enter and search the organization.) They used sledgehammers to break into the second-floor office, where they ransacked the Panthers' files and smashed their office equipment. They arrested eight Panthers, but they did not find Sams.

The FBI initiated a nationwide manhunt. The excuse of searching for George Sams enabled them to get search warrants for Panther offices all over the country. They searched offices in Chicago, Philadelphia, Kansas City, and more, but by the time they searched each office, Sams was nowhere to be found.

The timing of George Sams's appearance on the East Coast struck the Panthers as suspicious. How had the FBI become aware of Alex's murder so quickly, and how had Sams managed to get out of town just in time to avoid being arrested along with everyone else? Could it really be a coincidence that each Panther office he had visited was raided a few days later by police, shortly after he had left? They began to suspect that George Sams might be the real police informant.

TRAITORS IN THE RANKS

I routinely supplied whatever floor plans or diagrams I could to the FBI. That started in June 1969. I mean, they had a floor plan and keys to the Black Panther headquarters.

—WILLIAM O'NEAL

In the summer of 1969, FBI Director J. Edgar Hoover announced that the Black Panther Party was "the greatest threat to the internal security of the country." The statement cast a renewed, negative spotlight on the Panthers and their work. Most white Americans found Hoover's assessment easy to believe—all they had seen of the Panthers in the mainstream media involved images of scary-looking Black people carrying large guns and causing public disturbances.

Behind the scenes, COINTELPRO agents stepped up their attacks. They especially wanted to silence the Panther leaders who seemed most effective at getting the Panther message out to the public. The FBI had the stated goal of preventing violence, but their own actions led to more violence than anything the Panthers had done on their own.

◀ **Police outside the Panthers' L.A. office on December 8, 1969**

The day after Hoover's announcement, Bobby Seale contacted all the Panther offices nationwide and asked them to send representatives to Oakland. Once he had them together, he delivered a message: "The order of the day is to fortify Black Panther Party offices."

Raids were already a common occurrence, and now the Panthers feared police actions would grow even more intense. Panthers around the country worked to strengthen their office defenses. In Los Angeles, Geronimo Pratt led the Panthers in digging tunnels under the building and using the dirt to fill sandbags that they stacked against the walls and stuffed up into the rafters. Other chapters brought trucks of sand to the office and filled bags from there. Lining the walls with sandbags and replacing window glass with plywood were two common approaches to fortification. Sandbags offered a layer of protection because they would slow or stop bullets, and also make it harder for tear gas canisters to get through to reach the people inside.

The Panthers had now endured over six months of near-constant raids,

assaults, arrests, and other acts of aggression by local police and federal agents, and they had done very little to reciprocate the violence being directed at them by the government. Especially among the rank-and-file members, patience was wearing thin. Many wondered, how much longer would they have to endure this blatant disregard for their rights and their humanity? Weren't the Panthers supposed to be taking the fight to the powers that be? Did erasing "Self-Defense" from their name make the guns they carried lose their meaning?

At the end of July, just a few weeks after Hoover's announcement, the Chicago office was raided again. Two dozen police cars arrived on the scene, and three rank-and-file Panthers inside had to grapple with a dilemma Panthers faced often when presented with police violence: to fight back in self-defense or not to fight back? To the three young men in the office that day, the mandate to fortify and defend Panther territory seemed clear, and they engaged in a thirty-five-minute firefight with the officers.

When the Panthers ran out of ammunition, the police stormed inside. They struck the Panthers with rifle butts, knocking at least one of them unconscious, and arrested them for attempted murder. They set the building on fire and burned boxes of cereal that were being stored for the free breakfast program.

Afterward, the police boarded up the damaged building, labeling it a crime scene. At first, the Panthers weren't sure they could reenter the space. But leaving the office unoccupied felt like a symbol that the police had won and the Black Panther Party was over. The community would not stand for that. Neighbors, white anti-war activists, and other Rainbow Coalition members joined forces to rebuild and revitalize the Chicago office. Volunteers came in to paint, do repairs, and clean up the damage. "That's a heavy example of people in solidarity in the community," said Bobby Seale.

The community's rapid action sent a message loud and clear: *These are our Panthers. Don't mess with them.*

Panthers lined their office walls and windows with sandbags to protect against police assaults.

COINTELPRO agents actively looked for ways to undermine the powerful community support the Panthers had gained. They even worked to infiltrate the Black Panther Party itself. White FBI agents would stand out if they tried to join, so instead they carefully recruited Black citizens to help their cause. They paid people to join the Panthers and act like members, but secretly report back to FBI agents about what the Panthers were doing behind closed doors. These spies were known as informants because they carried information to the FBI. Some informants also acted as agents provocateurs, which means people who try to create distrust and chaos within the Panther ranks.

A young man in Chicago, William O'Neal, joined the Party as an FBI informant. O'Neal went through full Panther training, then worked his way up in the ranks to become chief of security for the Chicago chapter. His job involved managing the Panthers' weapons cache and serving as Fred Hampton's bodyguard. No one suspected O'Neal was working for the other side. They trusted him. But all along, he secretly tried to make trouble for the Panthers. He suggested violent activities, trying to get other Panthers to go through with his schemes, knowing that if they did, they would likely be caught or killed. Through it all, he reported to an FBI special agent named Roy Mitchell.

George Sams's behavior in New Haven also fits the profile of an agent provocateur. When he was caught in Nova Scotia three months after Alex Rackley's murder, in August 1969, Sams quickly turned state's evidence and told police that Bobby Seale had ordered him to kill Alex Rackley. Sams had also recorded the torture sessions that he led and left the recording behind in New Haven for police to recover when they arrested most of the chapter in May. These bizarre actions made it clear to the Panthers that Sams was out to frame them, whether or not he was working directly with the FBI to do it.

There was no evidence to support George Sams's allegations against Bobby Seale. Still, it offered police an excuse to arrest and investigate the Panthers' founder. Bobby was already under indictment with the Chicago 8, but he was out on bail until the trial would begin in September. In August 1969, the New Haven courts added an indictment for conspiracy to commit murder in the Alex Rackley case. Bobby was arrested on August 19 in California and brought to Chicago in September. The transport agents put him in a car in San Francisco and drove him across the country, locking him up in a different local jail every night as they made their way through the multi-day trip.

The Chicago 8 trial began in September 1969, and it showed yet again how racist the justice system could be. After being denied his legal right to the attorney of his choice, Bobby protested loudly from his chair while the trial was going on. In order to quiet him, the judge ordered that Bobby be handcuffed, tied to his chair with thick chains, and gagged. The white defendants also made multiple dramatic outbursts and created disruptions in the courtroom, but none of them were bound and gagged, even though all of the seven, and even their attorneys, were charged with contempt for their behavior during the trial.

Bobby was placed in a chair alone in the center of the courtroom. The chains around his wrists were tied so tight that he could feel his circulation being cut off. But the gag in his mouth

Courtroom sketch of Bobby Seale, bound and gagged, trying to write messages on a notepad to communicate

prevented him from speaking, even to ask for help when he was in distress. He managed to spit out the gag and shout. The next day, the guards tied his chains even tighter. They shoved the gag deep into his mouth, making it hard for him to breathe.

"I thought I was going to die," Bobby said. "I mean, really die, because of the way they were doing things." He struggled against the chains in court until he almost passed out in the chair. The other defendants spoke up on his behalf, and finally the guards loosened his bonds.

The judge severed Bobby's trial from the other seven defendants and sentenced him to four years in prison for contempt of court.

Much later, the contempt charges would be overturned on appeal because the judge had demonstrated bias in the trial process. Bobby said, "Anybody can read the court record and see that I wasn't trying to sabotage the trial, but that I was only trying to get my constitutional right—to either defend myself or have my lawyer present—recognized, but Judge Hoffman wouldn't recognize it."

At the time, with his trial severed from the rest of the group, his Chicago proceedings were placed on hold. Bobby was moved to New Haven, where he joined Ericka Huggins and her chapter members in awaiting trial in the Alex Rackley murder case.

ASSASSINATION

Chicago police had been trying for months to bring legal charges against Fred Hampton, but they could not get charges to stick. After repeated raids over the course of the fall, the informant William O'Neal helped Chicago police plan a raid that ended in tragedy.

On December 3, 1969, several members of the Chicago Panther chapter gathered at Fred Hampton's apartment. They ate dinner, drank Kool-Aid, talked about strategy for upcoming activities, and then lay down to sleep. Deborah

Johnson, Fred's fiancée, joined him in the bedroom, while the others spread out in the living room.

At four in the morning, a knock came at the door. Mark Clark, of the southern Illinois chapter, who was sitting on watch duty, stood up as if to respond. He received an immediate gunshot to the chest as Chicago police burst through the door and began firing. They possessed a search warrant for illegal weapons, but their actions showed that they never intended to use it for that purpose. They just wanted to get into the apartment to kill Fred Hampton.

The police fired over a hundred bullets into the apartment. Mark Clark was shot and killed immediately; he reflexively fired the shotgun in his hand one time. It was the only shot actually fired by Panthers that morning, though the police would later describe the assault as a "firefight" that the Panthers initiated.

Two more Panthers in the living room got shot; the rest managed to avoid the line of fire because it was mostly directed at Fred Hampton's bed, where he was sleeping. Deborah managed to scramble out of the way as the police burst through the bedroom door, firing wildly. Fred barely reacted, managing only to lift his head briefly before he was shot multiple times where he lay. It turned out that one of O'Neal's tasks earlier in the evening had been to dose Fred's glass of Kool-Aid with strong drugs to knock him out.

Fred's death broke the hearts of Panthers from coast to coast. In the hours and days after Fred's body was removed, people lined up down the block to walk through the shot-up apartment where he died to bear witness to the tragedy. One person who saw the hundred bullet holes called it "nuthin but a northern lynching."

Fred Hampton

Chicago police officers smiling as they carry Fred Hampton's body out of his apartment

The Panthers encouraged the parade of witnesses. It was important for people to see what happened, so that they understood the lengths to which the law would go to stop Black progress.

Hearing of Fred's death was "the most devastating piece of news I had heard since joining the party," said Aaron Dixon of Seattle. "Those who knew Fred Hampton knew intuitively that he was the next great Black leader . . . the most unselfish, the most principled, most prolific Panther around."

Aaron wasn't the only one who thought so. Bobby Seale had privately tapped Fred as his successor, to lead the national Party in his place if he was killed.

When the FBI declassified their COINTELPRO papers twenty-some years later, the paper trail revealed that a similar thought process had motivated Fred Hampton's murder. COINTELPRO agents had been tasked with "preventing the rise of a black 'messiah,'" a strong leader and speaker who had the potential to unite and motivate Black people. They looked at Fred and saw a future Martin Luther King Jr. or Malcolm X—someone who was perhaps even more dangerous than either of those icons before him because, under the Panther banner, Fred had found a way to bring together the best of both the civil rights and Black nationalist visions, as well as uniting people across racial lines. It was heartbreaking for Black America to be robbed of a leader with such potential.

PREDAWN RAIDS

Four days later, around dawn on December 8, 1969, L.A. police threw tear gas canisters through the windows of the BPP's Los Angeles office and prepared to storm the building. Eighteen Panthers had been asleep inside. They woke to the sound of machine gun fire cutting through the walls overhead.

The police no doubt thought it would be a straightforward raid, just like so many others had been. But Geronimo Pratt had spent months laying sandbags and turning the L.A. office into a virtual bunker. The Panthers returned fire from the protection of their walls, determined not to go quietly if the police breached their perimeter.

Neighbors came out into the streets, coughing and choking as the tear gas leaked through the walls into their homes. In a matter of minutes, the streets filled with bystanders, watching and waiting to see what was going to happen. Police shouted for the crowds to disperse. They refused.

The street full of witnesses prevented police from storming into the Panther stronghold. The eighteen Panthers fired back, defending their lives against the assault. Hunkered down in that office, guns in hand, "we were free for a while," said Panther Roland Freeman, who was seventeen at the time.

The Panthers were greatly outnumbered, and they knew it. Police reinforcements arrived with rows and rows of troops dressed in what would come to be known as SWAT gear, riding in armored personnel carriers that rolled through the L.A. streets like tanks. The cornered Panthers believed they were making a last stand and that they would die there in that office, fighting for what they believed in. They held off the police attack for five long hours.

With arms raised, Peaches (Renee Moore) was the first to surrender to police after the L.A. office standoff.

Eventually, however, the Panthers decided to live to fight another day. A brave sister nicknamed Peaches walked out of the office carrying a white flag. When she didn't get shot, the other Panthers followed suit. As they stepped into the light, police officers grabbed them, laid them on the sidewalk in a row, and proceeded to beat and kick them while the community watched in horror. They were arrested, along with a few others from Panther homes in the area that were also raided that morning. Several people sustained injuries from the gunfire and the beatings, but amazingly no one died.

When the police reported on the events, they said that the Panthers initiated the attack. But community members who witnessed these events knew that the police version wasn't true. They wondered at the audacity of the police to stage a raid and then say that the Panthers initiated an attack on them. It seemed the police continued to believe that the Panthers' very existence should be considered an attack.

Panthers heading into court on charges related to the December 8 standoff

A crowd of several thousand people gathered outside the L.A. Hall of Justice to protest the police assault on the Panther office.

A YEAR OF GROWTH AND TURMOIL

In many ways the intended damage had been done, but COINTELPRO actions also backfired in certain respects. Black Panther Party membership was near its peak, boasting thousands of members and supporters who had been driven toward the Party by the very police actions that were designed to drive them away. The Black community quickly recognized Fred Hampton's death for what it was: a targeted assassination. For some, it clarified the lengths the system would go to in suppressing Black progress. For others, it helped send any respect for law and order out the window. If those responsible for upholding the law could bend or break it to suit their own will, what was the meaning of law at all?

In 1969 alone, COINTELPRO resulted in the deaths of at least four key Panther leaders, facilitated the imprisonment of dozens more, and directly or indirectly contributed to the deaths of several rank-and-file Panthers. The killings of Fred Hampton, Mark Clark, John Huggins, and Bunchy Carter were U.S. government–sanctioned assassinations of U.S. citizens on U.S. soil. These were not simply bias-based shootings that could be explained away as the fault of dark alleys, snap judgments, or unconscious racism. They were political assassinations: the deliberate murder of individuals who couldn't be taken down using the law, even taking into consideration a justice system that was racially biased and in many cases outright corrupt.

The Panthers weren't breaking the law. They held views that challenged the status quo of American society, and they organized people to seek radical social justice. That was their crime.

POLITICAL PRISONERS

Deputy Chairman Fred has said, "You can jail a revolutionary, but you can't jail revolution." We, the people, are saying, "Pigs, we refuse to let you jail either."

—*THE BLACK PANTHER*

Evidence of state repression against the Panthers called the entire justice system into question. What was the meaning of law if those laws could be bent or broken to serve the will of the government? How could this system claim to achieve actual justice when it treated people differently based on their race?

The Panthers had addressed these issues from the start, as two key tenets of the Ten-Point Platform: calling for all Black people to be released from prison, and calling for all Black people to be able to be tried by a jury of peers from the Black community. Panther leaders' repeated imprisonments demonstrated this need on the national stage. The Panthers were continually being set up, framed, prosecuted for false or exaggerated charges, and imprisoned at length while

◀ **Angela Davis and Jonathan Jackson protesting the charges against the Soledad Brothers**

awaiting trial. The question loomed larger than ever: Could Black activists ever receive a fair trial in the United States?

As these high-profile arrests illuminated the systemic flaws in the justice system, it had implications not just for the Panther leaders in the spotlight, but also for thousands of ordinary Black citizens behind bars.

MORE THAN CRIMINALS

"Black men born in the U.S. and fortunate enough to live past the age of eighteen are conditioned to accept the inevitability of prison," wrote George Jackson as an inmate in Soledad Prison in California.

George Jackson

George himself had fallen victim to the broken system. He went to prison at age nineteen, in 1961, accused of stealing seventy dollars from a gas station. A court-appointed lawyer advised him to plead guilty to the charges so he would receive a lesser sentence. But instead of the light sentence George had been promised, the court sentenced him to "one year to life," with no indication of how long he would actually have to serve behind bars.

If George had pleaded innocent to the robbery charges against him, he would have had a chance to present evidence of his innocence in court. He might not have ended up in prison at all. His attorney gave him bad advice, possibly assuming he had committed the crime, and the judge probably took George's skin color into consideration when he sentenced him to such a long term.

The Panthers were thinking about people like George when they demanded the release of all Black prisoners in their Ten-Point Platform. How and why people went to prison concerned the Panthers. In a nation where only 11% of the people were Black, nearly 40% of prison inmates were Black, most from poor communities. Police were racially biased in making arrests, Black people were less likely to be able to afford the best legal representation, and judges and juries were racially biased in their verdicts and sentencing.

Of course, calling for the immediate release of *all* prisoners was a controversial and complicated issue. But to the Panthers, even those who *had* broken the law did not necessarily deserve to be locked up. Black people struggling with poverty, homelessness, or unemployment sometimes broke the law in an effort to survive. It was racism and classism that caused the legal system to view those people as criminals in need of punishment. If those same people were treated with kindness and given different opportunities to work, to learn, and to succeed, they might be able to turn their lives around. Prison took those opportunities away from people.

CONDITIONS INSIDE

The poor living conditions in most prisons made inmates feel even more desperate and less human. Panthers caught behind bars had to deal with the poor conditions of prison life, such as bad food and limited access to health care, and being political prisoners brought special challenges on top of that. Panthers often spent extra time in solitary confinement because the prison officials did not want them spreading their beliefs and converting other prisoners to the movement.

Many inmates, like George Jackson, gained political consciousness while in prison. George gathered a group of prisoners who also liked the Panther message and organized them into a prison chapter of the Black Panther Party. As a result of his organizing, the prison board denied him parole each and every time he became eligible.

Writing from behind bars, George became known as an important voice of the Panther Party. He wrote about the complicated reasons Black men ended up behind bars, emphasizing that it wasn't only a matter of who had committed crimes. He published two books, *Soledad Brother* and *Blood in My Eye*, that made

Angela Davis speaking

it onto the Panther reading list. His books meant a lot to other Panthers in prison and drew new recruits to the cause.

SOLEDAD BROTHERS

In 1970, prison officials charged George Jackson and two other inmates with the murder of a guard who had died during a low-scale prison uprising. There was no evidence to indicate George was involved, and most people believe that prison officials chose to blame these particular inmates simply to punish them for organizing prisoners to join the Black Panther Party.

George expected that he would be in prison for life either way, but if he was found guilty of killing the guard, he would receive the death penalty. The urgency of his case helped George's prison writings become more and more well known. The three accused men became known as the Soledad Brothers, as the Panthers and other people who believed in George's innocence worked to draw public attention to their case.

Angela Davis, a young college professor at UCLA, spoke up on behalf of the Soledad Brothers. She worked hard to get their case examined by legal experts, and to draw attention to the plight of other prisoners like them. Even though Angela did not officially join the Black Panther Party, she talked and worked with them because they agreed about the need for massive prison reform.

The police transferred George from Soledad State Prison to San Quentin State Prison in 1970, and he and the other Soledad Brothers prepared to stand trial for the guard's murder. But the transfer did not stop their political work. They talked to fellow inmates at San Quentin and gathered support for the Black Panther Party there, too.

FREE ALL POLITICAL PRISONERS!

All Panthers who spent time in jail or prison were considered political prisoners. This included groups like the New York 21 and the New Haven Panthers, as well as individuals like George Jackson and Huey P. Newton. In each case, their political views were the main reason they were locked up. In each case, false or exaggerated charges, provocation by police or police informants, and even fabricated evidence played a role. Political prisoners were frequently denied bail and held in jail for long periods while awaiting trial.

One journalist at the time wrote that it was difficult to imagine white activists ever being treated the way the New York 21 were, being "rounded up in the middle of the night, thrown into jails, dispersed around the city, kept under maximum security and even solitary confinement, detained in prison on exorbitant bail . . . and charged with plotting irrational actions." The same went for the other Panthers, who, it was clear, were unjustly targeted by the system.

Freeing these political prisoners was paramount for the Panthers. In the long

Courtroom drawing of members of the New York 21

term, the Party advocated for massive prison reform and a complete overhaul of the so-called justice system. In the short term, the Panthers' goals were to find excellent attorneys to handle their cases in court and to keep the Panther story alive in the media to drum up public support for those imprisoned.

FUNDRAISING FOR THE NY 21 DEFENSE

The task of fighting multiple legal battles at once was challenging. Trial attorney fees cost a lot more money than any individual Panther had. The Party was constantly raising money to pay members' bail and cover their trial costs. The Free Huey effort was still ongoing in Oakland, but now they were fundraising to support Bobby, Ericka, the New York 21, and others on trial as well.

Within a few months of their arrests, the Panthers managed to raise enough money to bail out a few of the twenty-one, including Michael "Cetawayo" Tabor, Afeni Shakur, and Dhoruba Bin Wahad. The three leaders dedicated their time to raising awareness and funds to support their collective defense. They hosted rallies and made speeches. The youngest defendants, including the teenage Jamal

Jamal Joseph speaking to a crowd at the University of Vermont

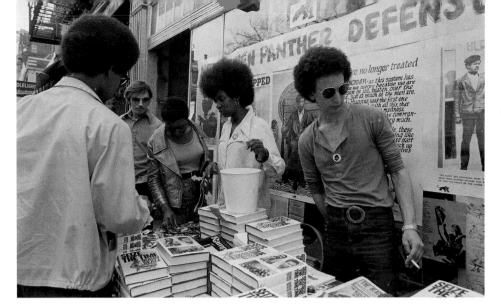

Selling books and buttons to raise money for Panther legal defense

Joseph, were charged as juveniles, so their trials were ultimately severed from the group. Jamal was released in February 1970 after spending almost a year in jail. He joined the Panthers' Speakers Bureau and worked to raise money to help the case. While he was profoundly relieved to be outside, Jamal still felt the echoes of imprisonment. He remained deeply tied to the group he'd been arrested with. As long as they were in jail, he felt he owed them his full 24/7 dedication. In jail or out, it was impossible to lose sight of the fact that they were all still fighting for their lives and their freedom.

COALITION PROTESTS IN NEW HAVEN

Fundraising to support the trials meant building coalition support, which the Panthers had proven very good at doing. While the New York 21 held rallies in the city, the community surrounding New Haven rose up in support of Ericka Huggins and Bobby Seale. Yale University hosted many political events and rallies. Women's liberation groups, predominantly made up of white women, stood outside the courthouse with FREE ERICKA signs. Students for a Democratic Society helped organize supporters, and two of the white members of the Chicago 8 came to support Bobby.

"Free Our Sisters, Free Ourselves" became a rallying cry, as they protested the treatment of women behind bars in particular. Ericka and the four young Panther women imprisoned with her endured gender-specific discrimination in jail. Ericka, a breastfeeding mother at the time of her arrest, was given pills to inhibit her milk production and only allowed to see her daughter once a week. One of her colleagues was pregnant and gave birth under harsh, unsanitary conditions, surrounded by leering FBI agents. The women were subject to strip searches and extensive isolation. They attempted to organize in prison and to call attention to the inhumane treatment afforded them as political prisoners, which certainly did not reflect their pretrial status of "innocent until proven guilty."

In March 1970, during pretrial hearings for the New Haven case, protests drawing 12,000 to 15,000 people occurred outside the jail and on Yale's campus. Yale University President Kingman Brewster made news for expressing support for the Panthers and concern for their ability to receive a fair trial.

This type of widespread, high-profile, cross-racial support was essential to the Panthers' defense funds. White people often had money, and inspiring them to support the cause was the only way the Panthers could see to survive. However, this put the organization in a tough spot with their Black communities because the Panthers began changing the way they protested in order to make themselves more palatable to these white audiences.

Liberal white people could embrace "All Power to the People" well enough, but the Panthers' most biting, anti-capitalist, "Off the Pigs" rhetoric made white audiences uncomfortable. This revolutionary rhetoric had built the Party and spoken to the brothers and sisters on the block. It had drawn them into the Party with the promise of real and lasting change, but now it seemed to some members that the Party was backing off from its own core mission.

Wealthy white people wanted to support breakfast programs and health clinics and see innocent activists free from prison. But the idea of true revolution,

while highly romanticized during the era, did not and could not resonate with white people who already sat in positions of power.

On top of the rank-and-file concerns, the New York 21 became critical of Panther fundraising tactics. The New York 21 case was pulling a lot of weight in the overall fundraising effort, partly because their story resonated extremely well with supporters, and they began to feel that funds they had raised for their own cause were being diverted to other Panther cases. In June 1970, an appeals court began considering Huey's manslaughter conviction, which energized the

Panther base but drew a lot of attention and resources away from New Haven and New York.

From jail, the New York 21 wrote letters of concern to the Central Committee in Oakland. They felt their needs were being ignored in favor of other causes, including Huey's own case.

UNDERGROUND!

Knowing that the police and the courts treated all Black people as criminals, some Panthers chose to "go underground" rather than risk more encounters with the justice system. This meant operating in secret, rather than openly organizing as most Panthers did.

Going underground was different from going into exile by leaving the country, as Eldridge Cleaver had done in 1968. Panthers who went underground stayed in the United States, and typically did so with the intention of continuing to pose challenges to the power structure. The court system and the FBI could not chase Panthers around the world, because they did not have jurisdiction in other countries, but they could hunt for Panthers hiding out within the United States. Panthers who left the country removed themselves from the battlefield, so to speak, whereas Panthers who went underground became fugitives, actively hunted by law enforcement.

A few New York 21 members were not caught in the initial roundup and immediately went underground or into exile. Some fled to places like Algeria, but others remained behind. Several among the twenty-one, including Jamal Joseph, went underground once they were out on bail, before the trial began. To them, it didn't make sense to keep following the letter of the law when the likely outcome for any Panther was only to be abused by the system in the long run. However, the Central Committee refused to support those who had gone underground, choosing instead to funnel all Party support to the Panthers on trial. This created additional tension in the ranks. The Panthers who went underground saw themselves as a vital part of the vanguard—they had put their lives and freedom on the line to support the Party and the people. Was the Party really going to abandon them now?

TAKING HOSTAGES

Panthers who went underground were often among those who felt that more extreme action was necessary to confront the justice system. What good was it doing the cause for them to rot in jail while they could be in the streets starting a revolution against those in power?

George Jackson's younger brother, Jonathan Jackson, was seventeen when the Soledad Brothers' trial approached. He wanted more than anything to help his brother get free. On August 7, 1970, Jonathan smuggled weapons to a group of three inmates on trial in the Marin County Courthouse in Northern California—the same courthouse where the Soledad Brothers' trial would soon take place. Using the weapons, the inmates helped Jonathan take hostages out of the courtroom, including the judge and three jurors. Jonathan put the hostages in a van, planning to drive to a local radio station and demand George be released in exchange for the hostages.

Jonathan's rescue attempt ended in tragedy. Security guards and police opened fire on the escaping prisoners as they drove away from the courthouse. Jonathan and two of the inmates were shot and killed, along with the judge they had taken hostage.

Authorities linked the guns Jonathan used in the action to Angela Davis, the young UCLA professor. The FBI put her on its Ten Most Wanted Fugitives list. She went underground for several months. The FBI caught up with her on the

East Coast and returned her to California for trial. Her supporters sparked a Free Angela movement similar to what the Free Huey movement was like several years earlier. Angela spent over eighteen months in prison before she was found innocent at trial. Her case became a national news story, as the woman who made a name for herself by defending political prisoners became a political prisoner herself.

Panthers across the country had divergent reactions to Jonathan Jackson's death. Some dismissed his action as a reckless stunt, entirely counter to the Party's principles. Others saw it as a powerful act of the revolutionary vanguard. They viewed Jonathan's sacrifice as a model for taking it to the Man, going out in a blaze of glory, and leaving a wake of destruction within the capitalist establishment. This dichotomy was quickly becoming the new fault line that would shake the entire Black Panther Party.

A CLASH IN THE CENTRAL COMMITTEE

On August 8, 1970, the day after Jonathan Jackson's tragic-heroic death, Huey P. Newton was released from prison. Two years into Huey's fifteen-year sentence, the appeals court had overturned his manslaughter conviction. Finally, the Panthers had a reason to celebrate.

But it was not so easy for Huey to walk back into the Panther leadership. Even though Huey had never stopped acting as the Panthers' Minister of Defense, in some ways the Party had moved on without him in the three years since his

Huey P. Newton addressing a crowd a month after his release from prison

arrest. It had grown from a small group of activists who all knew Huey personally into a national movement of people who saw him more as a symbol than a real person.

The turmoil of 1969 had made Huey more and more certain that the survival programs needed to be the centerpiece of the Panther movement. Armed revolution was a long way off. The people were not ready. They needed more education, more political power, and more unity before they could wage revolution.

Eldridge Cleaver, on the other hand, still wanted to incite an armed revolution in American streets as soon as possible. He remained in exile in Algeria but contributed from afar to the Party leadership. The more Huey talked about survival programs and voter registration, the more fiery Eldridge became about arming Black citizens. Rank-and-file Panthers listened to both leaders and understood their points, but many struggled to understand which strategy was the Panthers' priority.

COINTELPRO made matters worse. The FBI's misinformation campaign played upon this growing ideological divide in the Panther leadership and membership and, without Huey's or Eldridge's knowledge, planted more and more false communication to stir up the controversy. With so many Panthers dead, in prison, in exile, or underground, the remaining chapters and leaders grew confused about how to move forward.

"When the slave
kills the slavemaster,
it acts as a cleansing
process: Because then a
man is "born" and the
oppressor is gone."
HUEY P. NEWTON

"We shall h
our manhood.
shall have it or
earth will be leve
by our atten
to gain

ELDRIDGE CLEA

THE SPLIT

The idea of a Black Liberation Army emerged from conditions in Black communities. Conditions of poverty, indecent housing, massive unemployment, poor medical care and inferior education. The idea came about because Black People are not free or equal in this country. . . . And where there is oppression there will be resistance.

—ASSATA SHAKUR

Everyone in the Party knew that Huey and Eldridge were arguing, but they did not know how deeply the divide was going to cut the Party. At the Central Committee level, the concept of community-building versus insurrection was an ideological debate, colored by the leaders' individual needs and perspectives. Safely ensconced in Algeria, it was easy for Eldridge to advocate open revolution on American streets. In contrast, Huey had just gotten out of prison, an experience that rattled him deeply, and he had no interest in doing things that were likely to send him right back.

At the local chapter level, the debate posed very urgent, life-and-death questions about the focus and meaning of the revolution. Specifically, what did it mean to be the vanguard party? Did it mean taking care of the people, or taking things violently to the police? Or both?

◀ **Huey P. Newton and Eldridge Cleaver, from the front page of the *Black Panther***

"The party did not openly advocate attacks on the police," Aaron Dixon said. "We were supposed to be organizing the masses, helping them to prepare for self-defense and eventually guerrilla warfare, if it came to that." But in Seattle and other places, the anger and desire to act sometimes came to a head. "New chapters and branches all over the country were grappling with this same dilemma—to attack or not to attack."

DISILLUSIONMENT DILEMMA

In essence, the message out of Oakland was *Serve the people, be ready to defend the community against racist violence, and be ready to die for the people*. For Panthers around the country, this approach began to feel too similar to how things had felt back in 1966, right before frustrations with nonviolent civil disobedience boiled over into calls for Black Power. What had happened to the energizing rhetoric about offing the pigs? After years of ramping up toward revolution, being told to simply serve the community and wait to be attacked felt like the worst kind of gradualism—waiting on top of waiting.

The Panthers' profound commitment to serving the people still resonated, but the cost of upholding these services began to influence the Party's rhetoric and ideology. As the organization's fundraising needs intensified, the Oakland Central Committee Panthers felt they could not afford to appear as militant as they had set out to in the beginning. By the spring of 1971, fewer guns were appearing in the *Black Panther* newspaper. More articles focused on community services, legal defense, and political education, in addition to featuring members' art and poetry.

Many of the sisters and brothers on the block regarded this softening of the Panther platform as a failure. They felt that the Party had shifted its priorities from serving their community needs to trying to please the white establishment. They felt that too much money, energy, and focus was being spent on freeing the leadership, and not enough attention was being paid to rank-and-file Panther needs on the ground. Frustration grew. And with much of the national leadership either behind bars or struggling to keep the Party afloat, control over the rank and file dissolved.

Local chapters were largely left to their own devices. Many members and chapters continued to adhere to the Panther ideology and rules, but a few promoted illegal activities, which gave the Panthers a bad name. Some of the sisters and brothers on the block thought that freedom "by any means necessary" meant that the Panthers would back up whatever they decided to do, like robbing banks to get money for Panther programs or staging direct attacks on the police.

MILITANT CIVIL DISOBEDIENCE

Panthers learned in political education class that capitalist economic systems were literally robbing the Black community. Business owners were stealing wealth from workers by paying low wages, charging high rents, and increasing the retail cost of basic goods people needed to survive. The Panthers viewed prison as an updated version of slavery and working-class employment as an updated version of sharecropping—a system stacked against workers that gave them no opportunities for advancement and made building wealth difficult or impossible.

If the system was so corrupt, some Panthers felt it was their duty as the vanguard party to aggressively disrupt that system. If the capitalists were stealing the people's money, they felt it was the Panthers' duty to serve the people by taking that money back. Cisco Torres, who joined the Party in Denver, said they called it "'expropriating funds' from banks." In this view, robbing a bank was a political act, not a criminal one.

This belief represented a dramatic shift in attitude and behavior in a handful of Panthers, who adopted this stance of militant civil disobedience. The nonviolent civil rights movement had taught Black people that breaking segregation laws could be an effective path to creating awareness and change. What would it look like if other kinds of laws could be broken to serve the will of the people, too?

Intellectually, and in rhetoric, these questions were exciting to explore. Laws exist to control people's behavior, and to enforce or reinforce social behaviors and expectations. When the social expectations of behavior are biased against certain groups of people, the laws on the books are likely to be equally biased and/or selectively enforced. But throwing out the law book creates a new set of problems and considerations. If people stop drawing the line at the law, where should they draw the line? And how do they decide? If bank robbery in retaliation for capitalist theft was acceptable, what about killing a guard in the process?

The most extreme version of this perspective sent shock waves through the Party: *Not only must you be willing to die for the people, you must also be willing to kill for them*, some Panthers argued.

While laws are human made, most people agree that there are natural laws, inalienable rights that should not be violated, such as every human being's right to live. Every human society develops rules or laws against murder, though they also often allow exceptions, such as killing another person in self-defense or while fighting in a war.

The FBI seized these Panther weapons in April 1974 amid renewed city council campaigns by Panther candidates.

When police or federal agents attacked the Panthers, fighting back was clearly an act of self-defense. But some Panthers believed the revolution had begun, and they were already at war with the police, which meant the rules of engagement could be different. Some Panthers believed that *any* interaction with police should be considered self-defense, even if the Panthers were the ones attacking. They began to see themselves as soldiers, following the rules of war.

PURGES

Many Panthers debated these issues intellectually, but all were still expected to follow the law and the rules of the Black Panther Party. The Party routinely expelled members who broke the law or acted against the Panthers' rules and ideology.

Central Committee member David Hilliard and his brother June traveled to Panther cities around the country to remind people of the rules and to close Party chapters that did not have strong leadership willing to bring people back to the Black Panther Party's true vision.

They expelled people they suspected of being informants. They expelled people who promoted violence or displayed aggression against other Party members or the community. They expelled anyone they considered to be counterrevolutionary. This cleansing of the ranks was called a "purge."

These purges tightened up the ranks somewhat, but there was a larger public relations problem to contend with. Media coverage of the Panthers tended to focus on the more sensational aspects of Party life, like the police raids. A great deal of damage was done to the Panthers' reputation by members and former members who performed criminal activities in the name of the Party. Often these people turned out to be agents provocateurs rather than true Black Panthers, but in most cases, that truth came out much later. At the time, the Party's reputation took hit after hit.

Purging made sense at the local chapter level, as a way to ensure that the Panther rank and file was made up of loyal, hardworking members who had the community's best interests at heart. The situation became more complicated at the national leadership level, as the ideological divide intensified between Huey and Eldridge. The divide ultimately drew entire chapters, like the New York Panthers and the L.A. Panthers, into conflict with the Central Committee.

In January 1971, members of the New York 21 wrote an open letter to the Weather Underground, a white anti-war student group that was an offshoot of Students for a Democratic Society. The Weather Underground, also known as the Weathermen, had perpetrated several bombings and other acts of violence in the name of the revolution. The open letter criticized the Black Panther Party's national leadership, denouncing them as no longer the real vanguard of the revolution. They accused Huey publicly of mismanaging the funds that had been raised for their defense, and they declared that groups like the Weather Underground were the true vanguard because they were willing to take action in support of their beliefs.

In response, the Central Committee expelled the New York 21 from the Black Panther Party. This created significant chaos, as their trial, which had begun in September 1970, was still ongoing. The New York chapter was one of the largest in the country, and their rank and file still viewed the twenty-one as their leaders in the field. Panthers on the ground in New York City suddenly found themselves having to choose sides.

EXPELLED!

On March 4, 1971, a journalist named Jim Dunbar hosted a live broadcast of a phone conversation between Huey and Eldridge. The point was to air some of the troubles between the East Coast and West Coast Panthers, ideally reaching a consensus about the future direction of the Party. But the discussion soon became heated, and at the end of the interview, Huey expelled Eldridge from the Black Panther Party. "The Black Panther Party has reached a contradiction with Eldridge Cleaver and he has defected from the Party, because we would not order everyone into the streets tomorrow to make a revolution," wrote Huey in the *Black Panther.*

COMMITTING TO SURVIVAL

After Eldridge's expulsion, remaining Panther chapters added more and more social services. "To Serve the People" became the core goal and mantra of the Party. For the majority of Panthers (those who stayed with Huey), it always had been. The Split reaffirmed their belief in the Black Panthers' core goals and their willingness to put their lives on the line. They were not just standing up for what was right, not just defending against wrongs, but taking care of their communities out of love for the people.

The health clinics and food programs had already become key programs, nationally recognized as having a positive impact on Black communities. Now the Panthers introduced additional clothing banks, free shoe programs, prison busing to visit loved ones, ambulance services, and much more. They also took their commitment to education to a new level, by founding the Intercommunal Youth Institute in Oakland, a Panther Party–run elementary school.

Children at the Intercommunal Youth Institute

These quiet, yet revolutionary, projects did not receive much media attention from mainstream press. The newspapers seemed to prefer splashy headlines about gun caches and firefights and death and destruction. But from 1971 forward, the bulk of the Panthers' activities looked away from violence, toward creating lasting change. They still intended to overthrow the capitalist system—but they aimed to do it with their own hands, one community at a time.

RIFT IN THE RANKS

Eldridge did not go quietly. Most New York Panthers, among others around the country, sided with Eldridge after the Split, but a few Oakland Panthers had already come to New York to provide leadership in lieu of the twenty-one, and they remained loyal to Huey and the Central Committee. Additional Panthers from California, also loyal to the Central Committee, arrived on the scene to try to retain control of the rest of New York City.

This factionalism soon had life-and-death consequences. Just a few days after the Split, a twenty-three-year-old New York Panther named Robert Webb was shot and killed in Harlem, apparently during an altercation with Oakland-loyal Panthers over newspaper sales. That week's issue contained an unflattering article about Eldridge and Kathleen, and, according to other New York Panthers, Robert Webb was killed because he tried to seize copies of the *Black Panther* from a group of Huey's Panthers who were selling them.

The true story behind the shooting remains unclear. At the time, most Panthers believed Robert was killed by Oakland supporters, but many later came to believe that the shooters were police informants who wanted to intensify the Panthers' inner conflict.

However it happened, Robert Webb's death deepened the divide. A month later, a few New York Panthers retaliated against Oakland by killing

Samuel Napier, the *Black Panther* newspaper's distribution manager working out of New York. They shot him multiple times, left his body in the Corona, Queens, branch office, then burned the building down.

After the one-two punch of these shocking murders, Panther chapters around the country saw a sudden and extreme drop in membership, with perhaps as many as a third of their members leaving the Party. This type of infighting was not what people had signed up for, and the confusion made the organization less appealing to many.

Soon the Eldridge faction was producing its own newspaper, called *Right On!*, which continued the insurrectionary rhetoric that they valued. Safiya Bukhari served as East Coast communications secretary and editor of the new newspaper. Meanwhile, from the West Coast, the *Black Panther* continued to share news centering on education, survival programs, and political engagement.

The front page of the *Black Panther* after Napier's death

Many Eldridge-aligned Panthers, including Jamal Joseph, went underground for a while. "I kept moving from rundown tenements to dank basement apartments, always looking over my shoulder or lying awake, expecting the cops to show up with guns blazing," Jamal said. He was still underground when the New York 21 were acquitted in May 1971.

REVOLUTIONARY INTERCOMMUNALISM

Huey and most of the Panther leadership were still preparing the people for revolution, but they no longer had their sights set on the bloody kind, at least not in the short term. Huey introduced a new word into the Panthers' vocabulary: *intercommunalism*.

Revolutionary intercommunalism was a different way of thinking about how communities interact with one another. Instead of relying on nations to take care of people, Huey suggested that communities should come together and work on improving the world in ways that would help everybody. This idea built on Marxist theories that working-class people could take control of the economy.

The shift encompassed minor changes, like adjusting the *Black Panther* newspaper masthead ("Community News Service" became "Intercommunal News Service"), and bigger changes, like planning a Revolutionary People's Constitutional Convention to bring together people from all sides of the struggle. First, they held plenary sessions in Philadelphia. The plenary sessions allowed anyone who wanted to participate in the convention to come share ideas. Between 10,000 and 15,000 people—mostly Black people and young people—participated, holding sessions on race, class, gender,

sexuality, the environment, the economy, and more.

In theory, intercommunalism was a broad banner under which a lot of people could join. Unfortunately, Huey's new line of thinking didn't resonate with everyone. The highly intellectual rhetoric ultimately distanced many people rather than expanding the tent.

"People walked out in droves," said Assata Shakur. "Almost no one understood Huey's long speeches explaining intercommunalism." But "instead of criticizing what was happening, most Party members defended it." For Assata and others, this drove the divide deeper, as it seemed that to be loyal to Oakland meant bowing to Huey, no matter what.

Meanwhile, Huey remained convinced that the expansion of the Panther message was paramount. "We gather here to let it be known at home and abroad that a nation conceived in liberty and dedicated to life, liberty, and the pursuit of happiness has in its maturity become an imperialist power dedicated to death, oppression and the pursuit of profits," Huey said in a speech to the plenary convention. "Black people and oppressed people in general have lost faith in the leaders of America. . . . [A]nd we are here to ordain a new Constitution which will ensure our freedom."

BLACK LIBERATION ARMY

After the Split, some expelled factions of the Party began calling themselves the Black Liberation Army, or BLA. The BLA was a militant, underground wing of the vanguard. They took their name and inspiration from the Black Panther Party—after all, "the Black Liberation Army" was named in the Party Rules as the only army Black Panthers could fight in. Each BPP chapter had gone through military training and preparation for the time when its members might have to go underground and fight for the BLA. For many expelled Panthers, now was that time.

Being expelled hurt, but they still believed in the cause. "Rather than argue with black people about which faction of the Black Panther Party to follow, we needed to be talking about the path to revolution," Jamal said. He and the other members of the New York 21 had worked hard to raise the communities out of suffering. They did not want New York's Black neighborhoods to degenerate into drug dens and massive pockets of hopeless poverty.

"As Panthers," Jamal said, "we helped organize community marches and protests at known drug locations . . . to shame and intimidate drug dealers by the power of community action." As BLA fugitives, Jamal and his friends marched straight into the drug dens, armed, and demanded the dealers leave the neighborhood. They could no longer rely on a protest in the light of day to make change, but they still cared about protecting the community in the same ways.

Safiya Bukhari joined the BLA, too, but she was among a few leaders who were "elected to remain aboveground and supply necessary support." Even that role took a significant toll. "I had come to realize that nothing was permanent or secure in a world in which it is who you know and what you have that counts," she wrote. "I had seen friends and loved ones killed or thrown into prison. . . . I was receiving a great deal of flak from police."

Being a member of the BLA was even riskier than being a Panther. Police aggression became heightened, plus they had drug dealers, gang leaders, and organized crime bosses to contend with underground. "When you woke up in the morning as a Panther you had the thought that this might be the day that you went to prison or got killed," Jamal said. "When you woke up in the morning as a soldier of the Black Liberation Army you had the thought that this was definitely the day that you would die."

At least six BLA members did die fighting for their cause. And perhaps a dozen police officers died battling against them. Plenty more BLA members were caught in the act of trying to wage war against the establishment, or brought in by the police under suspicion of the same. They joined the rapidly increasing ranks of Panther political prisoners.

"Many different people have said and done many different things in the name of the Black Liberation Army," said Assata Shakur. "It is a concept, a people's movement, an idea." Assata, who became one of the best-known BLA members, spoke these words as a political prisoner, in her testimony when she was on trial for bank robbery in 1976.

"I wasn't one who believed that we should wait until our political struggle had reached a high point before we began to organize the underground," Assata later wrote. "And although i felt that the major task of the underground should be organizing and building, i didn't feel that armed acts of resistance should be ruled out. . . . Not any old kind of actions, but actions that Black people would clearly understand and support."

Like the Panthers, the BLA viewed themselves as engaging in self-defense. "A war between the races would help nobody and free nobody and should be avoided at all costs," Assata wrote. "But a one-sided race war with Black people as the targets and white people shooting the guns is worse. We will be criminally negligent . . . if we do not prepare to defend ourselves against it."

ASSATA SHAKUR: BLA WARRIOR

Assata Shakur joined the Black Panther Party in New York City in 1970. She worked in the medical cadre in Harlem, befriended members of the New York 21, and served in the Free Breakfast for School Children Program. Amid frustrations with the Party after the 1971 Split, she soon switched her allegiance to the BLA.

Assata was indicted ten times between 1973 and 1977, on charges varying from bank robbery to kidnapping to attempted murder of a police officer. In two cases, the charges were dismissed; in three cases, she was acquitted; and one trial resulted in a hung jury. Assata's only conviction occurred in 1977, for the murder of a New Jersey state trooper after a roadside stop in 1973.

On May 2, 1973, Assata and two others were pulled over for a broken taillight by a pair of state troopers on the New Jersey Turnpike. The routine traffic stop turned into a deadly shootout, leaving state trooper Werner Foerster and Panther Zayd Shakur dead, and Assata and the second officer injured. Assata was apprehended shortly after the shooting occurred and was held as a political prisoner thereafter. She was convicted in 1977 and was serving a sentence of thirty-three years to life when she escaped from prison in 1979.

It is difficult to know the relationship between Assata's activities in the BLA and the specific charges that were brought against her, but she maintains her innocence of these charges, including the death of state trooper Foerster. Assata and many Panthers believe she was targeted by COINTELPRO or similar operations.

After her escape, Assata sought asylum in Cuba, where she has lived in exile ever since. On May 2, 2013, the fortieth anniversary of her arrest, Assata was placed on the FBI's Most Wanted Terrorists list.

A relatively small percentage of Panthers took their actions to BLA-level extremes, even among Eldridge's militant-leaning faction. Even prison organizer George Jackson sided with Huey during the Split, which proved important for keeping the prison branches of the Party in the organization. George was known for powerful rhetoric around revolution, plus his brother had staged one of the more famous acts of violence against the state. The fact that he was willing to stick with Huey and the Central Committee through the turmoil carried weight with many Panthers who were otherwise on the fence.

But almost exactly a year after his brother's bold attempt to free him, George Jackson was shot to death by guards while allegedly trying to escape from San Quentin Prison. Many Panthers and fellow prisoners believed the escape was a setup, as part of the plot to stop George's prison organizing.

The Party's reaction to George's death was notably more muted than it had been to previous tragedies like the murders of Lil' Bobby Hutton and Fred Hampton. There was no sudden, dramatic rhetoric in the *Black Panther* about offing the pigs or waging revolution in the streets. The Panthers expressed sorrow and condolences, but the flames of their rhetoric had been turned down low. At George's funeral, Huey's remarks emphasized George's love for the people, saying very little about the idea of retaliation or revolution in response to this action by the state.

ATTICA!

Imprisoned people across the country took George Jackson's death quite hard. In upstate New York, inmates in Attica Correctional Facility were inspired by George's revolutionary message to stand up for themselves, and they staged a hunger strike in protest of George's death, demanding better food and care. The prisoners turned their shoelaces into black armbands, in honor of George.

Attica prison inmates negotiating with New York Corrections Commissioner Russell Oswald ▶

252 REVOLUTION IN OUR TIME

On September 9, 1971, the inmates' protest escalated. About a thousand of Attica's 2,254 prisoners took control of the southeast prison block. The spontaneous uprising resulted in the inmates taking hostages—thirty-nine guards and prison staffers—and releasing a list of demands to the prison warden. The demands included higher wages, better food, better medical care, religious and political freedom, and amnesty for the uprising itself.

Four tense days of negotiation followed. In the midst of the chaos, Panther members acted as civilian observers and helped relay communication between the inmates and the prison officials. Bobby Seale and Big Man Howard were two of the Panthers who went into Attica. Along with press, they were allowed inside to view the hostages and confirm to the prison officials that no one had been harmed.

Walking in there, down a long corridor, Big Man thought, "If ever there was a place that looked and smelled of death, this was it. It was just hours away." The inmates applauded when the Panthers entered. Bobby made sure they knew that the Panthers supported their demands. There was really nothing else they could do.

After the Panthers' walk-through, the standoff and negotiations continued. For a time, it appeared as though prison officials would meet some of the demands to end the standoff. But they chose to enact a tragedy instead.

"It's a scene not easily forgotten," said Big Man. A force made up of state troopers, sheriff's deputies, and prison guards launched an assault on the captured cellblock. Helicopters dropped firebombs, and guards with weapons fired down into the prison yard from high upon the walls. Ten hostages and twenty-nine inmates died in the assault, and eighty others were seriously wounded. "It was just an open fire order down into that yard," Big Man said. "The prisoners stripped off their clothes to show they were unarmed." But the guards just kept on shooting.

The Attica assault sent a now-familiar message loud and clear: the state would not tolerate any requests for humanity or any dissent against its authority. For the Panthers, it underscored the truth they had been grappling with for the past year: there could be no negotiation with the U.S. government. It was either play by the rules of society and accept a course of gradualism, or live as outlaws and fugitives and expect to be imminently destroyed.

◀ **Bobby Seale entering Attica state prison during the uprising to help mediate the dispute between guards and inmates**

LAST GASP

The thing I really loved about the Black Panthers was that they refused to be ignored.

—FATHER GEORGE CLEMENTS

The 1971 Split irreparably fractured the Black Panther Party. Rank-and-file members grew disillusioned as the chaos sown by the FBI carved deeper into the heart of the movement. Enough people had died that every chapter was affected by loss in one way or another. Dozens of people were in prison. Dozens more were out on parole, out on bail, awaiting trial, wanted, or living underground. Now that they understood that there were informants within their ranks, it was difficult to know who they could really trust. Panthers grew accustomed to sleeping with one eye open for fear of government bullets coming at them out of the night.

HIGH-RISE

The Central Committee was particularly worried about assassination attempts against Huey. According to Elaine Brown: "Wherever Huey was, it was certain the police would be. Outside his parents', there might be police in phony mail trucks. Police drove taxicabs behind the car he was riding in; police walked down

Two women partaking in the Black Panther–organized
People's Free Food Program, Palo Alto, California, 1972

Huey in the high-rise

whatever street he walked on. They were so invasive, it became necessary . . . to post a bodyguard overnight with Huey wherever he stayed."

In early 1971, the Central Committee moved Huey into an upscale apartment in a high-rise in Oakland. They claimed he was living there for security reasons, but the rank and file accused Huey of abusing hard-earned Panther funds. It was costing at least $600 per month to keep the penthouse, which was a huge sum in those days.

Regular Panther members, many of them living on the ten cents from their newspaper sales, survived by cramming several people into small living spaces. "Panthers who owned little more than the clothes on their backs were out in the street in the freezing cold weather selling papers, with big pieces of cardboard in their shoes and with flimsy jackets that did nothing to hold back the hawk," said Assata. They'd sacrificed everything short of their lives for the Panther movement—and most of them believed it was only a matter of time before they died in service to the cause. Seeing Huey living an extravagant lifestyle was disillusioning at best, and a betrayal at worst.

"I wanted to believe the security story, but it didn't fit my sense of logic," Assata said. The appearance of Huey's high-rise life, combined with his increasingly tight leadership style, led the rank and file to doubt his motives and judgment.

The accusations hit Huey hard, especially when the Department of Justice began investigating the Panthers' bookkeeping, too. Huey struggled in his personal life, especially with drugs and alcohol. Many Panther members turned to alcohol, in particular, to help cope with the uncertainty and pain and fear of day-to-day Panther life. Panther rules prohibited members from using alcohol or drugs while on duty, but some did use these substances off-duty. For Huey, the drugs and alcohol began to take over his life.

Huey's substance abuse affected the Panther organization. He was their co-founder and one of their leaders, and his actions upset many Panthers, including his closest colleagues and fellow leaders. He often stayed in his penthouse, taking interviews and issuing mandates. It was a far cry from the "live for the people, die for the people" hero the people had long rallied behind, but he still viewed himself as the absolute leader of the Party, even changing his title from Minister of Defense to Supreme Commander.

"There were great things about the brother," said Winston-Salem Panther Larry Little. "But then that mercurial personality of his and the drug abuse led to some God-awful decisions."

REGROUP IN OAKLAND

Huey's suspicion caused him to expel many members in the wake of the Split. With the Black Liberation Army staging assaults and going after police officers, and other Panthers (and provocateurs) committing crimes in the name of Black Power, the Party had descended into chaos. The national leadership was desperate to regain control. They theorized that if they could re-center the Party in Oakland, they could rebuild the movement from the ground up.

In 1971, Ericka Huggins and Bobby Seale were found not guilty (by hung jury) of the murder and kidnapping charges in Connecticut. The judge declined to retry them, and Ericka was released. Bobby still had time to serve on his contempt charge from the Chicago trial, but the court overturned his sentence in September 1972. Huey and Bobby reunited in Oakland, seeing each other again (outside of prison) for the first time in over five years.

Ericka also returned to the West Coast, this time to join the Central Committee in Oakland. Elaine Brown replaced Eldridge as Minister of Information and dug into reshaping the Party's political message.

The Oakland Panthers held a Black Community Survival Conference in March 1972. They gave away bags of groceries, registered voters, and talked to people about the importance of bringing the community together to help take care of those most in need.

Two months later, in May, Bobby Seale and Elaine Brown announced that they would run for political offices in Oakland. If lasting political change was going to happen in the country, with or without a violent revolution, it

A flyer for the Black Community Survival Conference

was essential to get Black people elected to positions of power. Bobby studied the demographics of political offices around the country. He discovered that there were around 500,000 elected official positions in the country, and fewer than fifty of those jobs were held by non-white people.

Revolution was a long way off, the Panthers now realized. But they could keep moving forward on some changes in the meantime. Surrounded by the thriving survival programs, amid this renewed political push, Panthers in Oakland likely thought things were looking all right for the movement.

Kids packing groceries in the Oakland Coliseum for the Black Community Survival Conference, 1972

THE VIEW FROM ELSEWHERE

The Central Committee closed Panther offices in other cities and redirected energy, personnel, and funds to Oakland to support the campaigns. The week Elaine and Bobby announced their candidacy, the Panthers gave away ten thousand bags of groceries to hungry families.

"Preparing the bags of groceries was a huge logistical feat," said Aaron Dixon, who came down from Seattle to help the campaigns. Volunteers gathered in a church basement, while others drove up in giant freezer trucks full of whole chickens, cartons of eggs, canned goods, bread, and potatoes. "There were many nights of no sleep and long hours of work, but this is what we lived for: meeting, planning, organizing, fighting, and serving the people."

But "it was difficult leaving Seattle," Aaron said. "We had established ourselves so firmly in the community. . . . In four short years, we had challenged the power structure, putting them on notice that they would have constant opposition when it came to making racist policies or committing brutal acts against Black people." Seattle had a health clinic, five breakfast programs, a free food program, a summer liberation school, and a campaign against forced school busing.

Only a handful of people were able to drop everything and rush to Oakland. Those who remained in their own cities floundered in the wake of the Party's withdrawal. Some chapters simply removed the Panther name and logo from their buildings and kept operating their survival programs, but many members felt disappointed and even betrayed by the Party. "It was like a bad, bad breakup," said Patrice Sims, of the Newark chapter. "Everything just stopped, the meetings, the teaching. Everybody just dissipated and went their own route."

A REVISED TEN POINTS

In 1972, the Central Committee updated the Panther Ten-Point Platform. One major change they made was to combine the original points eight and nine into one point that called for releasing all Black men from prison until they could get a fair trial by a jury of true peers. This made room for a new demand: for free universal health care to be provided for all citizens.

The other most significant change was in the language they used to describe the social problems they confronted. "White man" became "white capitalist," because their economic concerns as socialists extended beyond race. They broadened their description of themselves from "black people" to "all black and oppressed people." But the core of the platform remained the same.

Sickle cell anemia testing, 1972

HEALTH CARE ADVOCACY

In Oakland, new initiatives burgeoned. The Panthers understood what a challenge health care was to Black people, and they initiated an unprecedented level of health care advocacy on behalf of Black communities. The People's Free Medical Clinics were the first line of defense, but the organization confronted many related issues of access, education, and research.

In 1972, the Panthers' highest-profile effort was their advocacy around sickle cell anemia screening. Sickle cell anemia is a hereditary blood disease that causes blood cells to be curved instead of round, which makes them less efficient at carrying oxygen through the body. There is no cure for the disease, but it can be treated if it is diagnosed, which requires blood to be drawn and tested. If untreated, sickle cell anemia can be fatal. Sickle cell affects Black people at a much higher rate than other races, and because of racism in the health care system, it had not been significantly researched in the United States. Many Black children were not being tested due to the cost of the procedure and lack of education about the risk factors. The Panther clinics changed that.

Through their Sickle Cell Anemia Research Foundation, founded in 1971, the Panthers also pioneered research into the condition, advocating, raising funds, and promoting testing for the disease. Their efforts raised awareness and ultimately transformed the way that mainstream medical practitioners dealt with sickle cell screening and treatment: screening that was once overlooked became adopted as standard practice. From there, the Panthers' fight against medical discrimination gained momentum.

The Panthers fought against problematic clinical experimentation on Black subjects. Historically, medical researchers had used Black subjects to pioneer experimental medications that were not yet ready to try on white patients. Some researchers had even deliberately infected Black people with serious diseases, or withheld known treatments from them, simply to study disease progression. Black research subjects were sometimes treated as lab animals, like guinea pigs, whose suffering was considered acceptable as a tool to aid researchers in helping white patients in the future.

Medical discrimination was (and remains) a serious issue in the health care industry. Studies have shown that doctors prescribe less pain medication to Black patients, often dismiss their symptoms, or don't investigate symptoms as fully. For example, doctors may be less likely to order advanced screening or expensive medical tests for Black patients, based on assumptions of poverty. This can lead to serious conditions going untreated and, in the worst cases, can even result in deaths that could have been preventable. The Panthers worked to correct these biases, and to rebuild the trust that had long been broken between Black people and health care providers.

Health clinics opened, expanded, and thrived, continuing to provide basic primary care and family medicine. Often the Panthers named the clinics and community centers after slain Panthers, to honor and remember them. Philadelphia created the Mark Clark People's Free Medical Clinic, to honor the Panther who was killed in Chicago on the night of Fred Hampton's assassination. The Alprentice "Bunchy" Carter People's Free Medical Clinic opened its doors in L.A. Seattle had the Sidney Miller People's Free Medical Clinic, named for a local

A classroom at the Oakland Community School/Intercommunal Youth Institute ▶

Black youth killed by police. Chicago had the Spurgeon "Jake" Winters People's Free Medical Clinic, named for a young Panther who took a stand against police during the summer of 1969. The Panthers aimed to improve the health care system itself, as well as providing health education for Black people so they could be better equipped to advocate for themselves in a medical landscape.

OAKLAND COMMUNITY SCHOOL

The Panthers hoped to revolutionize education for Black children, and with that in mind they created liberation schools in communities across the country. Since many of their members came out of student organizing groups, the Panthers had already been working toward Black Studies programs and curriculum for higher education, but they felt that liberation education should start much younger. They believed that through such schools they could empower Black children and their families beyond the classroom, too.

In January 1971, they founded the Intercommunal Youth Institute, later renamed the Oakland Community School. Ericka Huggins took on leadership

for this program after her release from jail. The school served children from preschool through elementary school, and later expanded to middle school. They provided food and other services for the students, taking a holistic approach to education. They also employed progressive educational practices, such as building class groups based not on age but on ability. The school started small, but by 1973 the Panthers had acquired a dedicated building capable of serving 150 students.

"Oakland Community school was one of the most well-known and well-loved programs of the Black Panther Party," Ericka said. She described the school as "a small but powerful group of administrators, educators and elementary school students" who "challenged existing public education concepts for black and other poor and racially marginalized communities."

"Our model was to teach children how to think, not what to think," Ericka said. "The school's philosophy and curriculum have been replicated, which is what we wanted."

VOTE FOR BOBBY! VOTE FOR ELAINE!

In the spring of 1973, as planned, Bobby ran for mayor of Oakland and Elaine Brown for a city council spot. They campaigned hard, registered hundreds of new voters, and drew huge crowds of supporters. But despite all the work the Panthers put into their campaigns, Elaine and Bobby both lost their elections. The losses were very disappointing to the Panther leadership, very disillusioning to the remaining membership, and perhaps showed it had been a mistake to put all their eggs in the Oakland basket. The Panthers had been intent on capturing Oakland, creating a bastion of Black-controlled land somewhere within the American empire. Perhaps they had not given quite enough thought to how the organization would proceed if they could not win.

In the moment, though, they considered it a victory of sorts, as they'd received 40% of the overall vote and succeeded in creating a strong Black voting bloc that could be activated again in the future—a foundation to build upon, according to Elaine.

Then, in 1974, something occurred that caused Chairman Bobby Seale to leave the Black Panther Party altogether. Reports of what might have really happened between the founders are vague. Huey was in the habit of expelling members who displeased him, and some versions of the story suggest Huey expelled Bobby, for some sort of (real or perceived) infraction. The remaining Panthers felt stunned and confused at this unexplained development.

Later that year, Huey was accused of assaulting his tailor and a young woman. Rather than face the charges against him, Huey fled. He went into exile in Cuba, leaving his most trusted associate, Elaine Brown, in charge of the Black Panther Party.

Elaine and Bobby campaigning together in Oakland

(Photo: Ron Riesterer/ PhotoShelter)

Elaine Brown (*standing*) at a press conference

CHAIRWOMAN BROWN

When Huey left the country, and with Bobby already out of the picture, Elaine Brown stepped into the role of Chairwoman of the entire Party. Elaine raised the Panthers to a new level of organization and political power. Since she had run for city council the year before, she was a well-known person in Oakland, not just with Panther members but in the community as a whole. "Elaine paid much more attention to the needs of the troops than had the earlier leadership," said Aaron Dixon, who served as one of her right-hand staffers. "It looked like we had a very real chance of capturing Oakland."

The Panthers, in Oakland at least, began to breathe a bit easier. It no longer felt like they were at war with the police. Community services, electoral action, and behind-the-scenes political power became the most important elements of Panther life. The Party that had seemed to be dying got a surge of new life. As Aaron put it, "In effect we put our guns in the closet and instead drew upon the talents of our members to develop the programs and strategies for moving the community forward."

ELIMINATING THE OFFICES OF PRESIDENT AND VICE PRESIDENT

In 1974, President Richard Nixon was impeached by Congress and resigned after being implicated in a broad-scale political scandal known as Watergate. Nixon, a Republican, had broken the law by conspiring to, among other things, bug the Democratic National Committee Headquarters in the Watergate complex in D.C.

During the months of inquiry and investigation leading up to Nixon's resignation, the Black Panther Party released a position paper calling for the elimination of the offices of president and vice president. They wrote, "The expansion and consolidation of U.S. economic, political, and military force and power abroad has made the president of the United States more powerful than any king or tyrant in history. It has tricked the American people in to becoming coconspirators with the U.S. empire builders."

The position paper discussed how the powers of president and vice president could so easily be abused, using Nixon's administration as an example, and they argued that it took power away from the people to place so much authority in the hands of a single man. They advocated turning power over to Congress, as the "duly elected representatives of all the people."

From a historical standpoint, the Panthers argued, the intent of the checks-and-balances system made sense; however, the executive branch had strayed far from its original role in the structure of government. They wrote, "The executive branch has swollen, steadily usurping power from the courts. The kinglike executive has preempted the decision-making process inherent in the original checks and balances plan."

From a legal standpoint, they laid out their strategy for effecting this change at the highest levels of government. They argued that it was the sacred task of the people to stand up for themselves: "Let us be unafraid to meet the challenge laid before us by our founders, so long ago, to have such a government that derives its 'just powers from the consent of the governed.'"

Panther Chief of Staff David Hilliard (pictured here on the steps of the Lincoln Memorial in Washington, D.C.) calling for a new U.S. Constitution that would guarantee *all* Americans the rights to life, liberty, and the pursuit of happiness—rights that Black citizens had long been denied

Elaine led the Party from 1974 to 1977. In that time, the Party helped elect the first Black mayor of Oakland. Elaine worked within the political structures to secure a major highway construction contract that brought thousands of jobs to Oakland. The Oakland Community School grew to serve two hundred children and gained a reputation for excellence. "That school was an oasis for everybody who stepped into it," said Ericka Huggins. "[It] was a major pilot for what education could be."

Now stripped of their violent revolutionary rhetoric, the Panthers made progress toward the systemic change they had been aiming for all along. But at the same time, the lack of that rhetoric—and its exciting, provocative edginess—rendered the organization a shadow of what it once had been.

FINAL YEARS

Most storytelling about the Panthers ends with the 1971 Split, with a tiny coda about the next ten years, but that version only acknowledges the first four years of an organization that served the people for over a decade. With Elaine and Ericka at the helm, the Panthers became arguably more effective and certainly more sustainable than they had ever been. By consolidating in Oakland, they had lost their national reach, but there were hints that it could be rebuilt. Their hope was that, after building political power in Oakland, they could once again expand that model to other cities.

But Huey returned from exile to Oakland in 1977, and with Huey back, the mistrust, confusion, and paranoia that had accompanied the Party in the COINTELPRO days returned. "There's nothing that can change the brilliance of Huey Newton before he became really sick," said Ericka. But his substance abuse, and likely other factors such as post-traumatic stress disorder and/or other untreated mental illness, made him difficult to work with and to manage. He continued to expel people for unclear reasons or for minor infractions and was interpersonally volatile. Longtime committed Panthers like Aaron Dixon and even Elaine herself grew frustrated with the challenges of keeping the Party together. Huey's personality had changed so much that some members even wondered if he had somehow been deliberately targeted and compromised by federal agents, as a means of disrupting the Party.

The Panthers continued their community service work for the next several years, but their efforts lacked the energy and spark of the early years. Many of the programs slowly closed or became independent community-run services as the Panthers who led them left the Party or were cut off from the organization. The widespread coalition support the Panthers had built in the late 1960s–early 1970s began to dwindle. Advances in the women's movement and the U.S. withdrawal from Vietnam meant that women's groups and student groups were less active. Few could be motivated to support Black liberation with the same fervor once their own interests had been satisfied. Several historians have argued that the U.S. government made concessions to these interest groups partly to disrupt the Panthers' extraordinarily effective coalition-building.

The Panthers stopped printing their newspaper in 1980, when circulation had become so low, it no longer seemed worthwhile. In the final months, circulation of the *Black Panther*—once 400,000 copies per week—dwindled to only a few hundred copies per week.

The last Panther program to go was the Oakland Community School, which closed its doors in 1982. The Black Panther Party had breathed its last gasp.

Michael Brown. Eric
Garner. Trayvon Martin.
Oscar Grant. Renisha
McBride. Steven Washington.
Alonzo Ashley. Ronald
Madison. John Crawford.
Yvette Smith. Kendrec McDade
Ervin Jefferson. Rekia Boyd.
Sean Bell. Kimani Gray.
Amadou Diallo. Aiyana Jones.
HOW MANY
MORE?
No More Stolen Lives!
Trayvon Martin
killed by
wannabe cop vigilante
Feb 26, 2012

EMBERS

1982–Present

The thing about embers . . .
they can be rekindled.

THE POST-PANTHER DECADES

History is clear. Sacrifice, uplift, persuasion, and education have not eradicated, are not eradicating, and will not eradicate racist ideas, let alone racist policies. . . . Those who have the power to abolish racial discrimination have not done so thus far, and they will never be persuaded or educated to do so as long as racism benefits them in some way.

—IBRAM X. KENDI, *STAMPED FROM THE BEGINNING*

During the Panthers' last years, Americans had already begun to hold up the landmark legal and social achievements of the civil rights era as a total triumph over discrimination, prejudice, and racism. The country seemed eager to put the messy business of racial unrest behind it and declare victory.

Unfortunately, "racist progress has consistently followed racial progress," writes Dr. Ibram X. Kendi, a noted historian who studies race in America.

◁ Lisa Rae Gutierrez Guzman was arrested for striking at San Francisco State College in 1968. More than fifty years later, the struggle continues.

Previous spread: Seattle youth protesting against police brutality in August 2014, after Michael Brown was shot by police in Ferguson, Missouri

Whenever it appears that Black people have broken through barriers, white people have "created . . . new and more sophisticated barriers . . . [and] developed a new round of racist ideas to justify those policies."

Those who survived the Panther movement understood that Black Americans had only come so far. There was still much work left to do. And the decades that followed the Panther era brought a swift but subtle backlash against the advancements that a generation of young Black Americans gave up their lives to secure.

1980s: THE WAR ON DRUGS

As the United States emerged from a recession in the early 1980s, many Americans were concerned about the economy. President Reagan put in place a series of policies that he hoped would stabilize the economy. He cut taxes (primarily for wealthy business owners), cut government programs, and increased military spending. Instead of taxing its own wealthy citizens, the U.S. borrowed money from other countries, creating significant national debt but allowing a comfortable middle class to develop. Reagan-era policies also created new pathways for individuals and corporations to accumulate extreme wealth.

Echoing President Nixon, President Reagan spoke about law and order, prioritizing policies that would make life more comfortable for white middle-class people. Nixon had initiated the "war on drugs," a series of laws and law enforcement practices designed to stop the sale and use of illegal drugs like marijuana, cocaine, and heroin. Reagan deepened and expanded the effort. These drug laws disproportionately affected Black communities, as the "war on drugs" became the new catchphrase alongside "law and order" as coded language for suppressing Black people.

Nixon adviser John Ehrlichman later admitted that this practice was very deliberate. "We knew we couldn't make it illegal to be . . . Black but by getting the public to associate the hippies with marijuana and the blacks with heroin and then criminalizing both heavily, we could disrupt those communities. We could arrest their leaders, raid their homes, break up their meetings and vilify them night after night on the evening news. Did we know we were lying about the drugs? Of course we did."

Without examining the root causes of how drugs get into poor communities or why they are used, the Reagan administration criminalized drug *use* (not just selling or trafficking), effectively painting a huge swath of struggling people as criminals rather than being in need of help and support. Police descended on Black communities, claiming to be there to clean up the neighborhoods. In the process, they painted poor Black communities as drug-infested dens of poverty and crim-

First Lady Nancy Reagan championed a drug-free nation via the "Just Say No" campaign.

inality, unsafe and unclean. This intentional marketing campaign has had wide-reaching implications to the way Black people are perceived in the United States even today.

1990s: THE PRISON INDUSTRIAL COMPLEX

The war on drugs led to unprecedented rates of incarceration. The way that drug laws were written and enforced directly targeted Black people. For example, between the two types of cocaine, crack cocaine and powdered cocaine, crack was more common in Black communities, and powder was more common in white communities. A person caught with five ounces of crack immediately faced a minimum prison sentence of five years, while a person had to be caught with 500 ounces of powder cocaine to receive a five-year sentence.

Prison-reform activists began using the term "prison industrial complex" to describe the collection of systems that worked together to keep so many Black Americans imprisoned. The reasons people ended up behind bars were much more complicated than simply who had broken the law. Similar percentages of Black men and white men use drugs, and yet a Black man is five times more likely to be arrested for a drug charge. In 1998, Black people made up 13% of the U.S. population, yet approximately 45% of prisoners were Black. By 2010, a Black man was six times more likely to be incarcerated than a white man.

Americans' ingrained racial biases and fervent belief in the "innocent until proven guilty" stated value of the justice system make it hard for many to believe that the system can really be this unfair to Black people. It helps to start looking beyond the surface of things, toward the economic underpinnings of the justice system and the prison system.

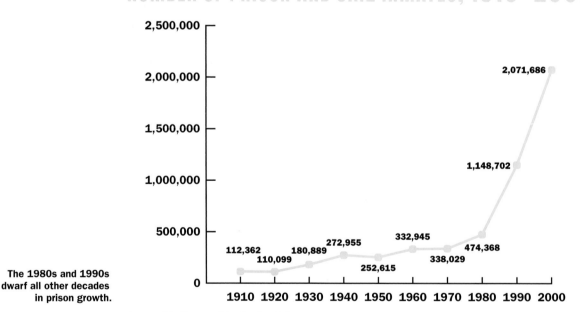

NUMBER OF PRISON AND JAIL INMATES, 1910–2000

The 1980s and 1990s dwarf all other decades in prison growth.

Source: **The Bureau of Justice Statistics**

Data points:
- 112,362
- 110,099
- 180,889
- 272,955
- 252,615
- 332,945
- 338,029
- 474,368
- 1,148,702
- 2,071,686

RODNEY KING

For decades, the justice system had unfairly targeted Black people, while frequently being exceptionally lenient to white people, especially white police officers. On March 3, 1991, a group of white police officers in Los Angeles pulled over a Black motorist, Rodney King. They arrested him and his two passengers. In the course of the arrest, the officers beat Rodney King with batons, used a Taser on him, and tackled him. The attack lasted several minutes, as the officers hit him until he was unable to get up.

A witness captured the assault on videotape. The brutality that Rodney King experienced was not new or surprising to Black people, but at that time, it was rare to have video evidence of the incident, rather than simply relying on witness statements. The police officers were charged with excessive use of force, tried, and acquitted on April 29, 1992.

When the verdict came down, Black and Latinx communities in Los Angeles rose up in rebellion. To many, the Rodney King verdict represented an open-and-shut case of police brutality. If the system couldn't offer justice in this case, how would it ever?

Sixty-three people died in the course of the uprising. People looted stores and set fires, causing property damage estimates of around $1 billion. For those who still remembered the Watts rebellion in 1965, it felt like a blast from the past.

White Americans shook their heads at the verdict, but more so at the unrest. The officers had been tried and acquitted. Wasn't that justice? In many ways, the violence seemed distant, restricted to Black and Latinx urban communities, whose members, white people decided, really were doing it to themselves.

Running a prison is expensive, and at the same time it can be a source of significant wealth for a business owner. Prisons receive more funding when they have more prisoners, and, in a modern-day echo of plantation slavery, incarcerated people's labor is owned and controlled by prison officials. In order to maximize their own profits, they need more prisoners. Always more.

Many people are employed based on the expectation that crimes will occur: police officers, defense attorneys, prosecutors, judges, administrators, prison guards and wardens, prison doctors, prison administrators, parole officers, and all the other staff involved from arrest to imprisonment. People in these jobs often have financial incentives to keep the system going.

The prison industrial complex exists because a series of connected policies and practices between law enforcement, the government, the courts, the prisons, and major corporations work together to make it financially advantageous to send more and more people to prison. When most of those people are Black (or simply non-white), ingrained racial bias makes it easier for white people to overlook the problematic practices of the legal system because they don't feel directly threatened by them. They convince themselves that those behind bars deserve to be there. Unfortunately, the core value at the heart of the American prison system is not the desire for justice, but the desire for money.

2000s: THE WAR ON TERROR

When two hijacked airplanes hit New York City's World Trade Center towers on September 11, 2001, killing three thousand people, white middle-class Americans were shaken out of their complacent bubble. A third plane struck the Pentagon, and a fourth, destined for the U.S. Capitol Building, crashed in a Pennsylvania field after brave passengers attempted to subdue the hijackers.

The attack ended two decades of white Americans pretending that everything was basically fine and they were untouchable. The towers fell, and suddenly white Americans were given new language for their racism and xenophobia: the war on terror.

September 11 inspired extreme nationalist fervor, along with outpourings of love and support for police officers and firefighters after so many first responders died in the twin towers. Deep fears about terrorism emerged among Americans. Because the hijackers claimed to be followers of Islam, Muslim communities were repeatedly targeted for bias and racism.

The U.S. government created a prison at a military base in Guantánamo Bay, Cuba, where they held individuals suspected of terrorism for months and years without due process. The Patriot Act introduced loop-

Smoke streaming from the World Trade Center towers on September 11, 2001

holes that allowed the government to deny people (mostly people of color) their right to trial, offering yet another example of the law and human rights being bent to serve the will of the state. While this law was ostensibly set up to respond to foreign threats, it affected plenty of U.S. citizens. If you so much as shared a common last name with a person suspected of terrorism, you could fall under suspicion yourself.

Policymakers, citizens, and the media alike openly discussed the balance between freedom and safety, between individuals' civil rights—like the right to free speech, freedom of assembly, freedom of association, and privacy—and the government's right to conduct surveillance, gather information, and use that information to protect the public. It was a big shift from previous attitudes toward individual civil rights, as people discussed when and how it was appropriate to violate a person's civil rights in service of national security. Historical patterns suggested that Black people, Muslims, indigenous people, and other people of color would be disproportionately affected by such policies. Many Americans seemed to believe that the government would use this power only to pursue a "genuine threat," while others questioned what criteria would be used to make that determination.

In this time of heightened fear, media representations of law enforcement played an insidious role in reinforcing pro-police biases. The proliferation of law enforcement television shows, where police often break the law for "good" reasons, failed to acknowledge how damaging this illegal behavior can be in real life. Such shows had always existed, but in the new climate of fighting terrorism, they became emblematic of something much more frightening, a factionalism that essentially placed white American police officers on the front lines of a race war.

Nightly, Americans could watch yet another bad-boy detective get slapped on the wrist for going in without a warrant in pursuit of justice. Audiences enjoyed watching police—the "good guys"—play games with suspects' civil rights and dance along the lines of legality to coerce a confession or trick a suspect into self-incrimination. Most white Americans absorbed this media without recognizing that the presumption that "the police are here to protect me" was not a view that could be shared by everyone.

THE FACADE OF POST-RACIAL AMERICA

In 2008, Barack H. Obama became the first Black person to be elected president of the United States. Even while being heralded as a triumph of racial progress, his election spurred a backlash of racism and white supremacy. In some white communities, explicit racist propaganda surfaced, bringing to light the presence of deep-seated racism that hadn't been so widely recognized by white Americans in decades.

Still, many Americans believed that the simple fact that the country's voters had elected a Black man president meant that the country had evolved beyond any concerns of racial bias. Conservatives and liberals alike dismissed the white supremacist resurgence as a fringe ideology, unworthy of mainstream recognition. Much like what had happened at the end of the Civil War and at the end of the civil rights era, Americans celebrated the public victory and congratulated themselves on their racial progress, while failing to properly address the deeper issues going on beneath the surface.

When President Obama was elected, Americans' primary concern was for the economy. During the election season, President George W. Bush was in the midst of solving an economic crisis that had occurred because of questionable (and even illegal) business practices among banks, investment firms, and mortgage lenders. Several of these multibillion-dollar businesses had gotten themselves into serious trouble, and, as a result, they had placed the entire nation's economic structure and prosperity at risk. The U.S. government decided to use taxpayer funds to "bail out" these major financial institutions, hoping to prevent a greater economic collapse. A massive recession would have been bad for all Americans, they argued, and yet many people found it shocking that the government felt such an obligation to support a handful of wealthy white men in their time of crisis, when it had been so challenging for decades to get anywhere near the same level of crisis support for poor people.

The first Black First Family: Malia, Michelle, Barack, and Sasha Obama with their family pets

Stability and opportunity for working-class and middle-class families remained the stated priority of most government efforts, but economic policies in the United States told a different story. With the "Wall Street bailout," as it was known, many people felt the U.S. government had proved that it cared more about wealthy white businessmen than the middle class, working class, or people living in poverty. Those latter three groups made up the vast majority of Americans—about 99%. Meanwhile, the top 1% of income earners in the United States held about 40% of the nation's wealth.

This represented a shocking degree of wealth disparity in a country designed as a democratic republic in which any citizen theoretically has the right and ability to pursue success and build wealth. It dramatically evidenced the uneven rewards of capitalism that the Panthers tried to draw attention to years earlier. Especially since of all the people in the top 1%, only 1.7% were Black. If hard work and merit were really the keys to profound economic success, it would stand to reason that about 13% of the top earners in the country would be Black, because Black people make up 13% of the total U.S. population. But that was far from the case.

Crowds of protesters gathered in Zuccotti Park in Manhattan during the Occupy Wall Street movement

In 2011, an economically inspired movement developed, seeking to call attention to the existence of this 1% and the imbalance of financial power they wielded as compared to "regular" Americans. In mid-September, activists set up tents in Zuccotti Park, a small green patch amid the towering corporate landscape of Manhattan's financial district. They pledged to Occupy Wall Street until the government acknowledged the wealth disparity and took systemic action to disrupt it.

The protest was met as anyone with a knowledge of American history would expect—with aggression and violence from law enforcement. Americans watched with shock on November 15, 2011, as police teargassed and arrested the young protestors, mostly white. Protestors had successfully occupied the park for nearly two months.

Former Panther Chairwoman Elaine Brown felt the Occupy movement "was powerful in that it established in the mass mind that there are two Americas— the very rich, the 1 percent, and the rest, the 99 percent—instigating an instant of outrage, leaving behind that consciousness." That type of mass-movement organizing continues to be needed, she argued, and hadn't been seen in recent years.

Since the Occupy movement, some activists have drawn their attention to an even smaller subset of the top 1%—the top .001%, which is the top one-thousandth of a percent. This handful of individuals—about 16,000 people/families—control approximately 11% of income in the United States. These individuals include people who run major corporations with thousands of minimum-wage employees, like Walmart and Amazon. Economic justice advocates point to the disparity, asking: *Why is this country perpetuating a system that allows one person to make billions of dollars a year that is earned from other people's labor, while paying the people who do the full-time work a wage so low they often have to take a second job to meet their basic living expenses?*

STAND YOUR GROUND

On February 26, 2012, seventeen-year-old Trayvon Martin was walking toward his father's fiancée's home in a gated community in Florida. A Neighborhood Watch member named George Zimmerman called the police, then followed Trayvon, because he felt a young Black man in a hooded sweatshirt walking in a predominantly white neighborhood appeared suspicious. The two apparently struggled, and George Zimmerman shot Trayvon Martin, killing him. He called it an act of self-defense. In most states, using lethal force in self-defense is acceptable only as a last resort, in a situation where you are unable to flee. Under Florida law, a person under threat has the right to stand their ground and fight rather than flee.

The Martin/Zimmerman case catapulted to national attention because of the moral questions surrounding the Stand Your Ground law. Many people wondered, did Trayvon Martin have to die? Should an armed person be able to shoot an unarmed person with no consequences? There were no witnesses to the encounter, so the only certain facts were that Zimmerman had followed Martin and ultimately shot him. Clearly bias had played a role in Trayvon's death—Zimmerman initiated the encounter because Trayvon looked suspicious to him.

As the court case progressed, Zimmerman received mail from white supremacists, praising him for his actions. Supporters set up fundraising efforts to help with his legal defense, and some of these people praised Zimmerman specifically for killing a young Black man. By the time Zimmerman was acquitted of charges against him, the whole country was paying attention to Trayvon's case.

BLACK LIVES MATTER

After Zimmerman was acquitted, three Black women began using the Twitter hashtag #BlackLivesMatter. Alicia Garza, Patrisse Cullors, and Opal Tometi hoped to draw attention to the fact that racism was causing young Black people to be targeted for death, whether due to deliberate acts of white supremacy or insidious acts of unconscious racial bias. They pointed to the long history of Black people being murdered by white people—from historical lynchings to modern-day police brutality—and the equally long history of society failing to hold

The hashtag has been used millions of times on Twitter, peaking at 8.8 million uses in a single day.

white people accountable for these actions.

Black Lives Matter became an extremely popular hashtag, and ultimately developed into a broad social movement against racially biased violence, the Black Lives Matter Global Network. The national movement continues, while satellite chapters work to deepen the organizing locally. As with the Panthers, this spread happened quickly, with thirty chapters established within two years. Unlike the Panthers, Black Lives Matter's founders embraced a more democratic, feminist, intersectional, grassroots style of leadership, allowing the movement to expand and decentralize rather than seeking to control or dictate every aspect of the movement. Critics suggest this makes the movement less organized and effective than prior movements, but Black Lives Matter supporters point out that those movements have often lived or died along with their leadership, making them easier to target and destroy.

As with every prior social movement to bring equality to Black people, Black Lives Matter experienced a harsh backlash. White people who were offended by the exclusivity of the phrase "Black Lives Matter" began using the hashtag #AllLivesMatter. Some argued that focusing on Black lives was unfair. But President Obama weighed in on the discussion, saying:

The reason that the organizers used the phrase "Black Lives Matter" was not because they were suggesting nobody else's lives matter. Rather, what they were suggesting was there is a specific problem that is happening in the African-American community that's not happening in other communities. And that is a legitimate issue that we've got to address.

Activists viewed the attempt to shift the conversation from "Black lives" to "all lives" as yet another erasure of the specific experiences and perspectives of Black Americans. Their argument is that this country has yet to recognize that Black lives matter *at all*. Even more insidiously, some people began using the hashtag #BlueLivesMatter, ostensibly in support of all police officers but with the disturbing implication of especially supporting officers who commit biased-based shootings out of fear for their own lives.

Protestors in Falcon Heights, Minnesota, marching in protest after police shot Philando Castile to death during a traffic stop

Black Lives Matter activists kept alive the vision of their movement by calling attention to lethal acts of bias, especially acts of police brutality, that occurred in the years following Trayvon Martin's sensationalized case.

On August 9, 2014, police officer Darren Wilson shot eighteen-year-old Michael Brown in Ferguson, Missouri, a suburb of St. Louis. Officer Wilson and witnesses reported the event differently, creating controversy about how and why Michael Brown was killed. It seemed as though Officer Wilson suspected Michael of participating in a convenience store robbery. He approached Michael and his friend in his police car, scuffled with Michael through the car window, and then fired at him. When the boys ran away, Officer Wilson got out of the car and fired several more times at Michael, striking and killing him in the process. The officer claimed self-defense, but people in the community didn't believe that the situation had escalated to the point of needing lethal force.

In November 2014, a grand jury declined to indict Officer Wilson for a wrongful shooting. The demonstrations in the street that followed echoed the Black community uprisings that occurred in 1964–1968 in cities around the country. Once again, Americans watched on television as a highly militarized police presence descended on a Black community, with tear gas and crowd-control gear.

A few months later, after twenty-five-year-old Freddie Gray died in police custody in Baltimore, that city, too, rose up in protest. Officers stopped Gray because he ran when he saw them coming, and then arrested him for carrying a knife in his pocket. He died due to injuries sustained during the arrest and/or during the van ride to the police station, including a severed spinal cord.

A protest held in downtown Baltimore on April 25, 2015, about a week after Freddie's death, turned toward rebellion, resulting in numerous arrests and injuries. Freddie's death was ruled a homicide, and six officers were charged in his death. All were eventually acquitted.

Michael and Freddie were but a few of the young Black people who had died that year due to police brutality and racial bias. Black Lives Matter protestors began carrying signs: HANDS UP, DON'T SHOOT, in honor of Michael Brown, and I CAN'T BREATHE, in honor of Eric Garner, who was choked to death in Staten Island in 2015 by Officer Daniel Pantaleo, with other officers on the scene. His crime: selling cigarettes.

More than a decade into the twenty-first century, amid headlines that continued to proclaim a post-race America, young Black people knew they were still fighting for their lives and freedom.

Crowds chanting "Hands up, don't shoot" during protests after Michael Brown was killed by police in Ferguson, Missouri

In light of these ongoing demonstrations and community uprisings, white Americans are quick to remind Black Americans that violence is not the answer. They are quick to say, *We know the world isn't fair, but we're working on it.* When Black people experience rage and frustration so strong it explodes out of their skin, white people see a lack of patience and moderation. When Black people act as if they have nothing to lose because all hope of equality is already lost, white people see misdemeanors and felonies. When Black people treat the law itself as meaningless because they are criminalized just for existing, white people see . . . criminals.

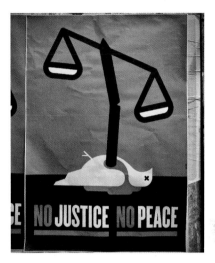

The Black Lives Matter movement spread worldwide. This poster appeared in Berlin, Germany, during protests in June 2020.

Black citizens are consistently shamed and criminalized for engaging in even peaceful demonstrations for civil rights. Asking to be treated as human in this society is, apparently, a bridge too far. When Black Lives Matter protestors stood in downtown Baltimore chanting, "No Justice, No Peace," the media reacted as though the protestors were promising destruction if the verdict did not go their way.

In fact, this chant is drawn from a quote by the Rev. Dr. Martin Luther King Jr. in which he expressed the reality that in a nation where we do not have a functioning justice system, peace does not exist. "No Justice, No Peace" is not a threat of violence, but a profound statement about the existing injustice that plagues American society. Most Americans, unfortunately, are far too steeped in the system to understand the deeper meaning of the chant.

THE NEW BLACK PANTHER PARTY

A group calling itself the New Black Panther Party came on to the scene around 1989. Like the original Panthers, they were a cadre of angry young Black people. Unfortunately, the New Black Panthers failed to pick up where the original Panthers left off. They twisted the meaning of the Panthers' militant voice into something hateful, all while using the Panther name and banner. Members of the original Panther Party worked to get the truth across to the media, saying, "There is no New Black Panther Party. . . . The Party operated on love for black people, not hatred of white people." But since history has so often overlooked the Panthers, few people understood the difference. It was all too easy for the New Black Panthers to confuse people.

WHITE SUPREMACIST BACKLASH

While police seem to view a group of Black demonstrators as a crowd that has the potential to be violent, similar assumptions are rarely made about a predominantly white crowd. In 2016, the crowds that flocked to campaign rallies for presidential candidate Donald Trump often carried explicitly racist signs. Trump and his supporters alike made repeated references to enacting violence against women and people of color, in addition to his central campaign promise to build a wall to keep new immigrants out of the country. These words and actions were consistently treated not as threats but as examples of free speech or even campaign hyperbole.

Many political analysts attribute the high voter turnout for Donald Trump in the November 2016 presidential election directly to the racist language he used in the campaign. Like previous "law and order" candidates, Trump used coded language to assure white Americans that he would work for them. Unlike previous candidates, he also used overtly racist language. His words empowered many people who openly identify as white supremacists to develop a bolder, more visible presence in the country.

On August 11, 2017, various white nationalist groups joined together for Unite the Right, a rally to protest the removal of a statue of Robert E. Lee (a famous Confederate general) from a Charlottesville park.

Shocked white Americans wondered what the response would have looked like if a group of young Black men marched through the streets carrying torches. Black Americans did not have to wonder.

White supremacist demonstrators marching through Charlottesville, Virginia, to protest the removal of a Confederate statue

MASS SHOOTINGS

One troubling effect of the white supremacy movement is the number of young white men who have turned to violence as an extension of their beliefs. In 2015, a twenty-one-year-old white man entered a Charleston church and murdered nine Black people attending a prayer service. In 2018, a former student returned to Marjory Stoneman Douglas High School in Parkland, Florida, and killed seventeen people on campus. In 2019, a white gunman motivated by anti-immigrant rage killed twenty-three people, many of them Latinx, in an El Paso Walmart. These are but a few of hundreds of examples. Between 1982 and 2019, 117 shooting rampages occurred in the United States, at least 64 of which were perpetrated by white men. Far from self-defense, these shootings represent deliberate assaults upon innocent members of the public. They are acts born of hatred.

There are more than a few remarkable things about this tragic trend. One, in responding to these scenes, law enforcement officers have repeatedly proved themselves capable of apprehending armed active shooters without using lethal force. This stands in sharp contrast to the viciously biased way Black suspects are treated when there is even a hint of suspicion that a gun could be present.

Two, the media coverage routinely humanizes and individualizes these white men, in an effort to explain their actions and choices. The legal and illegal actions of young white men who openly subscribe to a white supremacist belief system do not seem to reflect on the groups they belong to, no matter how violent their rhetoric. (In contrast, the legal and illegal actions of any member of the Black Panther Party reflected on not just the Party but the entire Black population.) In the moments when our society does recognize that there might be a pattern to these shootings, people usually look past race and suggest that the shooters are suffering from a mental illness. This excuses the individual's active racism and cruelty by suggesting that they didn't make a choice, but rather were acting from a diminished capacity, even though the overwhelming majority of people with mental illness do not commit mass shootings. When it comes to Black suspects, Americans are far less likely to leap to examine systemic issues like poverty, lack of opportunity, or even mental illness.

Three, there has been little meaningful gun rights reform in response to this movement of young white men arming themselves with the intent to inflict violence against innocent people. Public pressure from fearful students and concerned parents has increased, and yet significant legislative action toward gun control has stalled. In some corners, the response has even been to increase the presence of guns in schools and the volume of guns carried by private citizens. Even President Donald Trump said, "If you had a teacher who was adept with the firearm, they could end the attack very quickly." He continued, "They'd go for special training . . . and you would no longer have a gun-free zone."

This response stands in stark contrast to the immediate gun-control measures put in place when Black people began arming themselves against police brutality.

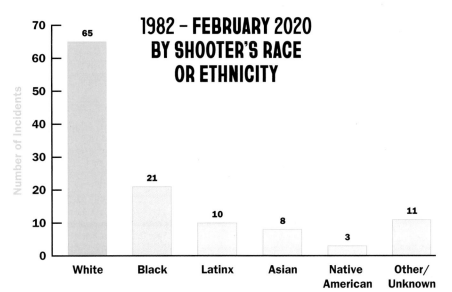

MASS SHOOTINGS IN THE UNITED STATES

1982 – FEBRUARY 2020 BY SHOOTER'S RACE OR ETHNICITY

Source: **Mother Jones**

The Mulford Act in California went into effect barely a year after the Black Panther Party was founded, and even the National Rifle Association supported that gun-control bill. Collective action by a very small number of Black people who planned to act only in self-defense was perceived as a significant enough threat to literally change the laws of the state. However, the same government struggles to see collective action by a growing number of young white men as anything more than a series of anomalies.

THE BIG PICTURE

When white Americans felt scared in the civil rights era, the country went after civil rights organizers and Black radicals, to the point of infringing their rights, to the point of imprisoning hundreds and killing dozens. When white Americans felt scared after September 11, the country went after Muslims here and abroad, to the point of infringing their rights, to the point of imprisoning hundreds and killing thousands. White Americans today could rightly feel scared of some of their own young white men, and yet still choose to turn that fear toward the Other, going after immigrants,[1] Indigenous people, and people of color, to the point of infringing their rights, to the point of imprisoning thousands and killing hundreds.

In this country, it would seem, white Americans can do no wrong and deserve to be protected at all costs. If the price of their comfort is the lives and liberty of Black Americans, this country is more than happy to pay. The Panthers' stories, and all these that followed, illuminate a shocking disparity in how people of different races are treated.

---

[1] The word *immigrants* as used today is sometimes a euphemism for people with national or ethnic origins outside of western Europe. Technically, the term applies only to people who were born outside the United States, but as a by-product of systemic racism, many white Americans label the descendants of non-white immigrants as "immigrants," too, while regarding themselves as American. This is a deliberate perversion of language, as all white Americans with European ancestry are either immigrants themselves or descended from immigrants, whether those who colonized this land on behalf of Europe or those who arrived later.

For those who live in the Black Lives Matter era, much of what the Panthers did—such as openly approaching police officers while visibly armed—seems shocking to the point of being unimaginable. Black people today find themselves at risk even when unarmed, and myriad examples from recent years indicate that police officers feel empowered to act with lethal force if they even *suspect* there might be a weapon, or if they simply feel afraid for their lives, a highly subjective judgment that is easily colored by racial bias. Is it possible that, despite all our claims of racial progress, police brutality has in some ways become even more of a threat to Black lives?

Just as the complex and intertwined forces of law, media, politics, economics, and bias combined to build the prison industrial complex, similarly insidious forces of white nationalism, the global war on terror, and even pop culture representations of Black people and law enforcement alike combine to create an atmosphere in which Black lives are systematically devalued and white people are given the benefit of the doubt.

Why does a Black man talking on a cell phone in his backyard get shot, while an armed white man actively committing a mass shooting can be brought in unharmed? Why do police armed with tear gas, wearing crowd-control gear, roll into Ferguson in tanks, while uniformed police stroll alongside the Unite the Right white nationalist demonstration in Charlottesville?

In America, who is allowed to freely exercise their rights to speech and assembly? Who is allowed to bear arms? Why does a white person's right to survive and thrive exceed a Black person's? In the United States of America, who is allowed to act in self-defense?

LEGACY

I have come to realize that picking up the gun was/is the easy part. The difficult part is the day-to-day organizing, educating, and showing the people by example what needs to be done to create a new society. The hard, painstaking work of changing ourselves into new beings, of loving ourselves and our people, and working with them daily to create a new reality—this is the first revolution, that internal revolution.

—SAFIYA BUKHARI

The story of the Panthers is not only an oft-overlooked chapter of history, but a potent reminder that there is still significant work to be done. The civil rights movement that we often call "past" remains very much part of the present. What does the future hold?

Among young Black people, there exists a renewed, ongoing churning toward justice. Perhaps that fervor never truly went away, but now, through organizations like Black Lives Matter and by harnessing the power of the internet, young activists are finding new ways to confront the systemic barriers to Black American survival and progress.

"Frantz Fanon said that each generation of youths will discover their mission, and upon discovering it they must decide to either fulfill it or betray it," Panther Larry Little reflected, adding that as a former Panther, "My job is to help them understand their mission so that they can fulfill it."

Ericka Huggins, 2015

Surviving Panthers hope that their story—the whole story: their victories, their mistakes, and the things they learned—can continue to inspire Black and oppressed communities. A new generation of young activists must pick up the mantle and become the vanguard of the revolution, whatever that looks like in their own time. *Our* time. Right now. Today.

"You can be inspired by what happened back then, but you can't duplicate what happened back then," said Emory Douglas. The Black Panther Party arose at a moment in time when all the elements appeared to be in place for the social, cultural, and political revolution that they promised. The American system withstood the Panthers' attempt, but surely now there is at least a crack in the foundation.

When young people ask her about the Panthers, Ericka Huggins says, the questions are never about the violence or the sensationalized tragedies. Instead, they ask: *How did you feed all those people? How did you start all those programs?* This is because "they can see past the media narratives to what we were really doing," she says. "That's really heartening."

TWENTY-FIRST-CENTURY PANTHERS (WHERE ARE THEY NOW?)

Former Panthers have gone on to do many great things to uphold the values they were willing to give their lives for in the heyday of the Party. Some, like Ericka Huggins, continued as educators. Some sought higher education themselves, like Huey Newton, who earned his PhD from the University of California, Santa Cruz. Some, like Bobby Seale and Kathleen Cleaver, found mechanisms to keep speaking out about their beliefs and to keep struggling for change. Others began careers as lawyers, nurses, engineers, journalists, or business owners. Several former Panthers founded nonprofit community organizations to continue work like the Panthers had done, such as converting old BPP headquarters into

Ericka Huggins and Jamal Joseph speaking in 2016

Bobby Seale in 2006. All surviving Panthers continue to carry the message forward.

community centers or running People's Free Medical Clinics under new names. A handful of former Panthers and BLA members remain incarcerated, while others, like Angela Davis and Safiya Bukhari, dedicated themselves to prison reform activism. Several former Panthers, like Jamal Joseph and Aaron Dixon, continued to work with youth, and former Panthers across the country participate in speaking engagements, panels, and documentaries to tell their stories and the story of the movement. A phenomenal archive maintained by Billy X Jennings in Sacramento and the efforts of the Black Panther Party Alumni Association keep the Party's legacy very much alive.

Panther alumni gather regularly to celebrate their victories, mourn the losses, and reconnect with old friends and comrades now scattered around the country. "We who survived these battlefields remain indebted to our sisters and brothers who are no longer with us, both the departed and the imprisoned, and to our fugitive and outlawed ancestors whose fighting spirit guided our course," Kathleen Cleaver said. "It's good that we come together to honor and to continue that attitude of devotion, love and sacrifice."

"We worked, ate, slept, laughed, and fought together for years and years," said Panther Steve Long. "To have it end so unceremoniously was difficult for a lot of people and a lot of people are still dealing with that separation."

Safiya Bukhari wrote about the disillusionment she and others faced over moving out of the Black Panther Party once it ended. The struggle continued, and yet the vanguard party that was supposed to lead the way was no longer there. "We sincerely believed that the Black Panther Party would lead us to victory," she said. "The only way we wouldn't live to see it would be if we died in battle."

Safiya and many of her friends suffered from post-traumatic stress disorder as a result of their lives as Panthers and in the Black Liberation Army. Jamal Joseph felt incredible relief the day he realized there was an actual clinical name for what he was experiencing. It helped to understand that "the last fifteen years had not been the fragmented episodes of a young man wrestling with beliefs and identity but rather a continuum of mind-engulfing and soul-deep pain," he said. "Like the person who can't afford medical care and learns to live with a toothache or back pain, I had ignored the forces that were tearing me apart."

The years of intense pressure from police, the violence they experienced and witnessed, and the constant fear of imprisonment or death created conditions very similar to the pressures soldiers face in a wartime combat situation. "We too are veterans," Safiya said, who have to contend with "our awareness that we are still alive while our people's conditions have grown worse despite all our sacrifices. . . . This is the ultimate shock."

Aaron Dixon (*at podium*) speaking alongside a group of former Panthers and fellow activists at a book event in 2012

Billy X Jennings and the It's About Time archive

The destruction of the Black Panther Party remains a source of grief to many former members, especially since all the information about COINTELPRO came to light in the 1980s, after the Freedom of Information Act forced federal authorities to release their records. Jamal Joseph was in prison when he saw COINTELPRO documents for the first time. "I cried as I read what had been done to us, realized how we were divided and manipulated and made to turn against one another." Former Panthers can now look back and realize that they were never as divided as they thought; in fact, it was the very power of their words and actions to unite Black and oppressed communities that brought their enemies forward.

Also particularly painful is the fact that there has been no end to the poverty, violence, and desperation within Black communities that the Panthers hoped to banish. Many Black children remain hungry. Underfunded schools struggle to educate students in predominantly Black communities. The prisons are overcrowded with Black men and women, whose circumstances are as much the cause for their imprisonment as their actions.

The Panthers who remain continue to carry the movement in whatever ways they can. "As members of an organization, many of us consider that we didn't complete our task," said Steve Long, who asserts that his formative experiences in the Party have "influenced everything I've done since."

Each Panther took a lifetime oath to love and to serve the people, and even though the structure for doing it has changed, they will not give up. The challenges remain severe, but true Panthers don't back down from a fight. Ericka Huggins said, "We wanted for people who have nothing to have something. And that doesn't compute for people who have everything."

The echoes of the Black Power movement continue to this day. Some of those echoes help us to understand the Panthers, and further illuminate who they really were and what they really did. Many Panthers, like Aaron Dixon, Assata Shakur, Safiya Bukhari, David Hilliard, Bobby Seale, Elaine Brown, Jamal

Joseph, and Huey Newton have written memoirs about their Panther days. Many speak and continue to share the message and the work they started decades ago. Thanks to their efforts, that message is now being heard in classrooms across the nation, in businesses and organizations in diverse communities, and even in the highest reaches of government.

REMEMBERING THE FALLEN

For thirty-five years, Lil' Bobby Hutton's grave in an Oakland cemetery had no headstone. His family could not afford the cost of even a modest plaque to honor his memory. On February 15, 2003, former Panthers gathered for a brief ceremony to finally mark his burial site. A local artist, Cheryl Parkins, designed the gravestone in Lil' Bobby's memory. Kathleen Cleaver called the occasion bittersweet. "We need to pause to appreciate it and to think back to where each of us was that dark night of April 6, 1968, when he was shot down by Oakland police bullets."

Fred Hampton's gravestone bears a spate of massive pockmarks, from bullets that have been fired at his final resting place. The first few times it happened, the headstone was replaced with a fresh one, but the new one would be shot up again. At some point the family decided to stop replacing it. This vandalism was integral to Fred's legacy, they decided. Racist violence was part of his life and led to his death, and the struggle deserved to be remembered.

Lil' Bobby Hutton's gravestone

Fred Hampton's gravestone, pockmarked by bullets

The Panther legacy has repeatedly been misunderstood and misrepresented even by those who wish to honor it. Like any organization this radical and complicated, the Panthers' legacy has many layers: layers of truth, of error, of beauty, of sorrow, and of struggle. There is a way to tell the story of the Panthers as one of violence, a way to tell it as one built entirely on love and care for the people, a way to tell it as a strange and complex mix of forces that led this group of young Black people to stand up, take arms, and fight.

It's not possible in this space to mention every Panther, known and unknown, who put their life on the line, or to enumerate each of their sacrifices. But each played an important role in the movement, however invisible to history. "What I'm most proud of is that I was able to be this back-office type person who helped build institutions to better the community," said Panther Norma Mtume, who ran the health clinic in Los Angeles. "A lot of people don't know about me and that's okay. I know what I did."

As sure as it died a bloody death, the Panther movement helped bequeath to a new generation of Black Americans the opportunities and education and knowledge we are afforded today. Elaine Brown said:

> In the long struggle of blacks in the United States for freedom, from the resistance of Angolan Queen Nzinga to the slave traders in the 1600s, to the slave ship rebellions of captured Africans headed for what would be the United States, through the myriad acts of resistance during the first 150 years of enslavement by the English and other colonialists, to the heroic rebellions during the nearly 100 years more of slavery, to the bloody efforts of blacks to survive the Black Codes and Plessy in the hundred years of struggle that followed, to the bloodshed that paid for the 1964/1965 civil and voting rights

legislation, and to the brutal struggle thereafter for human rights for blacks, there cannot be said to have been a more powerful or revolutionary effort by blacks for freedom than that of the Black Panther Party—dramatically evidenced by the fact that the United States government brought down upon it the full weight of its repression.

The Panthers excited people, scared people, challenged people, made them wonder what Black people were capable of—and it turns out that Black people are capable of anything, even when we have to build from scratch the infrastructure necessary to create opportunities. "It was the most amazing work I've ever done," Ericka Huggins said of her time in the Panthers. "Because we made something out of nothing."

"The Black Panther Party has attempted to provide an example to the community of what is possible," said David Hilliard, "and to raise the people's political consciousness so that we can all step forward with dignity and courage."

"It is the power of the people and the people only to whom we will be thankful, and in whom our faith rests for the future," Huey Newton wrote. Bobby Seale added, "At this time more than ever we need . . . creative Black youth who know our history and who understand that Black Unity is the catalyst to help humanize this racist world."

Although it was the culmination of endless eras of struggle, the Black Panther Party itself only survived a little more than a decade. In that time, the committed few who carried the Panther banner sacrificed everything—their time, their comfort, their families, their freedom, and their very lives in an effort to change the world they were born into. "Nothing will justify those years except the victory of the people," Huey said.

There are many who wish to erase this past, while others dedicate their lives to ensuring that America never will forget. The Panthers' stories live on, simultaneously soul-deep and soaring. The biggest question that remains is: *Who will succeed the Black Panther Party as the revolutionary vanguard, and what shape will the movement ultimately take?*

Many young Americans can feel the power of a contemporary, radical, fully intersectional vanguard forming right now, around us and within us. We are aware of the reality that after four hundred years on these shores, Black people in America are still enslaved. We must also be aware that we have fought our enslavement at every turn, and the struggle continues.

"We need activists who cross all ethnic and religious backgrounds and color lines who will establish civil and human rights for all," Bobby wrote. "We must create a world of decent human relationships where revolutionary humanism is grounded in democratic human rights for every person on earth. Those were the political revolutionary objectives of my old Black Panther Party. They must now belong to the youth of today."

Young members helped drive the Party to its peak. The Panthers invested in education and empowerment so that the youth in their communities would carry the movement forward.

REVOLUTION IN OUR TIME

The revolution has always been in the hands of the young.

—HUEY P. NEWTON

The Panthers' conviction that young people are the key to social transformation has always struck a chord with me. One of the strongest emotional memories I have from childhood is the frustration of constantly being told in one way or another, "Wait until you're older." Sometimes the sentiment was cast very dismissively, as in "You're not old enough to understand." Other times it was dressed as the well-meaning and hopeful "What do you want to be when you grow up?" Adults found myriad ways to underscore the message that I was merely in training to someday become a person who mattered.

The abject falsehood underpinning this way of thinking still bothers me. When I speak with people younger than me, I try hard to reframe that question. I ask, "Who do you want to be *right now*? What can you do tomorrow to push yourself one tiny step closer to your goals? What can you do today to help make the world a better place, whatever that means to you?" Not in ten years, not when you grow up—but *today*.

◀ **Young protestors in New Haven, Connecticut, during the New Haven 9 trial**

Because the truth is, so many of the movements that have shaped this country (and the world) have been led by young people. It is the vibrancy, vision, and commitment of teenagers, school-age children, and college students who put the civil rights movement in motion. The Rev. Dr. King and Malcolm X, the two most widely known and celebrated martyrs of the movement, were both assassinated at age thirty-nine, which means their ministry took place in their twenties and thirties. When I was a child learning about these leaders, I heard "thirty-nine" and thought of them as old. I now know the world regarded these men as young upstarts, shaking the foundations of society because they weren't "grown" enough to know better. More importantly, I now know that they were among the eldest of those doing the work of social change.

I'm now very aware that the whitewashed, adult-filled version of history I was taught obscured this facet of things on purpose. To perpetuate the narrative that young people are humans-in-waiting. To keep young people in their perceived place.

Ericka Huggins frequently reminds people that "the median age of Panthers was nineteen," which means many Panthers were even younger. We don't have to wait. We can change the world from the time we are very young, from the moment we realize there are injustices to correct. We can be brave like six-year-old Ruby Bridges, who integrated her elementary school all alone in 1960–1961. We can be confident like Lil' Bobby Hutton and Tarika Lewis, sixteen-year-olds who saw the Panthers in action and were among the first to step up and join.

When we do step up, we must start by learning what has gone before, by steeping ourselves in the history of revolutionary movements, until we understand the heart and soul of what it means to fight a revolution. It may not mean picking up a gun—the Panthers alone showed us that there are myriad ways to reimagine, transform, and, yes, revolutionize the communities, the nation, and the world we live in.

In October 2016, I attended the BPP Fiftieth Anniversary celebration in Oakland, California. I interacted with Panthers and Panther supporters, including having a brief conversation with Bobby Seale and a coffee outing with Ericka Huggins.

The first event was a luncheon celebrating Bobby Seale's eightieth birthday. It was a conference-style seated lunch event held on the second floor of a restaurant/event venue on the waterfront. Speakers on the dais included Ericka Huggins, recently released political prisoner Albert Woodfox, and of course Bobby Seale. It was by turns exciting and extremely humbling to be surrounded by a roomful of people much older than me who had actually lived this history that I have spent years studying. Speaker after speaker was someone whose story I was familiar with, people who had been shot, done time, risked their lives, and so on, for the movement. I spent most of the lunch slightly choked up.

When I finally got face-to-face with Bobby Seale, my mind filled up with images—him speaking in Oakland, him behind bars, him tied and gagged in the Chicago 8 trial courtroom. I felt unworthy to be in his presence. The work I was trying to do was but a pale imitation of the sacrifice and commitment of the Panthers. Did I even have the right to tell their story? It was difficult to speak. Bobby Seale signed my book and I managed to give him my card and tell him that I write books for children. He was

The Panthers' Fiftieth Anniversary celebration offered opportunities for protest and education as well.

Bobby Seale signing a book for me at the Fiftieth Anniversary luncheon

extremely receptive to me, his expression patient and open, even while I flailed for the right words.

In his gaze, I could feel the truth that the Panthers were (and are) driven by love for the people. I felt like he cared about me, and it would be okay to keep trying to tell this story. That it was important to keep this often mis-told history alive for the next generation. The Panthers were very much about education, empowerment, and truth for the next generation. In that room on that day, I got what I came for in more ways than one.

The main celebration the next night was a cocktail reception and seated dinner at the Oakland Museum, which also had a wonderful exhibit about BPP history. It was a very formal and institutional event, which struck me as interesting and even ironic, given the original revolutionary and countercultural style of the Black Panthers. It lacked the warmth and camaraderie of the birthday lunch. It felt more performative. I was seated next to elected officials and journalists from San Francisco who had come to support the event. I found myself wondering if we were all under FBI surveillance. The former Panthers at the front showed videos and made speeches. The event was held outdoors in the museum's courtyard and gardens, which made it feel more expansive but much less intimate.

The attitude of the attendees suggested a desire to see and be seen, not to really absorb the history. Parts of the speeches were hard for me to hear, because a group of guests at my table and the next table kept chatting through all the speeches. It was frustrating that the people around me weren't displaying anywhere near the reverence for the speakers or the event that I felt the Panthers' commitment and contribution inherently deserved. It renewed my belief that the Panthers have been so underrepresented, misrepresented, and belittled over time that few people really understand who they even were and what they did.

My other main takeaway was that it was an event perhaps too focused on the past, on what had occurred in the 1960s and 1970s. There was a conspicuous lack of youth representation in the speeches. When they pivoted to talk about the current events, it was much more focused on the release of political prisoners, which has been an ongoing battle for former Panthers all over the country. It's important work, of course, but for me it is not the whole picture, because so many of the social dynamics that the Panthers worked to overturn are still ongoing and perhaps even more entrenched than they were at the time. I felt a renewed sense of urgency to convey the Panthers' story to young readers, in a way that connects the work that happened back then with the work that is happening today.

LOOKING FORWARD: WHAT HAPPENS NOW?

I've written and rewritten this final chapter several times in the course of my work on this book, each time in a slightly different context. I penned reflections immediately after returning from the Fiftieth Anniversary celebrations in Oakland. I made repeated updates as the Black Lives Matter movement unfolded. As I write this now, it is the spring of 2020 and I am working from my house in Vermont, under self-isolation during the COVID-19 pandemic. As the country faces a global health crisis, we also struggle through a shortage of masks for health care workers, a government "stockpile" that doesn't seem to be getting to the citizens who need it, and an increasingly impatient population of (predominantly) white people who advocate for personal freedom without regard for personal responsibility.

This very spring, a Black woman, Breonna Taylor, was shot to death in her bedroom when police executed a no-knock warrant on the wrong home. A Black man, Ahmaud Arbery, out for his daily jog, was followed by two armed white men, who assaulted him and shot him to death. These tragedies occurred against the backdrop of white citizens bearing legal arms and marching on statehouses to protest social distancing orders. When these white citizens began issuing death threats to lawmakers, an armed unit of young Black people stepped forward to escort a Black lawmaker to her office. Watching these race and class disparities play out once again in the streets of our nation, it is clear to me that the history we study is still happening right in front of our eyes, just as it was happening in front of the Panthers. They took action. Will we?

Of course we will. In the weeks since I wrote the two paragraphs above, a Black man, George Floyd, died with a white police officer's knee on his neck on a street in Minneapolis. The community took to the streets in response, despite the looming threat of the pandemic, to demand justice for George and accountability for the police officers who killed him. That peaceful protest was answered with tear gas and rubber bullets. In the following days, Minneapolis and cities around the country exploded with protests, uprisings, and chants of "Black Lives Matter," "No Justice, No Peace," and "Abolish the Police." Predictably, these demonstrations were also met with continued repression and violence at the hands of law enforcement. We have been here before, and we'll be here again.

By the time this book comes out, it is a near certainty that we will have endured other painful moments as a people, as a nation. There is a constant stream of new context informing and illuminating this history. What will we do with this knowledge, and how will we use it to shape the movements for justice yet to come?

I discovered an archival video in the course of my research, with former civil rights movement leaders who were looking back in the early 2000s at their own words and convictions of the 1960s. They declared in retrospect that the biggest mistake of the civil rights era was to believe that all the problems could be solved in their lifetime, and they failed to train the next generation to take up the mantle in the necessary ways to maintain the struggle. My own life experience bears this up in a lot of ways: young people are often underestimated and excluded from challenging conversations. Whether it's to protect the children, or due to a misguided faith in their own power to solve everything, the perennial mistake of elders is to dismiss the power and potential of youth. On the flip side, the mistake of youth is often to dismiss the wisdom and experience of those who have gone before. In their day, the Panthers didn't make either of these mistakes. They placed the core of their emphasis on building a cadre of revolutionary youth, and they promoted empowerment through education about Black history. They were undermined and overturned at every stage, perhaps partly because of the truly systemic nature of the change they envisioned, and the fact that they made real progress in these directions in a very short time frame.

Can we achieve such a thing again? I believe we can, and I particularly believe that the Panthers' legacy will speak to the Black Lives Matter generation of young activists already working today. Perhaps we do not need to entirely reinvent the wheel, if we can be brought to understand the mistakes and successes of the activists who've gone before us. We deserve access to this history, as well as the opportunity to build our own future.

ACKNOWLEDGMENTS

I began researching and writing this book over a decade ago, so a proper acknowledgments section would include pretty much everyone I've ever met. Or so it seems. It has been a journey. I'm grateful to the many helpful librarians and staff at the archives I visited all across the country. I'm grateful to the former Panthers I've met and studied for so generously and repeatedly sharing their stories with the world. I'm grateful for every article and anecdote and archival film clip I stumbled across that helped me put the pieces of this puzzle together.

I'm grateful for the dear friends who listened to me talk at them while I honed my arguments and worked toward deeper understanding, especially Will Alexander and Alice Dodge, Sarah Albee, Tracey Baptiste, Martha Brockenbrough, Emily Kokie, Kerry Land, Kobi Libii, Cynthia Smith, Linda Urban, Nicole Valentine, and Renée Watson. Ann Jacobus kindly opened her home to me several times to enable me to do extensive research in the Bay Area, which would not have been possible without her support. Thanks also to Nancy Hobson, Janet Fox, Shawn Jordan and Amelia Lo, Kiara Koenig, Tami Lewis Brown, Tara Mack and Gary Younge, Bich-Van Pham, and Zu Vincent for similarly taking me in. I'm grateful to Professor Pam Harkins for consistently sharing books and wisdom, and my colleagues at Vermont College of Fine Arts for their support. My parents remain my biggest fans, and they have always been there for me in times of challenge and joy.

I appreciate my editor and friend Andrea Tompa more and more with each passing book. The entire team at Candlewick Press has embraced this challenging project with enthusiasm, including book designer Nathan Pyritz, cover designer Matt Roeser, publicist Jamie Tan, copyeditors Erin DeWitt and Hannah Mahoney, and Erin Farley, who helped with photos. My agent, Ginger Knowlton, is a tireless advocate as well. So many wonderful people have put love, wisdom, and energy into this book, and I am forever grateful.

KEY PEOPLE

The story of the Black Panther Party intersects with the life stories of many individuals. It was ultimately a global movement that engaged thousands of people, but this book could only capture a few of their names and a small portion of their experiences. Many Panthers have written their own autobiographies or shared their stories in articles and interviews. Here are some of the key players in BPP history who appear in this book.

ELAINE BROWN: A member of the BPP Central Committee and eventual Chairwoman, Elaine grew up in Philadelphia and attended Temple University before moving to Los Angeles. She held several roles in the BPP, from a leader in the L.A. chapter, to Minister of Information, to taking over as Chairwoman when Bobby Seale left the Party and Huey Newton went into exile. She has been a candidate for local and national offices ranging from Oakland City Council to president of the United States. After leaving the Party, Elaine lived abroad for a time before returning home to continue her work in racial and economic justice. Through her nonprofit corporation, she provides legal aid and economic development opportunities for incarcerated and

formerly incarcerated people. She has written several books and created albums of her own music.

H. RAP BROWN (now Jamil Abdullah Al-Amin): A SNCC leader and BPP member, Jamil served time in Attica Correctional Facility in the early 1970s, converted to Islam, and changed his name. After his release, he opened a mosque in Georgia, but after a murder conviction in 2002, Jamil remains a political prisoner.

SAFIYA BUKHARI: A New York Panther, Safiya sold newspapers and worked at a free breakfast program site for the BPP before joining the BLA and acting as a support for underground members. Arrested in 1974, Safiya spent nine years as a political prisoner. Released in 1983, she spent the rest of her life advocating for political prisoners. She died in 2003 after an illness.

STOKELY CARMICHAEL (Kwame Ture): Elected Chairman of SNCC in 1965, Stokely popularized the slogan "Black Power" after a 1965 speech. His leadership of voter registration efforts in Lowndes County, Alabama, inspired the Black Panther Party and its name. Stokely eventually became Field Marshal of the BPP. Later he moved to Guinea, West Africa, and changed his name to Kwame Ture. He continued writing and advocating for international cooperation among Black people until he died, in 1998.

ALPRENTICE "BUNCHY" CARTER: One of the L.A. chapter leaders, Bunchy had served time in Soledad Prison with Eldridge Cleaver. He worked within the coalition of Black student organizers across Los Angeles to recruit members for the Party. Bunchy was murdered on January 17, 1969, as part of a COINTELPRO plot to disrupt and destroy the Panther leadership.

ELDRIDGE CLEAVER: A journalist by training, Eldridge became BPP Minister of Information, overseeing communications and publication of the *Black Panther* newspaper. Eldridge served time in prison before joining the BPP. His book *Soul on Ice* was a national bestseller, though controversial due to the extreme sexist views he portrayed. Eldridge went into exile in 1968 and spent the rest of his time in the movement leading the International arm of the BPP from his home in Algeria.

He was expelled from the Party in 1972 after an ideological clash with Huey Newton. Many Panthers followed him, and Eldridge continued leading the East Coast branch of the Party, dedicated to pursuing immediate armed insurrection. When he and his wife, Kathleen, left the Black Panther Party, they moved to France but eventually returned to the United States, where

he faced the charges he had evaded. Eldridge underwent a religious and political conversion, denouncing many of his earlier views. He and Kathleen separated in 1981, later divorcing. Eldridge died in 1998.

KATHLEEN NEAL CLEAVER: Central Committee member and Communications Secretary for the BPP, Kathleen began organizing as a leader in SNCC, then joined the BPP after forming a connection with Eldridge, who became her husband. When he went into exile in Algeria in 1968, Kathleen joined him, helping to build and lead the International BPP. When they left the Black Panther Party, the couple moved to France but eventually returned to the United States. Kathleen separated from Eldridge after his political beliefs evolved toward extreme conservatism. They divorced in 1987. Kathleen went to law school, then went on to teach. She continues her work, living and teaching on the East Coast.

ANGELA DAVIS: A prominent activist, writer, and educator, Angela became a symbol for the Black Power movement when her name appeared on the FBI's Most Wanted list in connection with Jonathan Jackson's tragic rescue attempt. The Free Angela movement galvanized support for Black Power, and her eloquent speeches and writings positioned her as the voice of a generation. She was acquitted of murder and kidnapping charges after a high-profile trial. Angela was a student organizer with SNCC before becoming involved with the Panthers and the Communist Party. She later returned to academia as a professor at University of California, Santa Cruz, and remains a leader in the prison reform movement, as there are still a number of political prisoners behind bars in the United States. Many former Panthers join her in those efforts.

AARON DIXON: The leader of the Seattle chapter, Aaron was one of the first to help organize a chapter outside of California. Extremely dedicated to the BPP, he continued to serve in Oakland during the Party's declining years. Aaron founded a youth service organization in Seattle to continue educating and inspiring new generations.

EMORY DOUGLAS: The BPP Minister of Culture, Emory created hundreds of visual art pieces for the *Black Panther* newspaper and oversaw its production. He continued working in arts and journalism after his time in the Party.

FRED HAMPTON: Fred began as an NAACP youth organizer before joining the BPP. He was known for powerful public speaking and community-organizing ability. The Rainbow Coalition that he founded brought together activists from a range of diverse backgrounds to work collectively. He was assassinated in his bed on December 4, 1969, by Chicago police as part of a COINTELPRO operation.

DAVID HILLIARD: A student and longshoreman, David joined the party in the early days and became a member of the Central Committee. His leadership helped keep the Party going through the key growth years of the movement when other leaders were in prison or in exile. David later took an active role in preserving the Panthers' legacy. He published a memoir and served as director of the Dr. Huey P. Newton Foundation, in addition to teaching and writing.

ELBERT "BIG MAN" HOWARD: One of the founding members of the BPP, Big Man grew up in Tennessee and served in the U.S. Air Force before attending Merritt College, where he joined the Panthers in 1966. He worked at the Panther National Headquarters in a variety of roles, from working the phones to contributing to the newspaper. He wrote a memoir, contributed articles to the BPP alumni's online archives, and helped organize reunion events. He died in 2018.

ERICKA HUGGINS: A leader in the L.A. and New Haven chapters and director of the Oakland Community School, Ericka began as a student organizer on the East Coast and came to California in 1968, around the time of the murders of the Rev. Dr. Martin Luther King Jr. and Lil' Bobby Hutton. Ericka helped establish the L.A. chapter before returning to the East Coast and leading the New Haven chapter. Ericka spent nearly two years in prison awaiting trial in the Alex Rackley case, was tried, and was released after a hung jury. Ericka directed the Oakland Community School even after the rest of the Black Panther Party had largely folded. She became the first woman and the first Black person appointed to the Alameda County School Board. After leaving the Party, Ericka continued her work as an educator and speaker.

JOHN HUGGINS: A leader of the L.A. chapter, John served in the U.S. Navy before attending Lincoln University, where he met his best friend and eventual wife, Ericka. The couple moved west to participate in the Panther movement, helping to build the L.A. chapter. John was killed on January 17, 1969, by US Organization members who later turned out to be participating in COINTELPRO operations.

ROBERT JAMES (LIL' BOBBY) HUTTON: Lil' Bobby was the first person to join the BPP in 1966, at age sixteen. Lil' Bobby, unarmed, was killed by police on April 6, 1968.

GEORGE JACKSON: The BPP's Field Marshal within the U.S. prison system, George was convicted of robbery at age nineteen and spent the rest of his life in prison. He published two popular books for the movement and was killed by prison guards in 1971.

JONATHAN JACKSON: Brother of George Jackson, Jonathan died on August 7, 1970, during a failed attempt to liberate prisoners from the Marin County Courthouse and negotiate for George's release.

JAMAL JOSEPH: The youngest member of the New York 21, Jamal was acquitted of those charges but later served two additional prison sentences for his activities in the BLA and for helping other fugitives. In prison, he developed a love of theater; he later founded a theater company and went on to teach film at Columbia University. He continues to work with young Black people, inspiring and educating them to be the best they can be.

JOAN TARIKA "MATILABA" LEWIS: The first woman to join the BPP in 1967, Tarika helped open the doors of the party to those other than young Black men. She created a lot of art for the *Black Panther*. After leaving the BPP in 1969, she continued to create art and music and speak about her experiences.

SAM NAPIER: The BPP newspaper distribution manager, Sam was murdered in New York in April 1971, likely in retaliation for the murder of Robert Webb.

HUEY P. NEWTON: Co-founder and Minister of Defense of the BPP, Huey was born in Louisiana and moved to California as a small child. He attended Merritt College, where he met Bobby Seale in the course of Black student organizing, at which point they decided to form their own organization to take the work beyond the campus. He became the international symbol of the Panther movement during his high-profile murder trial, which galvanized the Free Huey movement.

After the Party disbanded, Huey earned a doctorate from the University of California, Santa Cruz. He struggled with drugs and alcohol and lived a tumultuous few years after the Black Panthers ended. Early in the morning of August 22, 1989, Huey was shot to death on the sidewalk outside his Oakland apartment, likely over a drug dispute. Huey's friends and followers felt shocked and saddened by his death, as well as by the harsh turns his life had taken since the Panther days.

WILLIAM O'NEAL: An FBI informant in the BPP's Chicago chapter, O'Neal served as Fred Hampton's personal bodyguard while secretly providing information and floor plans of Panther properties to the FBI. His cooperation helped facilitate the assassination of Fred Hampton. He later admitted his actions and appeared to wrestle with a balance of pride and guilt about his role. O'Neal died in 1990.

ELMER "GERONIMO JI-JAGA" PRATT: A member and ultimately the leader of the L.A. chapter, Geronimo served in Vietnam, after which he attended UCLA, where he met Bunchy Carter and joined the Panthers. He took over as chapter leader when Bunchy was killed in 1969. Framed for murder under another COINTEL-PRO operation, he spent twenty-seven years in prison, released after his conviction was vacated in 1997. He moved abroad to Algeria, where he died in 2011.

ALEX RACKLEY: A New York Panther who was tortured and murdered by BPP members in 1969, under the direction of BPP member and likely police informant George Sams. Nine BPP members, including Ericka Huggins and Bobby Seale, stood trial for his murder but were ultimately released.

GEORGE SAMS: The BPP member who orchestrated the torture and murder of fellow Panther Alex Rackley, Sams was initially expelled from the Party for bad behavior but later reinstated. He may have been a police informant or undercover agent provocateur.

BOBBY SEALE: Co-founder and Chairman of the BPP, Bobby was born in Texas and moved to California as a child. He served in the U.S. Air Force before attending Merritt College, where he met Huey Newton. Bobby's work with youth at a local community center inspired the pair to shift their focus from student organizing to community organizing.

Bobby led the demonstration at the state legislature in Sacramento that elevated the Panthers to the national scene. He was charged with conspiracy alongside white anti-war organizers in the high-profile Chicago 8 trial, and later charged with murder in the death of Alex Rackley in New Haven. He spent two years in jail on trial and awaiting trial, as well as serving time for contempt of court, but was ultimately released.

He ran for mayor of Oakland in 1973. Bobby left the Party before it ended, but he continued working in the spirit of the movement. He continues to speak, write, and educate people about the systemic challenges facing Black Americans and oppressed people throughout the world.

ASSATA SHAKUR: A New York Panther and BLA member, Assata lived underground as a wanted fugitive for a time before being arrested in connection with a roadside shootout with New Jersey state troopers. She was tried and convicted, but she escaped from prison in 1979 and returned to life underground. She now lives in exile in Cuba.

ROBERT WEBB: A New York Panther, Robert was killed in 1971 amid the escalating dispute between splitting factions of the Party.

Numerous other Panthers appear in anecdotes in the text or are briefly quoted. Many of their stories—including those of **Claudia Chesson-Williams**, **Ronald Freeman**, **Cyril "Bullwhip" Innis**, **Phyllis Jackson**, **Billy X Jennings**, **William "BJ" Johnson**, **Larry Little**, **Steve Long**, **Thomas McCreary**, **Steve McCutchen**, **Norma Mtume**, **Margo Rose-Brunson**, **Madalynn "Carol" Rucker**, **Patrice Sims**, and **Ajamu Strivers**—can be found in Shih and Williams, *Portraits from an Unfinished Revolution*.

The text also mentions several members of the New York 21, including **Afeni Shakur**, **Michael "Cetawayo" Tabor**, and **Dhoruba Bin Wahad**. More of their story can be found in Sekou Odinga et al., *Look for Me in the Whirlwind: From the Panther 21 to 21st-Century Revolutions* (Oakland, CA: PM Press, 2017).

TIME LINE

PROGRESS

Policing the police is a key Panther program

Panthers run political education classes

The *Black Panther* newspaper in publication

Black Panther chapters established nationwide

Free Huey movement

Panthers maintain People's Free Medical Clinics

Panthers offer Free Breakfast for School Children Program

Free Ericka movement

Panthers offer Free Clothing Program

Additional survival programs operate

International arm of the BPP active

Panthers lead sickle cell anemia awareness campaign

Oakland Community School in operation

Elaine Brown and Bobby Seale run for office in Oakland

Elaine Brown is Chairwoman of the Party

Following Panthers' lead, U.S. government initiates free breakfast programs in schools

① ②③④ ⑤ ⑥⑦ ⑧ ⑨ ⑩ ⑪

| 1967 | 1968 | 1969 | 1970 | 1971 | 1972 | 1973 | 1974 | 1975 |

❶ ❷❹❸ ❺ ❻❼❽❾ ❿⓫ ⓬ ⓭

BACKLASH

Frequent arrests of Panthers

COINTELPRO targets the Panthers

False letters incite conflict between SNCC leaders and Panthers

False letters and propaganda inflame tension between U.S. Organization and Panthers

False letters urge Jeff Fort to kill Fred Hampton

Panther offices raided regularly

Panther survival programs targeted for disruption

New Haven Panthers trial

False letters fan the flames of the split between
Huey Newton and Eldridge Cleaver

New York 21 trial

PROGRESS

BACKLASH

GLOSSARY

PANTHER VOCABULARY

acquit: to find not guilty

avaricious: greedy

boycott: to refuse to use a particular service (like city buses) or to refuse to buy from a particular business in order to make a political statement

capitalism: a political and economic ideology that emphasizes individualism, private property ownership, and a free market in which goods and services are privately controlled

Central Committee: the national BPP leadership team, operating out of Oakland, California

chapter: a local BPP office and its membership

coalition: a partnership or alliance among groups, often for political organizing

coded language: words or phrases that might seem to mean one thing on the surface but have a second layer of meaning; particularly effective when large groups of people understand the second meaning but agree to pretend that only the surface meaning exists. An example is politicians using the phrase "law and order" when they really mean "policing and controlling Black communities."

colonialism: the act of exerting social and political control over a region, community, or group of people, occupying their land, and exploiting them economically

communism: a form of socialism; a political

theory that advocates for collective ownership of property and other shared resources across society

counterrevolutionary: acting against the interests of the revolution

exile: the state of having been forced to leave the country due to political pressure and/or for the purpose of evading law enforcement

ideology: a system of beliefs and ideals that express a certain political or social or economic philosophy

imperialism: a system that exerts a nation's power over others through force, often in the form of a military presence

incarceration: imprisonment

indict: to bring a formal criminal charge against someone who has been arrested; used in relation to serious crimes that will be tried by juries; often done by the determination of a grand jury

informant: an individual who secretly reports to the police or FBI; may also act as an agent provocateur, inciting violence or causing trouble

intercommunalism: a theory, introduced by Huey Newton, that globalization represents an opportunity for oppressed people across identities to unite in common revolutionary aims

Jim Crow: Originally a minstrel character designed to mock enslaved Black men, Jim Crow also appeared in cartoons and thus became a generic, derisive term for a Black man. Due to this pop culture inspiration, segregation laws in the South were often referred to as Jim Crow laws.

liberation: freedom, or the process of becoming free

lynching: a form of vigilante justice in which someone is murdered, usually in punishment for a perceived crime or infraction, without due process of law

Marxism: the political and economic theories of Karl Marx and Friedrich Engels, first published in the *Communist Manifesto* and later built upon by thinkers such as Vladimir Lenin

militant: strident and aggressive in support of a political viewpoint, including a willingness to use violence to achieve it

misogynoir: dislike, distrust, and/or prejudice against Black women specifically

misogyny: ingrained hatred or prejudice against women in general, regardless of race

the movement: a phrase used to broadly refer to the effort of organizing for civil rights, Black Power, social justice, and/or social transformation

neutralize: to get rid of or to render ineffective; this language was used often by the FBI under COINTELPRO when they discussed strategies for disrupting Panther leadership

oppressed: held subservient, treated harshly, and controlled or suppressed by those in power

pig: a police officer

platform: the stated beliefs or goals of a political organization

proletariat: workers or working-class people, collectively

purge: to remove undesirable or problematic members from a group

racism: discrimination against an individual or group of people based on their race

raid: an aggressive armed visitation by police or the FBI; a frequent tactic used by law enforcement to enter Panther property with or without a warrant; meant to be intimidating and create fear and insecurity

rank and file: the majority of an organization's members; used by the BPP to describe those who did not hold an explicit leadership position within the Party but who worked hard and often tirelessly doing the daily work of the movement

repression: active efforts to prevent progress, often using force

revolution: transformation; the forceful overthrow of a government or political system in favor of change

revolutionary: used by Panthers to refer to a person who has dedicated their life to the movement or to describe something that supports or furthers the movement

rhetoric: a way of using language; the use of specific language to achieve a certain effect

section leader: used by the BPP to refer to a Panther who has been placed in charge of a specific section of the community and assigned a group of rank-and-file members to manage; section leaders familiarized themselves with the residents, businesses, landscape, and all other facets of their area in order to identify challenges, problems, and opportunities and to provide direct support for the people

sexism: discrimination against a person or a group of people based on their sex or gender

socialism: a political and economic theory that emphasizes shared resources and community control of the means of production

survival programs: community services established by the Panthers to help care for the basic needs of Black people in poor communities, such as health care, food programs, and support for housing and employment justice

systemic: relating to an entire structure and its processes; particularly used to refer to issues that are embedded within a system or facets that cause it to operate in a certain way

underground: operating in secret or in hiding, typically to avoid arrest or capture

vanguard: the group who leads the way toward change

visionary: being able to see, imagine, or describe a future, change, or possibility that is original, powerful, or intriguing

warrant: a document signed by a judge giving law enforcement officers permission to enter and/or search someone's private property

FURTHER READING

These are the books I enjoyed most and found particularly useful in the course of my research, as well as additional resources I would most recommend to readers.

Want to know more about something else you read in this book? Check out my source notes and bibliography. They contain dozens of additional references, as I relied upon a wide variety of sources for the factual underpinning of this history.

BLACK PANTHER PARTY HISTORY

Joshua Bloom and Waldo E. Martin Jr., *Black against Empire: The History and Politics of the Black Panther Party*

> An incredibly well-researched and well-documented history of the Panthers that covers a wide range of topics and angles. This is the number-one must-have text I would recommend to anyone wanting a serious study of the Panthers.

Elaine Brown, *A Taste of Power: A Black Woman's Story*

> A memoir beginning with her childhood and detailing her development as an activist, up through her time as Chairwoman of the Black Panther Party and the aftermath of the Party's decline.

Emory Douglas, *Black Panther: The Revolutionary Art of Emory Douglas* (edited by Sam Durant)

> This collection offers dozens of samples of Emory Douglas's artwork that appeared in the *Black Panther* over the years, in addition to essays reflecting on the newspaper and art in the Panther movement.

Jamal Joseph, *Panther Baby: A Life of Rebellion and Reinvention*

> A memoir of his time in the Black Panther Party and the Black Liberation Army. Very engaging to read, and emblematic of what a young Panther's recruitment and training looked like.

Bobby Seale, *Seize the Time: The Story of the Black Panther Party and Huey P. Newton*

> Bobby Seale's early memoir of the Black Panther Party founding offers numerous powerful narratives about the need for the movement and its early actions and reception by society. He wrote most of it during his time behind bars during his trial in New

Haven. It's particularly interesting to read because it was written and published during the height of Panther activity and is sharp with rhetoric, but doesn't yet have the long view of the movement that Bobby would come to have later.

Stephen Shames and Bobby Seale, *Power to the People: The World of the Black Panthers*
> A photo-essay and interview collection published in conjunction with the Panthers' Fiftieth Anniversary featuring many powerful Panther leaders reflecting on the movement.

Bryan Shih and Yohuru Williams, eds., *The Black Panthers: Portraits from an Unfinished Revolution*
> This is a gorgeous photo-essay and interview collection featuring recollections from former Panthers from chapters across the country, including well-known leaders and lesser-known foot soldiers of the movement. It's full of incredibly dynamic portraits of the activists as they appear now, with powerful narratives about their past experiences and current views.

CIVIL RIGHTS MOVEMENT HISTORY

Melba Pattillo Beals, *March Forward, Girl: From Young Warrior to Little Rock Nine*
> Billed as a prequel to *Warriors Don't Cry*, this memoir covers Pattillo's early childhood and the path that led her to be one of the nine teens making history in Little Rock.

——, *Warriors Don't Cry*
> The powerful memoir of one of the Little Rock Nine students who integrated Central High School in Little Rock, Arkansas, in 1957.

Phillip Hoose, *Claudette Colvin: Twice toward Justice*
> This biography is really part memoir, as it contains significant segments of direct transcripts from Claudette remembering her pivotal role in desegregating the Montgomery bus system.

Ellen Levine, *Freedom's Children: Young Civil Rights Activists Tell Their Stories*
> A collection of interviews and firsthand recollections of civil rights organizing by some of the youngest participants in the movement.

John Lewis and Andrew Aydin, *March* (illustrated by Nate Powell)
> This trilogy of graphic novels follows John Lewis through his years as a SNCC activist, participating in the Freedom Rides, the March on Washington for Jobs and Freedom, and the infamous Bloody Sunday march across the Edmund Pettus Bridge in Selma, Alabama.

BLACK AMERICAN HISTORY

Tonya Bolden, *How to Build a Museum: The Smithsonian's National Museum of African American History and Culture*
> A chronicling of the process of creating the long-awaited museum honoring Black American life.

Henry Louis Gates Jr. with Tonya Bolden, *Dark Sky Rising: Reconstruction and the Dawn of Jim Crow*

> Gates is a renowned Black history scholar who teamed up with a prolific children's writer to bring this story to young readers.

Walter Dean Myers, *Now Is Your Time! The African-American Struggle for Freedom*

> A lyrical and thoughtful summary of Black history by one of our greatest authors.

Kadir Nelson, *Heart and Soul: The Story of America and African Americans*

> This book offers a brief general overview of Black American history and is beautifully illustrated.

Jason Reynolds and Ibram X. Kendi, *Stamped: Racism, Antiracism, and You: A Remix*

> Jason Reynolds remixes Ibram X. Kendi's National Book Award–winning history text (*Stamped from the Beginning: The Definitive History of Racist Ideas in America*) for a teen audience. A quick and engaging read with a striking voice.

YOUNG ADULT FICTION

Kekla Magoon, *Fire in the Streets*

> A companion to my first novel, *The Rock and the River*; the story follows a fourteen-year-old girl who wants to join the Black Panther Party in 1968 Chicago.

———, *The Rock and the River*

> My first novel was, to my knowledge, the first middle-grade/young adult book to address the Black Panther Party in a significant way.

Mildred D. Taylor, *Roll of Thunder, Hear My Cry*

> My favorite novel from childhood (and a Newbery Medal winner to boot) kicks off a powerful series of novels about a Black family's struggles and triumphs in mid-twentieth-century America. (Check out the whole Logan family saga.)

Rita Williams-Garcia, *One Crazy Summer*

> In this Newbery Honor–winning novel, the Gaither sisters attend Black Panther Party youth programs in Oakland, including the Free Breakfast for School Children.

WEBSITES

Black Past: blackpast.org

> Black Past is a nonprofit organization dedicated to creating a unified repository of Black history materials online. The site offers comprehensive introductory information about a wide range of Black history topics, with source citations for each article, as well as speech texts and other primary source material.

Education for Liberation Network: EdLiberation.org

> A national network led by educators and activists of color that seeks to engage, educate, and empower young people in social justice movements.

It's About Time: itsabouttimebpp.com

> The official website of the Black Panther Party Alumni Association features archival and contemporary photos of life in the Party and after. The organization sponsors the

Black Panther Party reunions and publishes occasional issues of the *Commemorator*, a modern incarnation of the *Black Panther* newspaper for alumni.

Slavery and Remembrance: A Guide to Sites, Museums, and Memory: slaveryandremembrance.org

This site offers information about the transatlantic slave trade and the harsh reality of chattel slavery in the American colonies and the Caribbean.

SNCC Digital Gateway: snccdigital.org

A fabulous interactive history of the Student Nonviolent Coordinating Committee and related civil rights movement activities, full of archival links and media to explore.

Zinn Education Project: zinnedproject.org

This site offers classroom resources for teaching history while pushing beyond the lens of whiteness.

DOCUMENTARY VIDEOS

The Black Panthers: Vanguard of the Revolution. Directed by Stanley Nelson Jr.

A good overview of the Panther movement, with archival footage and contemporary interviews.

The Black Power Mixtape, 1967–1975: A Documentary in 9 Chapters. Directed by Göran Olsson.

This documentary by Swedish filmmakers captures the story of the movement from an international perspective, with interesting archival footage and modern voice-over commentary by artists and activists.

Eyes on the Prize: America's Civil Rights Movement. Produced by Henry Hampton et al.

This award-winning fourteen-part documentary covers many facets of the civil rights struggle from the 1950s through the 1980s.

Free Angela Davis and All Political Prisoners. Directed by Shola Lynch.

Angela Davis's story is fascinating. The film covers the history of her activism as well as bringing us up-to-date on her efforts in the prison reform movement.

Merritt College: Home of the Black Panthers. Directed by Jeffrey Heyman and James Devin Calhoun.

Archival footage of the Panthers interspersed with modern-day reflections by Party leaders. The focus here is on the Panthers' origins, their Black Studies organizing, and the social context in which their movement emerged.

SOURCE NOTES

p. v: "The revolution . . . hands of the young":
"Huey Newton Talks to the Movement," 11.

1. SHATTERING THE STATUS QUO

p. 3: "Radical simply means . . . at the root':
"Angela Davis Quotes."

p. 5: "Well, you aren't violating . . . can go inside":
An extensive recap of the Panthers' march
on Sacramento, including descriptions and
dialogue, is found in Austin, xiv.

p. 6: "Anybody here know . . . making these
laws?" and "Upstairs on the next floor":
quoted in ibid.

p. 7: "Am I under arrest? . . . my gun back!":
quoted in ibid., xv.

p. 7: "The Black Panther Party . . . repression of
Black People": quoted in Major, 77.

p. 7: "Black people have begged . . . their total
destruction": quoted in Foner, 40–41.

p. 8: "a tinge of pride and amazement" and "The
image stayed . . . my mind": Dixon, loc. 1026
of 5536.

p. 8: "Look at those dudes . . . to join": Joseph,
36.

2. THE DARK PAST

p. 13: "For most of us . . . stories begin or end":
Dixon, loc. 132 of 5536.

p. 14: one out of ten ships . . . : "Slave Ship
Mutinies."

p. 14: over one million kidnapped black
people . . . an unknown number died fighting
for their freedom: ibid.

p. 14: Eleven million survived, traumatized . . . :
ibid.

p. 15: Queen Nzinga: Protecting Her People
(sidebar): For more on Queen Nzinga, see
Bortolot; Snethen; and "Angola, Southern
Africa."

p. 16: one goal was to abolish slavery: The First
Continental Congress laid out a series of
declarations in a document dated October 20,
1774, including a commitment to ending the
slave trade as of December 1, 1774. But the
delegates ultimately removed this assertion
from later versions of their documents,
including the Declaration of Independence.
See "The Continental Association, October
20, 1774."

p. 18: Native people were also denied citizenship rights: The three-fifths clause includes language excluding "Indians not taxed" from the count entirely, which referred to Native people living on reservations and those who remained under tribal jurisdiction. However, there was some debate about the meaning of this clause, and it was exercised differently under the U.S. Census over the years. See Russell. Essentially, Indigenous nations fought to retain their sovereignty, while the U.S. government sought greater control over land and people. The complicated history of the debate over Native Americans' citizenship status is further discussed in Tennant.

p. 18: Many Native people were enslaved . . . on the three-fifths clause: Though the three-fifths clause excludes from the count Native people who remained under tribal jurisdiction, there were also many who were held in slavery, who would most likely have been considered among the "all other persons" portion of the clause. See "Slavery, Within and Without" and "Colonial Enslavement of Native Americans Included Those Who Surrendered, Too."

p. 19: Out of about three million enslaved people . . . 100,000 managed to successfully escape: Statistics around escape from slavery are imprecise because the number of enslaved people in the country is generally given as an annual statistic (such as 3.2 million slaves working in the fifteen slave states in 1850, according to *The Root*),

but the number of slaves who escaped might be referring to total numbers over a longer period of time. Plus, it is difficult to determine how many people escaped because they were breaking the law and had to flee in secret. See www.slaveryandremembrance.org and Mitchell.

p. 19: an enslaved man named Gabriel . . . could try again: For more information on Gabriel, see Reed, "Gabriel Prosser (1775–1800)."

p. 20: Denmark Vesey, a free Black man . . . : For more about Denmark Vesey's rebellion, see Sutherland.

p. 20: Nat Turner succeeded in rallying . . . : For more about Nat Turner's rebellion, see Reed, "Nat Turner (1800–1831)."

p. 24: "The way we can best . . . make it our own": The details of this meeting with Black and white leaders are discussed in Gates.

3. SEPARATE BUT EQUAL

p. 27: "The chasm . . . wide and deep": Terrell, "What It Means to Be Colored in the Capital of the U.S."

p. 28: Black Codes (section): For an example of black codes, see "(1866) Mississippi Black Codes."

p. 31: Seven out of the nine justices decided . . . : In the majority decision, the justices wrote that making "a legal distinction between the white and colored races" did not "destroy the legal equality of the two races," because the law was not meant to "enforce social, as distinguished from political equality, or a commingling of the two races upon terms unsatisfactory for either." Plessy v. Ferguson, 163 U.S. 537 (1896).

p. 31: "Our Constitution is color-blind . . . the Constitution": Justice Harlan's dissent can also be found in Plessy v. Ferguson, 163 U.S. 537 (1896).

p. 33: Negro Improvement (section): A comparative summary of the lives and views of Booker T. Washington, W. E. B. DuBois, and Marcus Garvey can be found in "Three Visions for African Americans."

p. 33: Booker T. Washington: For more information on his life and his ideas, see "Dr. Booker Taliaferro Washington."

p. 34: W. E. B. DuBois: For more information on his life and his ideas, see "NAACP History: W.E.B. DuBois."

p. 35: Marcus Garvey: For more information on his life and his ideas, see Robert A. Hill, "Marcus Garvey, 'The Negro Moses,'" Africana Age: African and African Diasporan Transformations in the Twentieth Century, Schomburg Center for Research in Black Culture, https://wayback.archive-it.org/11788 /20200108191454/http://exhibitions.nypl.org /africanaage/essay-garvey.html.

p. 36: Black Wall Street: For more information, see https://www.tulsahistory.org/exhibit /1921-tulsa-race-massacre/.

p. 37: "Here we were as a nation . . . second-class citizen": quoted in Hampton and Fayer, xxv.

p. 37: "There was extreme resentment . . . anymore over here'": quoted in ibid., xxiv.

p. 39: "You can resist . . . fist at them": Lawson. James Lawson was a leader in SNCC and SCLC who became a key theorist and teacher about nonviolent resistance.

p. 39: "Americans will <u>always</u> fight for liberty": This 1943 poster is in the Smithsonian's collection of war propaganda posters: https:// amhistory.si.edu/militaryhistory/collection /object.asp?ID=558&back=1.

p. 40: "separate educational facilities are inherently unequal": Brown v. Board of Education of Topeka, 347 U.S. 483 (1954), supreme.justia.com/cases/federal/us/347/483 /#tab-opinion-1940809.

p. 40: "with all deliberate speed": When many southern states were slow to integrate their schools in the wake of the initial *Brown v. Board* ruling, the court heard new arguments in 1955 and issued a second ruling that integration must happen "with all deliberate speed." This declaration seemed to mean they wanted states to take immediate but thoughtful action, but in attempting to acknowledge the complexity and controversy around school integration in some communities, the court chose rather ambiguous language that didn't help matters. Many schools were not integrated until 1960 or later. The second ruling, Brown v. Board of Education of Topeka, 349 U.S. 294 (1955), can be read here: supreme.justia.com/cases /federal/us/349/294/#tab-opinion-1940989.

p. 40: "Rebellion was on my mind that day": quoted in Hoose, 30.

p. 41: "The bus boycott . . . system at last": quoted in ibid., 63.

p. 42: "I'm not walking for myself . . . my grandchildren": quoted in ibid., 67.

p. 42: The boycott cost . . . $3,200 per day: ibid., 69.

p. 43: "Those were hard, fearsome days": quoted in ibid., 98.

p. 43: Collective Action (sidebar): For more information about these key civil rights groups, some of which still exist today, see McCurdy and visit the following websites: SNCC: https://snccdigital.org; SCLC: https://nationalsclc.org; NAACP: www.naacp.org.

p. 44: "Your House Is Gonna Be Blowed Sky High!" (section title): quoted in ibid., 97. A caller to Aurelia Browder's house (one of the participants in *Browder v. Gayle*) made this threat over the phone.

p. 44: nine Black students in Little Rock, Arkansas . . . : For more information about the Little Rock Nine, see Beals.

p. 45: The NAACP began leading nonviolent resistance training programs . . . : *Life* magazine published a fascinating photo-essay about civil rights organizing, which includes a discussion of a passive resistance training program called "social drama"; see Cosgrove. Some of the images shown in the online photo-essay appeared in the *Life* issue dated September 19, 1960.

p. 46: "a feeling of liberation, restored manhood": from a display at the Greensboro Historical Museum, located on the site of the Greensboro sit-ins, in the former Woolworth's building.

p. 47: In the spring and summer of 1961 . . . pipes and bats: The Anniston, Alabama, incident is only one of many examples of Freedom Riders being threatened, attacked, or put at risk. For more information about the Freedom Rides, see Bausum.

p. 48: Over two thousand . . . dragged off to jail: A massive civil rights demonstration took place in Birmingham, Alabama, over the course of eight days, beginning May 2, 1963. The infamous instances of dogs and fire hoses being turned on the crowd took place on May 3. Over the course of those few days, thousands of arrests occurred, filling Birmingham jails. For more information, see Momodu.

p. 52: Lost in the Struggle (sidebar): Information about the Civil Rights Memorial and a link to brief biographies of the civil rights martyrs named on the monument can be found at "Civil Rights Memorial," Southern Poverty Law Center, www.splcenter.org/civil-rights-memorial.

5. THE AGGRESSIVE ALTERNATIVE

p. 55: "A Winchester rifle . . . refuses to give": Wells, *Southern Horrors*.

p. 56: nearly all of whom were white: Sklansky, 1213, reports that in 1970, in the largest three hundred police departments in the United States, only 6% of police officers were Black.

p. 56: "getting his head banged in . . . because he was Black": former Panther William Calhoun in the 2015 documentary *The Black Panthers: Vanguard of the Revolution*.

p. 56: many officers abused the power of their position: Nodjimbadem.

p. 58: At least one person . . . to local property: According to Stultz, the overall damage included 1 killed, 100 wounded, 450 arrested, and $1 million property damage.

p. 60: "It would be almost impossible . . . freedom can come": Malcolm X, *Autobiography*, 387.

p. 61: A City Exploding (section): For more information about the Watts uprising, see "Watts Rebellion (Los Angeles)."

p. 64: Stokely Speaks (section): For a really comprehensive look at Stokely Carmichael's leadership and organizing with SNCC in Lowndes County, see Jeffries.

p. 64: "What's happening is rebellions, not riots": "'Black Power' Speech (28 July 1966, by Stokely Carmichael)."

p. 64: "We must think politically . . . Black Power": ibid.

p. 65: The population of Lowndes was 80% Black: Woodham.

p. 66: "Stokely believed . . . power base": Stokely says this explicitly in his speeches. He also talks extensively about the goal of a political power base for Black people in the Student Nonviolent Coordinating Committee's "What We Want," reprinted in Carmichael, 17.

p. 66: "That's the first time . . . register to vote": quoted in Hampton and Fayer, 180.

p. 67: "My father was concerned . . . Lowndes County": quoted in ibid., 271.

p. 67: "When we chose that symbol . . . to survive": quoted in ibid., 277.

p. 68: "Those of us who carried guns . . . wasn't violent": quoted in ibid.

p. 68: Nine hundred Black voters . . . : Jeffries, 173.

p. 69: This initial Panthers image . . . : https://designobserver.com/feature/the-women-behind-the-black-panther-party-logo/39755.

6. PICKING UP THE GUN

p. 73: "It is criminal to teach . . . obeying the law": from remarks given March 12, 1964; Malcolm X, *Malcolm X Speaks*, 22.

p. 73: "We had seen Watts . . . rule by force?": Newton, *Revolutionary Suicide*, 115.

p. 74: "We had seen the Oakland Police . . . at the point of explosion": ibid.

p. 74: "Everything we had seen . . . time had come": ibid.

p. 74: "ivory towers of the college": Seale, *Seize the Time*, 34.

p. 74: Most of their fellow . . . getting things done: ibid.

p. 75: "I never wanted to use . . . young brothers rejected": ibid., 36.

p. 75: "to think in ways related . . . black community unifying": ibid., 35.

p. 75: "We got five thousand . . . ignored us": quoted in Hampton and Fayer, 352.

p. 76: "the police . . . the city council": quoted in ibid., 351.

p. 76: "Don't anybody say nothing! . . . inform on ourselves": Seale, *Seize the Time*, 48.

p. 76: "Man, those kids tore . . . stories they'd heard": ibid., 53.

p. 76: "Now, do you think . . . beating on no woman": quoted in ibid., 54.

p. 77: "if a policeman unjustly . . . brutalizes them": ibid.

p. 77: "I have never witnessed . . . knew cases": ibid., 55.

p. 77: "We had to start a new organization": Seale, "Interview."

p. 77: "I was determined . . . my own self": Shames and Seale, 22.

p. 77: They gathered all of their ideas . . . : The Ten-Point Platform and Program was one of Huey and Bobby's first efforts with their new Black Panther Party for Self-Defense, but sources vary in reporting the exact timing of the writing of the platform. In *Seize the Time*, 59, Bobby Seale indicates it was the first thing they did together in September/October 1966. In *Revolutionary Suicide*, 120–122, Huey Newton also writes that it was the first thing they did, and that the ten points came together very quickly. However, Bloom and Martin (70 and 413) suggest that the platform was more likely first written several months later, in May 1967, which is when the first written version of the platform appeared in the second issue of the *Black Panther*, published May 25, 1967.

Given that both Panther leaders discuss the writing in parallel ways, it seems most likely to me that Huey and Bobby began hammering out the language in October 1966 and pulled the complete draft together over the next few months, prior to starting the newspaper. After that point, they would make a few minor edits to the platform, such as adding the plebiscite language to point ten in May 1967. Several varying versions of the platform can be found in different publications, all labeled "October 1966 Platform and Program," up until 1972, when the Panthers formally adjusted the language to be more inclusive across racial lines and to add a demand about universal health care.

p. 78: Malcolm X's nine-point list detailing "What Muslims Want": The text of the list can be found in Marsh, 46.

p. 78: "I found the Declaration . . . typed it up": Shames and Seale, 23.

p. 78: "Huey went upstairs . . . his duty": ibid.

p. 79: "We flipped a coin . . . won chairman": quoted in Hampton and Fayer, 353.

p. 79: All they needed now was a strong name . . . : Both Huey and Bobby discuss the founding process and the naming procedure in their autobiographies (*Revolutionary Suicide* and *Seize the Time*). Huey discusses it again in Hampton and Fayer, 350–356.

p. 82: The first person to join . . . got right to work: Lil' Bobby Hutton is consistently described as the first person to join the BPP. The first six members of the Party were Huey and Bobby, Lil' Bobby, Elbert "Big Man" Howard, and brothers Sherman and Reginald Forte. Bobby Seale discusses these early members of the party in Shames and Seale, 62, and Seale, *Seize the Time*, 65, 78.

p. 82: Policing the Police (section): The action and quoted dialogue in this sequence are drawn from Bobby Seale's accounts of this early encounter while policing the police, found in Shames and Seale, 25–26. An account of a similar incident appears in Seale, *Seize the Time*, 85–99.

p. 84: "I actually think that . . . and false arrests": quoted in Shames and Seale, 25.

p. 84: "We want land, bread, housing . . .": This is the final point of the Black Panther Party's Ten-Point Platform and Program; Bloom and Martin, 70–72.

p. 85: What We Want, What We Believe (sidebar): The Panthers' platform and program is framed around the dual concepts of "what we want, what we believe." For each point on the Ten-Point Platform ("what we want"), there is an associated explanation of why ("what we believe"). Sometimes, as in the *Black Panther* newspaper itself, the platform is presented in two separate sections: first the full list of ten wants, followed by the list of ten beliefs. Sometimes it is presented with the two integrated and paired, as it is here. I find it clearer and easier to see the connections between the two halves of the platform when they are presented in an integrated way. This list is based on Seale, *Seize the Time*, 66–69.

7. A COLD RECEPTION

p. 89: "I'm one of the 22 million . . . American nightmare": Malcolm X, "The Ballot or the Bullet." Malcolm apparently gave this speech at least a few times; there are transcripts available of the version he gave in Detroit as well as this version from Cleveland.

p. 89: "We're not a self-defense group . . . to the people": Newton, *To Die for the People*, 14.

p. 90: "It is . . . the people that will . . . liberate themselves": Huey wrote and made statements similar to this in a number of places, but this quote comes from Shames and Seale, 24, based on archival footage of Huey found in "Black Panthers—Off the Pig," www.youtube.com/watch?v=-7oBlwr_Qjw.

p. 93: nearly 500,000 American troops . . . : Taylor, "The Vietnam War, Part I."

p. 95: "What has been amputated . . . that law book": *Merritt College: Home of the Black Panthers*.

8. FILLING THE RANKS

p. 97: "No political party . . . practical movement": Mao Tse-tung, *Quotations from Chairman Mao Tse-tung*, Beijing: Peking Foreign Languages Press, 1966, Marxists Internet Archive, www.marxists.org/reference/archive/mao/works/red-book/ch01.htm.

p. 98: The Panthers sold red books at Merritt . . . : Bobby Seale discusses the Panthers' early moneymaking scheme in Seale, *Seize the Time*, 79–85.

p. 98: "That was important . . . could relate to it": ibid., 77.

p. 99: "We had to transform . . . brothers on the block": quoted in Austin, 33.

p. 99: "We painted a sign . . . opened that office": Seale, *Seize the Time*, 77.

p. 99: "because they were used . . . the revolutionary ": quoted in Hampton and Fayer, 351.

p. 100: Panther Fashion (sidebar): The quotes and information are drawn from Bobby

Seale's discussion of the Panther uniform in Shames and Seale, 42.

p. 101: Tarika Lewis became the first woman . . . fighting for their community: Austin, 57, 63; see also Wells, "Untold."

p. 101: In one instance early . . . signal was installed: Austin, 63.

p. 103: The Widow Shabazz (section): Bloom and Martin, 48–50.

p. 104: "Frightening 'Army'": "Frightening 'Army' Hits the Airport," *San Francisco Chronicle*, February 22, 1967.

p. 104: Denzil's story was all too familiar . . . : This paragraph recounts the generally acknowledged details surrounding Denzil Dowell's shooting death. Accounts of the case appear in Seale, *Seize the Time*, 134–139; Newton, *Revolutionary Suicide*, 145–152; and Bloom and Martin, 50–57.

p. 105: "I was really impressed . . . what they were doing": quoted in Bloom and Martin, 53.

p. 106: The Pocket Lawyer of Legal First Aid (sidebar): Newton, *Revolutionary Suicide*, 167–168.

p. 108: Negotiations and Potential Alliances (section): Bloom and Martin, 91–92, 111–114, details some of the back-and-forth between the Panthers and SNCC. The debates between these organizations (and others) were ongoing and complex.

p. 108: "The Panthers were the first group . . . impressed with that": quoted in Shames and Seale, 69–70.

p. 108: "We were essentially in compatible . . . same place": quoted in ibid., 70.

p. 109: Executive Mandate #2: Bloom and Martin, 92.

p. 111: The proposed gun-control law would . . . stop them from policing the police: In an April 1967 article in the *San Francisco Chronicle*, Rep. Don Mulford is quoted addressing the need to stop the "increasing incidence of organized groups and individuals publicly arming themselves" (quoted in Bloom and Martin, 57).

p. 111: Twenty-four Panthers were arrested: ibid., 60.

p. 112: "racism was not out . . . it was there": Dixon, loc. 899 of 5536.

p. 112: "We had gone out . . . had now surfaced": ibid., loc. 1051 of 5536.

p. 113: Fred Hampton, also eighteen . . . the value of self-defense: Haas.

p. 113: Nearer to Oakland . . . their presence and platform: Brown, 118.

p. 113: Alprentice "Bunchy" Carter . . . Los Angeles: Bloom and Martin, 143–145; Brown, 118–130.

9. OFF THE PIGS!

p. 115: "If violence is wrong . . . this country": Malcolm X, "Message to the Grassroots."

p. 116: "All power comes from . . . Anything else is theft": Newton, *Revolutionary Suicide*, 178.

p. 117: "We recognize the significance . . . for liberation": Newton, *Revolutionary Suicide*, 173.

p. 117: "What is a pig? . . . an unprovoked attack": *Black Panther*, September 7, 1968, 6; Foner, 14, also shows the full quote, cited to a May 1967 issue of the newspaper.

p. 117: Its first known use occurred in 1902: Demby.

p. 117: people tended to speak in terms . . . views and uses the word: McWhorter discusses the transition from "prejudiced" to "racist," which occurs so specifically around the time when the Panthers were using this rhetoric in their speech and writing that it is reasonable to conclude that their influence significantly aided (or perhaps even precipitated) the transition.

p. 118: "Words could be used . . . unthinkingly accepted": ibid., 177.

p. 118: "We must recognize the difference . . . courageous manner": Newton, *To Die for the People*, 101.

p. 119: "We were taught that . . . not even be necessary": Joseph, 62–63.

p. 120: "Am I under arrest?" . . . "No": Austin, 87, explains that "Huey asked whether he was under arrest and was told no." The surrounding text, 86–88, discusses the incident in full.

p. 121: Free Huey! (section): Many books about the Panthers discuss the events of October 27–28, 1967, in some detail. In this section, I'm presenting the relevant facts that are generally agreed upon. Certain things remain unknown about the incident, and the text addresses the various theories in the subsequent section. See Bloom and Martin, 99–102; Newton, *Revolutionary Suicide*, 173–178; and Austin, 86–88.

p. 122: the very night Huey's probation for a previous incident had expired: Huey had served probation for an assault conviction that occurred a few years earlier, after a fight with a man named Odell Lee. His probation term expired at 11:59 p.m. on October 27. When Huey and Gene were pulled over at four a.m. the following morning, his probation had been up for about four hours. They went out late that night, in part to celebrate his freedom. See Austin, 86, and Newton, *Revolutionary Suicide*, 173–174.

p. 122: "I wanted to use the trial . . . our revolution forever": Newton, *Revolutionary Suicide*, 201.

p. 123: "the ideological and political significance" and "I needed to know . . . advance their struggle": ibid., 201–202.

p. 123: "Free Huey or the sky's the limit!" signs are visible in photographs: Shames, 18–19.

p. 124: "A lot of grassroots . . . sea of type": Shames and Seale, 109.

p. 124: "was basically done by hand . . . afford a computer": quoted in ibid., 110. Emory's reference to computers likely relates to a later time in the newspaper production, as computers for home and office use were not commercially available until the mid-1970s.

p. 124: "I did my art . . . needed to be done": quoted in ibid., 110.

p. 124: "Emory's images . . . attacked our people": quoted in Douglas, 14.

p. 125: "The Black Panther newspapers . . . anger and hope": quoted in ibid., 93–94.

p. 125: "The Black Panther Black Community News Service . . . spirit of the people": Landon Williams, "The Black Panther: The Mirror of the People," *Black Panther*, January 17, 1970, quoted in Foner, 14.

p. 126: When the Federal Bureau of Investigation

(FBI) discovered this plan . . . : The story of the newspaper shipments being destroyed by federal agents is discussed in Shames and Seale, 110.

p. 127: as many as 400,000 copies per week: The FBI says circulation of the paper was at least 139,000 in 1970, and an Intelligence Committee report suggests circulation of 150,000 in 1970 (Bloom and Martin, 392), but Douglas, 14, 96, estimates they were putting out 400,000 total copies per week in 1970–1971.

p. 128: On January 16, 1968 . . . : The events of this morning are discussed in Seale, *Seize the Time*, 225, and Austin, 116–117.

p. 128: A month later . . . ultimately deemed illegal: Austin, 118–119.

p. 128: "Whenever I got arrested . . . homes or offices": Howard, 62.

p. 128: Huey, for example, spent ten months in prison . . . : Newton, *Revolutionary Suicide*, 215.

p. 128: "If you go to jail . . . born in jail": Malcolm X, "The Ballot or the Bullet."

p. 129: "We draw the line at the threshold of our doors" and "Our organization has received . . . as evil-doers": Executive Mandate #3, in Newton, *To Die for the People*, 12.

10. DEATH OF THE KING

p. 133: "When he died . . . died in America": "Reflecting on Martin Luther King's Legacy 50 Years After His Death."

p. 134: "an *eerie* scream . . . they killed him!": quoted in Austin, 162–163.

p. 134: "All hell broke loose": quoted in ibid.

p. 134: "protestors and rioters swarm . . . white-owned businesses": Joseph, 28.

p. 135: people in over one hundred cities took to the streets: Braimah.

p. 135: "Almost all were arrested . . . family could make": Haas, 35–36.

p. 135: "I kicked and banged the steel . . . on the streets": Dixon, loc. 1324 of 5536.

p. 135: "Anger filled me . . . would be the gun": ibid., loc. 1332 of 5536.

p. 136: The Kerner Commission: Why Do They "Riot"? (sidebar): Bloom and Martin, 86–90.

p. 136: "feel it is legitimate and necessary . . . subordinate status": quoted in ibid., 86.

p. 137: Ambush! (section): Reports vary about exactly what happened on the night of April 6, 1968. The Panthers initially said that they were taken off guard by the police, but David Hilliard and Eldridge Cleaver both later suggested that the Panthers had been considering an ambush of their own, in retaliation for Dr. King's assassination. The discussion of the events included here is described in Bloom and Martin, 118–119; Austin, 164–168; and Seale, *Seize the Time*, 234–235.

p. 137: On April 5, . . . police the next night: Big Man Howard describes his encounter with Lil' Bobby in Howard, 30–31.

p. 139: "There was no discipline . . . acting the fool": Bobby Seale discusses how Panther discipline and training evolved in the wake of Lil' Bobby's murder in Shames and Seale, 51.

p. 140: "Looking into the casket . . . romanticized": Dixon, loc. 1417 of 5536.

p. 140: "The sudden arrests . . . anger, violence and love": quoted in Douglas, 58.

p. 140: Bobby Seale brought a small group . . . but also exciting: Dixon, loc. 1452 of 5536.

p. 141: Ericka and John committed their lives to the movement: Bloom and Martin, 139.

p. 141: "Nonviolence was dead . . . Hutton was killed": Brown, 131.

p. 141: "The murder of King changed . . . attention as they got": quoted in Hampton and Fayer, 514.

11. GOING NATIONAL

p. 143: "There is a world of difference . . . methods of liberation": Newton, "In Defense of Self-Defense," *Black Panther*, June 20, 1967, reprinted in Newton, *To Die for the People*, 83.

p. 143: Within the space of two years . . . thousands of members nationwide: Bloom and Martin, 2–4.

p. 144: A crowd of about five thousand people: Information about the size of the crowd and other facts of the case appear in Newton, *Revolutionary Suicide*, 216, and Austin, 113–114.

p. 144: especially with white activists: A number of wealthy white people contributed to the Panthers' efforts, including some famous people like Jane Fonda and Donald Sutherland. Bloom and Martin, 295.

p. 144: Charles Garry mounted a passionate defense . . . : Seale, *Seize the Time*, 244.

p. 145: "By framing the practice . . . from non-blacks": Bloom and Martin, 160.

p. 146: The entire nation watched . . . no one was killed: Astor.

p. 146: On September 8 . . . remain behind bars: Bloom and Martin, 199; Newton, *Revolutionary Suicide*, 260–265.

p. 146: Two Oakland police officers . . . entered a café next door: The two officers' assault on the Panther office is discussed in Bloom and Martin, 199–200, and Seale, *Seize the Time*, 245.

p. 147: "These dudes keep breaking the law . . . where people are living": Seale, *Seize the Time*, 245.

p. 147: The officers were suspended . . . : ibid., 246.

p. 147: "All that stuff exposed . . . and attacking cats": ibid., 246.

p. 148: Eldridge Cleaver was still in serious legal trouble . . . : ibid., 256.

p. 148: The Peace and Freedom Party . . . overlooking civil rights efforts: Bloom and Martin, 107.

p. 149: Organization (section): Austin, 38, presents a flow chart of Panther leadership hierarchy. See also pages 36–40 for discussion of Panther leadership roles and organizational structure.

p. 150: nineteen-year-old Fred Hampton: Haas, 15–20, provides information on Hampton's early organizing.

p. 151: "We had many recruits . . . in the long term": Dixon, loc. 1998 of 5536.

p. 151: Joudon found himself needing the whole auditorium: Bloom and Martin, 149.

p. 151: "emerging consensus . . . Black Power": ibid., 150.

p. 153: Olympic athletes Tommie Smith and John Carlos: Davis, "Olympic Athletes Who Took a Stand."

p. 155: "There is no single . . . Panther histories": Shih and Williams, 51.

p. 155: Fifteen-year-old Jamal Joseph . . . : Jamal Joseph discusses his path to the Panthers in his memoir *Panther Baby*.

p. 155: "Man, you gotta kill . . . young brother, I just did": Joseph, 45–47.

p. 157: "Guns were around . . . ready to engage in revolution": ibid., 62.

p. 157: "At each Wednesday-night meeting . . . the discipline and the reading": Brown, 137.

p. 157: the Central Committee developed . . . twenty-six rules: Bloom and Martin, 343.

p. 158: "When I came out of high school . . . meaning of that paragraph" and "It gave me more . . . wasn't like that": quoted in Shih and Williams, 195–196.

p. 161: Jamal and other recruits . . . ever needed to: Joseph, 53.

p. 161: "what happened from the time . . . end of the day": Bukhari, *The War Before*, 22–23. In addition to the quote, this section further discusses the Panthers' values around discipline.

p. 161: Day-to-day work . . . done at the moment: The relentless pace of work for rank-and-file Panthers is described in Joseph, Bukhari, Brown, and many of the essays in Shih and Williams.

p. 161: "Your role was to do . . . had done previously": quoted in Shih and Williams, 95.

p. 162: "The easiest way . . . worker bees": quoted in ibid., 12.

p. 162: The chapters varied widely . . . members on duty: I make the estimate about chapter membership based on several in-person anecdotes contained in Shih and Williams and the numbers Bobby Seale offers in Shames and Seale, 128.

p. 162: For each paper she sold . . . : Safiya Bukhari says Panthers earned ten cents per paper, as does Lipsky, while Joseph, 134, says Panthers earned five cents per paper. It seems possible that Bukhari is referring to a later time than Joseph, since they both served in New York, but it's also possible that different chapters/offices operated with different rules. The sale price of the paper was initially fifteen cents but later went up to twenty-five cents, so that could also account for the difference.

p. 162: "I was told to get off the corner . . . to tell people": Bukhari, *The War Before*, 27.

p. 163: 10-10-10 Rule: Reference to the 10-10-10 Rule appears in "Rules of the Black Panther Party." It is defined in Bukhari, "Kamau Sadiki."

p. 163: Back in Oakland . . . mail or death threats: Big Man describes his role and routine in Howard.

p. 164: Jamal Joseph rose quickly . . . high-school-aged Panthers: Joseph, 63.

p. 164: "It all started by going door-to-door . . . who was in your section?": quoted in Shih and Williams, 113.

p. 164: "The Panther office became . . . they would come to us": quoted in Austin, 283.

p. 165: "We had a grievance board . . . to settle the argument": quoted in Shih and Williams, 113.

p. 165: "this idea of love . . . for the people": quoted in ibid.

p. 165: "It's love that would . . . your brother or sister": quoted in ibid.

p. 166: "I knew I was fighting . . . believed in my heart": quoted in ibid., 17.

p. 167: "When you joined . . . willing to have theirs": quoted in ibid., 43.

p. 167: Full-time Panthers . . . devote themselves fully to the movement: Joseph, 163.

p. 167: The median age of Panthers was nineteen: Ericka Huggins says this in Shih and Williams, 85, and Shames and Seale, 52.

p. 167: "you would eat . . . pot of food": quoted in Shames and Seale, 128.

p. 167: "I set up cooking crews . . . their own meals": quoted in ibid.

p. 167: "He was a parent . . . a family": quoted in ibid., 47.

p. 168: "there were times when . . . the party's baby": quoted in Shih and Williams, 108.

p. 168: "In a time when the other . . . but by ability": Bukhari, *The War Before*, 56.

p. 169: "Men and women don't stop . . . we joined the BPP": quoted in Shih and Williams, 107.

p. 169: "Whatever was going on . . . members of the Party": Bukhari, *The War Before*, 55.

p. 169: "We used criticism . . . chauvinist activity" and "If I made a mistake . . . 'Chairman, you shouldn't . . .'": Shames and Seale, 41.

p. 170: "In changing this society . . . how we think of each other": Bukhari, *The War Before*, 58.

p. 170: "There were too many different . . . laid back": quoted in Shih and Williams, 129.

p. 170: "I got arrested a lot . . . good business for them": quoted in ibid., 152.

p. 170: "worked so hard . . . bring about social change": quoted in ibid., 74.

p. 171: "We thought about death . . . that's what revolution is": quoted in ibid., 20.

p. 171: "It was an honor . . . to die as a Panther": quoted in ibid., 17.

13. SURVIVAL PENDING REVOLUTION

p. 173: "If we suffer genocide . . . change things": Newton, *To Die for the People*, 66.

p. 174: "we must concentrate . . . meet the needs of the people": *Black Panther*, 1969.

p. 174: "The legacy of . . . we organized people" and "participate in their own upliftment": quoted in Shih and Williams, 85.

p. 175: "Our children need . . . they can learn": *Black Panther*, January 1969.

p. 175: A typical breakfast . . . up and running: Dr. Huey P. Newton Foundation, 30.

p. 175: "I got up early . . . and got them off to school": Bukhari, *The War Before*, 19.

p. 176: When breakfast programs . . . each day nationwide: Bloom and Martin, 13.

p. 177: Each family would receive . . . and canned goods: Dr. Huey P. Newton Foundation, 35.

p. 177: SUPPORT THE STORE . . . : The Panthers' picket signs are visible in photographs, such as those in Shames and Seale, 123–124, and the *Black Panther*, August 9, 1971, 1 ("SUPPORT THOSE WHO SERVE THE PEOPLE").

p. 178: "lower their prices . . . economic exploitation": Dr. Huey P. Newton Foundation, 39.

p. 178: "While I was working . . . and hurts people": Bukhari, *The War Before*, 20.

p. 180: Black people have consistently been a medically underserved population: Shih and Williams, 176. Alondra Nelson, who wrote the essay in Shih and Williams from which this statement is drawn, also wrote a book about the Panthers' medical activism; see Alondra Nelson.

p. 180: within a year the Panthers had opened . . . : According to Alondra Nelson, 75–77, the first clinic opened in Oakland in 1969, and in April 1970 Bobby Seale issued instructions for every chapter to create a People's Free Medical Clinic.

p. 180: "They were leaving a lot of people . . . who died": quoted in Shih and Williams, 169.

p. 181: A Multitude of Needs (section): Dr. Huey P. Newton Foundation's *The Black Panther Party: Service to the People Programs* is a guide to many of the Panthers' community initiatives: SAFE, 17–19; People's Free Shoe Program, 61–65; People's Free Clothing Program, 66–68; legal aid and prison busing, 78–80.

p. 182: Jamal Joseph was serving . . . children and staff: Joseph, 156–158.

p. 182: police raided a breakfast . . . and set fire to it: There were multiple food-destruction incidents with police. This one is detailed in Shames and Seale, 129.

p. 183: "We say that the survival programs . . . out of that situation": Dr. Huey P. Newton Foundation, 4.

p. 183: "We did everything we did . . . It was brilliant": quoted in Shih and Williams, 86.

p. 183: "When consciousness and understanding . . . an incredibly rich land": Dr. Huey P. Newton Foundation, 4.

14. ALL POWER TO THE PEOPLE

p. 185: "A chicken just . . . revolutionary chicken!": from Malcolm X's speech on May 29, 1964, at the Militant Labor Forum Hall in Harlem; *Malcolm X Speaks*, 68–69.

p. 185: the Panthers began talking less . . . human rights for all: The shift in rhetoric can be seen clearly in issues of the *Black Panther* newspaper and in early Panther speeches and writings versus later speeches and writings. Executive Mandate #1, for example, primarily uses the language of "black People" and "black communities" and was delivered in 1967 (Foner, 40), whereas the call for a Revolutionary People's Constitutional Convention, issued in 1970, states: "Black people are not the only group within America that stands in need" and explicitly discusses the need for broader human rights across numerous marginalized groups (Foner, 267–269). See also Austin, 249.

p. 186: Marxist-Leninist Theory (section): Clearly the most direct source to learn more about Marxist theory is *The Communist Manifesto*; however, you can also find a brief introduction to the ideas in Corcione. For a parallel brief introduction to capitalism, see Kelly.

p. 187: Vladimir Lenin offered his own spin on Marxism: Le Blanc.

p. 189: Rainbow Coalition (section): Haas discusses Fred Hampton's work in great detail. Also, see Ganeva for a great article summarizing the spirit of the coalition effort, featuring interview clips from former coalition participants and links to archival video and other further reading.

p. 190: The Rangers ultimately renamed . . . about community organizing: Churchill and Vander Wall, xi, mention the Blackstone Rangers' name change to Black P. Stone Nation. They don't suggest that the name change occurred to bridge the Panthers and the Rangers, as the groups never fully and formally allied, but remained on friendly ground.

p. 191: The U.N. had intervened . . . violence from the state: The plebiscite concept excited the Panthers, but it is hard to say more specifically what it would have looked like. The U.N.'s prior interventions and plebiscites looked different in different places; in fact, part of the process of hosting a plebiscite was to determine needs, then develop and implement a popular consultation, or vote, among the constituency in question. See United Nations Department of Political Affairs.

p. 192: "Our struggle was not . . . as human beings": Bukhari, *The War Before*, 58.

p. 193: "Black women are oppressed . . . That has got to go": quoted in Bloom and Martin, 303.

p. 193: Some even suggested . . . to advance the movement: Panther women at all levels— from the Central Committee down to paper sellers and breakfast volunteers—describe facing pressure from Panther men to have sex, ostensibly for the good of the revolution. Some describe experiences of assault or rape.

While this was a dynamic that was clearly ever present in the Party, it is my belief that this behavior speaks to cultural biases, individual dysfunction, and preexisting trauma rather than being a value of the organization. Thus, I have chosen not to detail this aspect of life in the Party further.

It is true that we as a society need to become more transparent about violence against women, and at the same time I am aware that Black men as a group are often (and too easily) demonized as sexual predators. To emphasize that women were assaulted within the Party would imply that this happened because they were Panthers—and, in fact, this very argument has been used to demonize and discredit the Panthers for years. However, I have found no evidence to suggest that women in the Party were raped, assaulted, or pressured at a higher rate than women across society. Violence against women is a far deeper, more systemic problem, and to lay it at the feet of the Panthers does a disservice both to the Panthers and to the larger issues in play. For anecdotes and analysis of sexual aggression and sexual violence in the Party, see Bloom and Martin; Shih and Williams; and Brown.

p. 193: "The liberation of women is one . . .": quoted in Bloom and Martin, 305.

p. 193: Huey addressed the (white) women's movement . . . : The text of a 1970 speech Huey gave to this effect can be found in Quintard Taylor.

p. 194: "But the enemy . . . a thousand cuts": Bukhari, *The War Before*, 61.

p. 194: By 1970, women made up a significant majority: Tillet. In Seale, *A Lonely Rage*, Bobby estimates that within three years of founding, at least 60% of Panthers were women; see also Alondra Nelson, 93.

p. 194: "Women *were* the party": Ericka Huggins, in conversation with the author, October 25, 2016.

p. 195: "We worked closely with teacher . . . unions is rarely covered": quoted in Shih and Williams, 116.

p. 195: "The power of the oppressor . . . strength to smash injustice": Newton, *The Huey P. Newton Reader*, 136.

15. THE WRATH OF COINTELPRO

p. 197: "A top secret *Special Report* . . . against it": introduction to *COINTELPRO: The FBI's Secret War on Political Freedom*, by Nelson Blackstock (New York: Monad, 1975), 17.

p. 198: Between 1963 and 1971, the FBI ran nearly three hundred . . . targeted the Black Panther Party: Bloom and Martin, 210, note that 295 actions were initiated to destabilize Black nationalist organizations, and 233 of those (79%) targeted the Black Panther Party. The surrounding section of the book, 200–215, discusses COINTELPRO operations more broadly, including the time line of the FBI's surveillance and intervention efforts. On page 200, they state that efforts to discredit the Rev. Dr. King began by the end of 1963, although they elaborate on pages 201–202 that more

explicit memos regarding Black nationalists under COINTELPRO were written on August 25, 1967; March 4, 1968; and thereafter.

All FBI COINTELPRO operations reportedly ceased in 1971, and although Churchill and Vander Wall present compelling evidence that certain activities did continue, the majority of the damage done to the BPP was completed by that point.

p. 198: The program's major goals . . . increasing their membership base: The COINTELPRO goals outlined here are paraphrased from an FBI internal memo dated March 4, 1968, quoted in Churchill and Vander Wall, 255.

p. 200: The FBI kept this program top secret . . . to get to the Panthers: Churchill and Vander Wall's *Agents of Repression* is the source that discusses the COINTELPRO operations in the most detail. Several additional sources refer to the FBI and local police operations overstepping their legal bounds in an effort to surveil and interfere with Panther programs. According to the FBI website, COINTELPRO was "later rightfully criticized by Congress and the American people for abridging first amendment rights." See "COINTELPRO."

p. 200: "submit imaginative and hard-hitting . . . crippling the BPP": quoted in Churchill and Vander Wall, 41.

p. 201: Before Nixon's election . . . multiple offices were raided: This pattern of raids and its relationship to Nixon's election is discussed in Bloom and Martin, 212–214.

p. 201: at least forty-three separate FBI field offices . . . : Churchill and Vander Wall, 38.

p. 202: Throughout the month of December . . . and the resulting fire: Attacks on Black Panther offices are discussed in Bloom and Martin, 212–214.

p. 203: "A black brother you don't know" and "I know what I'd do, if I was you": quoted in Churchill and Vander Wall, 65. According to Austin, 205, the false letter was approved by Director Hoover on January 30, 1969.

p. 204: "Consideration has been given . . . violence prone": Chicago FBI field office to Director Hoover, January 10, 1969, quoted in Churchill and Vander Wall, 397.

p. 204: They sent false letters . . . between SNCC and the Panthers: COINTELPRO operations against the Panthers (along with other groups like SNCC) are discussed in Churchill and Vander Wall, chapters 2–3. Mention of the false letters between Stokely and Rap appears in ibid., 50.

p. 204: "capitalize on BPP and U.S. differences . . . ranks of the BPP": According to Austin, 240, the memo was drafted on November 8, 1968.

p. 205: Black Studies Organizing (sidebar): Chapter 12 of Bloom and Martin discusses nationwide Black Studies organizing efforts in detail.

p. 205: the United States' first Black Studies program: A lot of student organizing was happening concurrently around the country, but Austin, 378 n39, states that San Francisco State's program was the first one established.

p. 205: Similar protests took place . . . country in 1969: Bloom and Martin, 286.

p. 205: The Panthers gained support . . . and justice: ibid., 286.

p. 206: The disagreement reached . . . fled the scene: The incident surrounding John Huggins's and Bunchy Carter's deaths is discussed in Bloom and Martin, 219–220, and Austin, 225–228.

p. 207: Over one hundred police . . . eventually dropped: Bloom and Martin, 219.

p. 207: After all, U.S. cooperated with law enforcement . . . the power structure: "A Political Assassination," *Black Panther*, January 25, 1969, quoted in Bloom and Martin, 220.

p. 208: They even appeared at John's funeral . . . : Brown, 179.

p. 208: The Chicago 8 (section): For more information about the Chicago 8 trial (sometimes referred to as the Chicago 7 trial because Bobby Seale's case was severed from the group), see Levine; McNamee; and Greenberg.

p. 209: "I was a little shook up . . . to come after you": Joseph, 75–76. For the full narrative of Jamal's arrest, see ibid., 72–81.

p. 209: The New York District . . . City landmarks: ibid., 79; Bloom and Martin, 213–214.

p. 209: There was no evidence of such a plot . . . : The trial created almost two years of distraction for the Party and effectively hobbled the New York chapter leadership. In the end, the jury deliberations on the eight-month trial lasted barely three hours before they returned with "not guilty" verdicts on all charges, saying, "There just wasn't enough evidence"; see Asbury.

p. 210: Suspicious Behavior (section): Bloom and Martin, 248–251, and Austin, 289–293, discuss George Sams's actions and the suspicions around him. Churchill and Vander Wall, 53, conclude that Sams was indeed a paid FBI informant, while other sources are less definitive.

p. 210: Into this leadership vacuum . . . previous year: According to Bloom and Martin, 248, after Sams was expelled, Stokely Carmichael vouched for him to be reinstated, based on their days working together in the past.

16. TRAITORS IN THE RANKS

p. 213: "I routinely supplied . . . headquarters": quoted in Hampton and Fayer, 534.

p. 213: "greatest threat to the internal security of the country": quoted in Austin, xxvi, 169.

p. 213: The FBI had the stated goal . . . actions led to more violence . . . : In 1975–1976, the U.S. Senate's Church Committee examined law enforcement behavior under COINTELPRO and concluded that their actions not only violated the law but were also designed to precipitate violence; see Kifner. For more information about the Church Committee, see U.S. Senate, "Senate Select Committee to Study Governmental Operations with Respect to Intelligence Activities."

p. 214: "The order of the day . . . Party offices": Shames and Seale, 129.

p. 215: At the end of July . . . firefight with the officers: Bloom and Martin, 234.

p. 215: When the Panthers ran out . . . the free breakfast program: ibid.; Shames and Seale, 129.

p. 215: "That's a heavy example . . . in the community": Shames and Seale, 130.

p. 216: A young man in Chicago . . . FBI agent named Mitchell: William O'Neal's activities are discussed in detail in Churchill and Vander Wall, 65–68.

p. 216: George Sams's behavior . . . FBI to do it: Bloom and Martin, 251.

p. 217: Free Bobby! (section): Bobby Seale offers a firsthand account of his experiences of being arrested, transported to Chicago, and placed on trial in Seale, *Seize the Time*, 289–361. Details of Bobby's arrest and the Chicago and New Haven cases can also be found in Bloom and Martin, 250–266.

p. 218: "I thought I was going to die . . . were doing things": Bobby gives this quote and discusses his experience of being bound and gagged in court in Seale, *Seize the Time*, 342.

p. 218: "Anybody can read the court record . . . recognize it": ibid., 347.

p. 218: Assassination (section): Haas, 75–87, examines the lead-up, the incident, and its aftermath in detail. See also Bloom and Martin, 237–246, and Churchill and Vander Wall, 64–77.

p. 218: Chicago police had been trying . . . charges to stick: Bloom and Martin, 229–236. Chicago authorities tried Fred Hampton for robbery and assault in April 1969. They arrested and indicted him, along with fourteen other Panther leaders, for kidnapping in June 1969, and also raided the Panther office numerous times in the course of 1969. Despite a conviction for the assault and robbery charges, Hampton was no longer behind bars.

p. 219: They possessed a search warrant . . . to kill Fred Hampton: The scale of the assault was immense, and the FBI showed advanced planning by having Fred drugged. It was later revealed that the supposed raid was intended to result in Fred's death. Witnesses in the apartment heard the policemen standing over Fred's body speculate on whether he could survive his injuries and then shooting him again for good measure. They also dragged his body out of bed to the doorway to make it appear as though he'd been fighting back. Fred Hampton's family (along with Clark's and the surviving Panthers) ultimately received a $1.85 million settlement from the government. Churchill and Vander Wall, 64–77.

p. 219: It turned out that . . . knock him out: According to Bloom and Martin, 245, Fred Hampton's autopsy revealed a heavy dose of Seconal in his system. Many historians and former Panthers believe that William O'Neal drugged Fred to ensure the success of the assassination.

p. 219: "nuthin but a northern lynching": quoted in Haas, loc. 401.

p. 220: "the most devastating piece of news . . . most prolific Panther around": Dixon, loc. 3059 of 5536.

p. 220: Bobby Seale had privately tapped Fred . . . : Seale, *Eyes on the Prize* Interview."

p. 220: "preventing the rise of a black 'messiah'": quoted in Churchill and Vander Wall, 255.

p. 221: Predawn Raids (section): The L.A. office raid and its aftermath are discussed in Bloom and Martin, 222–225. In addition, a short clip of archival footage of the shootout and subsequent arrests on December 8 are available at www.youtube.com/watch?time_continue=95&v=xwQI79lYsTI&feature=emb_logo.

p. 221: "we were free for a while": Roland Freeman said this at an event in Harlem where he spoke in 2011, when he appeared on a panel at the Black Panther Film Festival following a film screening. This phrase was also a headline in the *Black Panther* in the days after the L.A. office shootout.

p. 221: Police reinforcements arrived . . . streets like tanks: Both Bloom and Martin, 223, and Fleischer cite this as the first use of SWAT teams.

p. 222: But community members who witnessed . . . attack on them: Witnesses rapidly spread the word about the assault on the L.A. office. On December 11, 1969, a crowd of three to four thousand gathered outside the courthouse to protest the police treatment of the Panthers. This included support from mainstream/moderate Black leaders and citizens. See Bloom and Martin, 224–225, and Fleischer.

p. 223: "In 1969 alone . . . cases outright corrupt": Use of the term *assassination* to describe these Panthers' deaths may be controversial. Fred Hampton's murder is widely acknowledged to have been deliberate and premeditated by the FBI and Chicago police. Mark Clark's death was likely an unplanned consequence of the same raid. The shooting of John Huggins and Bunchy Carter may or may not have been planned or orchestrated by law enforcement; however, the FBI had targeted them for "neutralization" and stoked tension between the U.S. government and the Panthers with the hope of causing violence, so it seems fair to categorize these deaths as "government-sanctioned."

17. POLITICAL PRISONERS

p. 225: "Deputy Chairman . . . jail either'": *Black Panther*, June 7, 1969, 6.

p. 226: "Black men born in the U.S. . . . inevitability of prison": Jackson, 4.

p. 226: instead of the light sentence . . . serve behind bars: Churchill and Vander Wall, 94.

p. 226: 11% of the people were Black: Specifically, 11.2%, according to the U.S. Census Bureau, "1970 Census."

p. 226: nearly 40% of prison inmates were Black: Lanagan.

p. 227: Panthers often spent extra time in solitary . . . to the movement: Political prisoners spending lengthy stretches in solitary confinement remains a fact of the prison system even today. For example, in 1995 the Angola Prison warden stated that several Black Panthers in his care (known as the Angola 3) were being held in solitary because they were "still trying to practice Black Pantherism." Placed there in 1971, the

Angola 3 each spent around forty years in solitary. See Pilkington.

p. 227: As a result of his organizing . . . he became eligible: Pilkington comments on Panthers being denied parole generally; with regard to George Jackson specifically, see Churchill and Vander Wall, 94–95.

p. 228: In 1970, prison officials . . . join the Black Panther Party: Kendi, 411–412, mentions the Soledad Brothers case and community protests. The source notes in Churchill and Vander Wall, 410, also offer a summary of the inciting incidents, along with additional sources to draw upon for more information.

p. 228: Angela did not officially join the Black Panther Party: It's a common assumption that Angela Davis was a Black Panther, but my research indicates that she was never a member, despite being politically allied with the Panthers' mission and ideals, and even working closely with them at times. In *Stamped from the Beginning*, for example, Kendi focuses an entire section on Angela and her activism but barely mentions the Panthers. In "Angela Davis on Feminism, Communism and Being a Black Panther during the Civil Rights Era" (www.youtube .com/watch?v=x3q_qV5mHg0), Davis says she was "involved with the Black Panther Party" before joining the Communist Party.

p. 229: "rounded up in the middle . . . irrational actions": quoted in Austin, 285–286.

p. 230: Within a few months of their arrests . . . Dhoruba Bin Wahad: Bloom and Martin discuss the New York 21 arrests and bail and re-arrests in various places, including 213–214 and 360–361. Austin, 286, and Joseph, 159–162, talk about some of the twenty-one being released on bail.

p. 230: The youngest defendants . . . lives and their freedom: Jamal Joseph dedicates a significant portion of his autobiography to his experiences in the New York 21. Chapters 5–8 discuss his arrest and imprisonment. Chapter 9 discusses his reentry into Panther life post-incarceration (126). Chapter 10 discusses his role in the National Speakers Bureau (147–148). Chapter 11 mentions his trial being severed from the group (159) and discusses the release of other members of the twenty-one (160–162).

p. 231: Yale University hosted . . . to support Bobby: The Free Ericka movement and New Haven protests are discussed in Bloom and Martin, 254–256. Yale University Library archives hold records and ephemera related to the Free Ericka protests that took place on campus, in the Catherine Roraback Collection of Ericka Huggins Papers (call number: JWJ MSS 96), https://archives.yale.edu/repositories/11/resources/996.

p. 231: gender-specific discrimination . . . "innocent until proven guilty": Phillips, 191–192.

p. 232: In March 1970, during pretrial . . . receive a fair trial: Austin, 293.

p. 233: In June 1970 . . . Huey's own case: The tension between the New York 21 and the Central Committee in Oakland is discussed in ibid., 300–301.

p. 234: A few New York 21 members . . . before the trial began: Several New York 21 members escaped arrest; see Austin, 285. Jamal Joseph describes his underground life in *Panther Baby*, beginning in chapter 12.

p. 234: the Central Committee refused to support . . . tension in the ranks: The Party felt it could not support Panthers underground without risking its own reputation and status; see Bloom and Martin, 357.

p. 235: Taking Hostages (section): Jonathan Jackson's rescue attempt is discussed in Kendi, 412–413, and Churchill and Vander Wall, 95–96.

p. 236: A Clash in the Central Committee (section): Bloom and Martin, 339, 358–371; Austin, 297–325.

p. 237: The turmoil of 1969 . . . the Panther movement: Austin, 297.

p. 237: Eldridge Cleaver . . . soon as possible: ibid.

p. 237: COINTELPRO made matters . . . stir up the controversy: Bloom and Martin, 366.

18. THE SPLIT

p. 239: "The idea of . . . will be resistance": "Opening Statement by Assata Shakur (Joanne Chesimard)."

p. 239: Huey had just gotten out . . . send him right back: The Panthers had always advocated following the law, but there are a lot of hints that Huey's time in prison made him more fearful of the possible consequences of Panther actions. The Panthers' rhetoric always included the expectation of future insurrection, yet when many in the Party began moving in that direction, Huey pressed for patience in the extreme, even to the point of minimizing the violent, visionary rhetoric that had put the Panthers on the map (Bloom and Martin, 369).

Huey's intent focus on putting off armed revolution may have been motivated by more than ideology. Several sources suggest that post-prison Huey was skittish, radically self-protective, and far more concerned with keeping order in the Party than ever (Austin, 287, 296; Brown, 243–244). His insistence on having a more secure place to live than other Panthers despite the damage to Party cohesion (Brown, 262) and the fact that Huey later fled the country to avoid facing renewed criminal charges (Brown, 356–357) both underscore this conclusion.

p. 240: "The party did not openly advocate . . . to attack or not to attack": Dixon, loc. 2250–2266 of 5536.

p. 240: By the spring of 1971, fewer guns were appearing . . . : Interesting statistics on the reduction of violent imagery in the *Black Panther* can be found in Bloom and Martin, 369.

p. 240: Many of the sisters . . . rank and file dissolved: This tension between the national leadership is covered extensively in many sources, including Bloom and Martin, 354–359. Several anecdotes in Shih and Williams reflect it from a rank-and-file perspective (see, for instance, 132).

p. 241: a few promoted illegal activities . . .

attacks on the police: Bloom and Martin, 342–343, 353.

p. 241: "'expropriating funds' from banks": quoted in Shih and Williams, 224.

p. 242: The most extreme version . . . some Panthers argued: This phrasing represents the logical extreme to which the Panthers' insurrectionary rhetoric could be taken. Many Panthers and BLA members believed that Black Americans were already at war and that killing in the name of the cause was, at a minimum, justified and sometimes even necessary. Some factions developed a goal to proactively seek and destroy "undesirable elements," which meant attacking anyone and anything that posed a threat to Black lives and liberty. See Austin, 98–99.

p. 243: Purges (section): The purges that took place in 1969–1971 are discussed in detail in Bloom and Martin, 342–346.

p. 244: In January 1971 . . . having to choose sides: A scanned version of the New York 21's open letter to the Weather Underground appears at https://issuu.com /librarymachinebroke/docs/ny21. See also Bloom and Martin, 358–362.

p. 245: "The Black Panther Party has reached . . . make a revolution": quoted in Foner, 277–278.

p. 245: Now the Panthers introduced . . . elementary school: A thorough exploration of the many survival programs the Panthers founded and operated can be found in Dr. Huey P. Newton Foundation.

p. 246: a few Oakland Panthers . . . and the Central Committee: Austin, 300.

p. 246: That week's issue contained . . . who were selling them: Bloom and Martin, 363.

p. 246: At the time, most Panthers . . . Panthers' inner conflict: Austin, 314.

p. 246: Robert Webb's death deepened the divide . . . less appealing to many: Bloom and Martin, 364. Three Panthers eventually pleaded guilty and served time for manslaughter in the Napier case. Webb's killer remains unknown, and no one was ever prosecuted for the crime.

p. 247: as many as a third of members leaving the Party: Bobby Seale estimated a 30–40% membership drop after Webb and Napier were killed (ibid., 373).

p. 247: Safiya Bukhari served . . . the new newspaper: Bukhari, *The War Before*, xxix.

p. 247: "I kept moving from rundown . . . with guns blazing": Joseph, 190.

p. 248: Revolutionary Intercommunalism (sidebar): Some scholars (like Bloom and Martin, 312, 468 n13) argue that the introduction of this language was merely that— new language to describe what the Panthers were already doing. Still, the linguistic shift affected a variety of things within the life of the Party. Newton, *The Huey P. Newton Reader*, 181–199, outlines Huey's theory.

p. 248: Between 10,000 and 15,000 people . . . the economy, and more: "Flyer for the Revolutionary People's Constitutional Convention," Berkeley Revolution website, revolution.berkeley.edu/flyer -revolutionary-peoples-constitutional -convention/.

p. 248: "People walked out in droves . . . members defended it": Shakur, 226.

p. 248: "We gather here . . . pursuit of profits" and "Black people and oppressed people . . . our freedom": Newton, *To Die for the People*, 161–163.

p. 249: "Rather than argue with black people . . . path to revolution": ibid., 198.

p. 249: "As Panthers . . . community action": ibid.

p. 249: "elected to remain . . . flak from police": Bukhari, *The War Before*, 6–7.

p. 250: "When you woke up . . . that you would die": Joseph, 202.

p. 250: At least six BLA members did die . . . battling against them: It's hard to say exactly how many BLA members died, due to the underground nature of the group. They took credit for some of their actions, but police also attribute actions to them that they did not claim. Bukhari, 138–153, lists many who died in the struggle, including at least six people she cites as BLA members. There are academic discussions of the BLA in both Austin and in Bloom and Martin, with personal reports of life in the BLA contained in Shakur's *Assata* and Joseph's *Panther Baby*. Naturally some elements of these autobiographies are vague around the BLA's specific activities, as it would be unwise to confess in writing to breaking the law or to directly discuss actions that law enforcement might interpret as crimes.

p. 250: "Many different people . . . people's movement, an idea": Shakur, 169.

p. 250: "I wasn't one who believed . . . clearly

understand and support": ibid., 243. Assata employs several rhetorical strategies in her writing that are meant to convey subtle meaning and disrupt expectations, including the use of a lowercase *i* to downplay individualism and emphasize that she considers herself no greater than any other person.

p. 251: Assata Shakur: BLA Warrior (sidebar): Assata Shakur's autobiography discusses her life in the Panthers and the BLA.

p. 251: Assata was indicted . . . stop in 1973: Jill Nelson.

p. 251: Assata was placed on the FBI's Most Wanted Terrorists list: According to the FBI website (www.fbi.gov/wanted/wanted _terrorists /joanne-deborah-chesimard), Assata was the first woman to be placed on the list.

p. 252: "A war between the races . . . defend ourselves against it": ibid., 139–140.

p. 252: At George's funeral, Huey's remarks . . . action by the state: Bloom and Martin, 374–379, discuss the political implications of this moment at length.

p. 253: Attica! (section): Elbert "Big Man" Howard discusses the Panther role at the Attica uprising in *Panther on the Prowl* (72–76), as well as in the article "Slave Revolt at Attica" on It's About Time, the Black Panther Party Legacy and Alumni website: www.itsabouttimebpp.com/Big_Man/Slave _Revolt_at_Attica.html.

p. 254: "If ever there was a place . . . just hours away": Howard, 72.

p. 255: "It's a scene not easily forgotten" and "It was just an open fire order . . . they were unarmed": ibid.

19. LAST GASP

p. 257: "The thing I really loved . . . be ignored": quoted in Hampton and Fayer, 523. Clements was the activist pastor of the Holy Angels Church in Chicago, site of a BPP free breakfast program.

p. 257: "Wherever Huey was . . . wherever he stayed": Brown, 256.

p. 258: It was costing at least $600: Brown, 258–260, alternately says the penthouse was $600 per month and $12,000 per year, while Shakur, 230, says it was $650 per month.

p. 258: "Panthers who owned . . . hold back the hawk": Shakur, 230.

p. 258: "I wanted to believe . . . sense of logic": ibid.

p. 259: the Department of Justice began investigating the Panthers' bookkeeping: Bloom and Martin, 211, cite IRS and FBI cooperation to gain intelligence on Panther finances. Brown refers to this investigation in a couple of places, including 263–264, which mentions the FBI reviewing Panther bank accounts.

p. 259: Many Panther members turned to alcohol . . . Panther life: Though Panther rules prohibited drinking and drug use on duty, anecdotal mentions of drinking wine and liquor, going to bars, smoking marijuana, and so on, occur with some regularity in Panther memoirs and narratives. These anecdotes do not imply any significant pattern of alcohol abuse or drug addiction among members; though there were exceptions, like Huey, overall most Panthers' relationship to these substances was likely comparable to that of adults outside the Party. See, for example, Joseph and Brown.

p. 259: he still viewed himself as . . . supreme commander: Shakur, 230; Brown.

p. 259: "There were great things . . . some God-awful decisions": quoted in Shih and Williams, 172.

p. 259: They theorized that . . . from the ground up: Bloom and Martin, 380.

p. 259: In 1971, Ericka . . . : Oelsner.

p. 259: Bobby still had time to serve . . . court overturned his sentence: "U.S. Is Dropping Action on Seale."

p. 260: Ericka also returned to the West Coast: Huggins, "An Oral History."

p. 260: The Oakland Panthers held . . . those most in need: Shames and Seale, 218.

p. 261: Bobby studied the demographics . . . held by non-white people: Bobby Seale said this in his speech at the BPP Fiftieth Anniversary Celebration luncheon, which I attended.

p. 261: The Central Committee closed . . . to support the campaigns: Dixon, loc. 3643 of 5536, discusses this consolidation to Oakland, as do several essays in Shih and Williams. Not all of the offices actually closed or left the Party at this point, but numerous leaders reported to Oakland to support the campaigns.

p. 261: "Preparing the bags of groceries . . . serving the people": Dixon, loc. 3886 of 5536.

p. 261: "it was difficult leaving . . . Black people": ibid., loc. 3648 of 5536, which also mentions the various Seattle programs Aaron felt sad to leave behind.

p. 262: Some chapters simply removed . . . their survival programs: Alondra Nelson, 180, gives the example of Seattle keeping its health clinic running and eventually changing the name and affiliation.

p. 262: "It was like a bad . . . went their own route": quoted in Shih and Williams, 132.

p. 263: Health Care Advocacy (section): Alondra Nelson explores the Panthers' health care advocacy in great detail, including the establishment and operation of the People's Free Medical Clinics, their sickle cell anemia advocacy, and more.

p. 264: Historically, medical researchers . . . patients in the future: One famous case of medical discrimination occurred at the Tuskegee Institute, from 1932 to 1974, where a group of about six hundred Black men were the subject of experiments to study syphilis, a sexually transmitted infection. As part of the experiment, doctors and researchers denied medical treatment to Black men known to have syphilis in order to study the disease progression. Information about the Tuskegee Study can be found in "U.S. Public Health Service Syphilis Study at Tuskegee."

p. 264: Medical discrimination was . . . health care providers: Several studies document the phenomenon of racial biases in medical practice. Holpuch discusses some of the findings.

p. 264: Philadelphia created the Mark Clark . . . summer of 1969: These health clinics are mentioned by name in Alondra Nelson, 90–111.

p. 265: The Panthers hoped to revolutionize . . . communities across the country: Bloom and Martin, 192, say the Panthers established at least nine liberation schools, from Seattle to the Bronx.

p. 265: Since many of their members . . . serving 150 students: Shames and Seale, 93.

p. 266: "Oakland Community School was . . . racially marginalized communities": quoted in ibid.

p. 266: "Our model was to teach . . . what we wanted": quoted in ibid.

p. 266: In the moment, though . . . according to Elaine: Brown, 327.

p. 268: "Elaine paid much more attention . . . capturing Oakland": Dixon, loc. 4264 of 5536.

p. 268: "In effect we put our guns . . . community forward": ibid., loc. 4184 of 5536.

p. 268: Elaine led the Party . . . reputation for excellence: Bloom and Martin, 383–385.

p. 269: BPP Position Paper: Eliminating the Offices of President and Vice President (sidebar): The position paper appears in full in Dr. Huey P. Newton Foundation, 91–98.

p. 269: a broad-scale political scandal known as Watergate: For more about the Watergate scandal, see the *Washington Post*'s collected coverage at www.washingtonpost.com /watergate/.

p. 270: "That school was an oasis . . . education could be": quoted in Shih and Williams, 87.

p. 270: Their hope was that . . . model to other cities: Bloom and Martin, 385–386.

p. 270: "There's nothing . . . became really sick": quoted in Shih and Williams, 86.

p. 270: Longtime committed Panthers . . . keeping the Party together: see Dixon, loc. 4108–4109, 4603–4606 of 5536, and Brown, 441–443.

p. 271: Some members even wondered . . . personality was so different: Shih and Williams, 123–124.

p. 271: Several historians have argued . . . successful coalition-building: Bloom and Martin, 390–401. Bloom and Martin draw a fascinating conclusion about one of the reasons such a deeply felt, broadly appealing revolutionary movement like the Panthers' might fall apart. Their conclusion essay as a whole is worth reading, but essentially they argue that the overall national climate for revolutionary action has diminished, perhaps largely because other interest groups received concessions to their agenda. Black communities received the fewest of these concessions and in many ways have gone on to be more heavily targeted, but it is harder to achieve coalition support because we no longer have as broad a sense of discontent to the level that inspires revolution. Or we didn't at the time that book was published in 2013. Who's to say what happens next?

p. 271: circulation of the *Black Panther*—once 400,000 copies per week: Douglas, 14, 96, estimates they were putting out 400,000 total copies per week in 1970–1971.

20. THE POST-PANTHER DECADES

p. 275: "History is clear . . . in some way": Kendi, 508.

p. 275: "racist progress has consistently . . . justify those policies": ibid., x.

p. 276: 1980s: The War on Drugs (section): "A Brief History of the Drug War."

p. 276: "We knew we couldn't . . . Of course we did": quoted in ibid.

p. 277: 1990s: The Prison Industrial Complex (section): For more about the prison industrial complex, see Alexander. Online introductions can be found in Schlosser and in Vagins and McCurdy.

p. 278: In 1998, Black people . . . were Black: Angela Davis.

p. 278: 45% of prisoners were Black: Beck and Harrison. In 2017, Black people made up 12% of the U.S. adult population and 33% of the sentenced prison population. See Gramlich and Drake.

p. 278: Number of Prison and Jail Inmates graph: Bureau of Justice Statistics, https://www.bjs.gov/content/pub/pdf/p00.pdf.

p. 279: Rodney King (sidebar): The archival video of police officers assaulting Rodney King is posted online. An excerpt of it can be seen in this brief ABC News report, which also discusses the charges pending against the officers and the history of police brutality in Los Angeles (please note: the video is grainy but still disturbing): "3/7/91 Video of Rodney King Being Beaten Released." For more information about the court case and the subsequent uprising, see Anjuli Sastry

and Karen Grigsby Bates, "When LA Erupted in Anger: A Look Back at the Rodney King Riots," NPR, April 26, 2017, https://www.npr.org/2017/04/26/524744989/when-la-erupted-in-anger-a-look-back-at-the-rodney-king-riots.

p. 280: 2000s: The War on Terror (section): For more about the impacts of the 9/11 attacks, see Green.

p. 281: While this law . . . under suspicion yourself: The American Civil Liberties Union examines the effect of the PATRIOT Act on U.S. citizens in "Surveillance Under the USA/PATRIOT Act," www.aclu.org/other/surveillance-under-usapatriot-act.

p. 281: If you so much as shared . . . suspicion yourself: See "Traveling While Muslim Complicates Air Travel."

p. 282: media representations of law enforcement played an insidious role: Recent studies have examined the role of police in media as it relates to Americans' understanding of law enforcement. These pervasive representations undoubtedly have an impact on how we view the police in complicated and controversial real-life incidents like the shootings of unarmed Black people; see Donovan and Klahm. Another recent study by Color of Change analyzed racial bias in television representations of law enforcement and found that the majority of fictional police are represented as white, while the majority of fictional perpetrators are represented as people of color; see "Normalizing Injustice."

p. 282: The Facade of Post-Racial America (section): For a look at the dialogue around "post-race" America, see Hannah-Jones.

p. 282: explicit racist propaganda surfaced: Samuel.

p. 283: The U.S. government decided . . . economic collapse: For more context on the 2008 economic bailout, see Herszenhorn, as well as Mike Collins, "The Big Bank Bailout," *Forbes*, July 14, 2015, www.forbes.com/sites /mikecollins/2015/07/14/the-big-bank-bailout /#3fe4ac242d83.

p. 284: 2010s: Occupy Wall Street (section): Coverage in the *Atlantic* offers a glimpse of the Occupy movement in action and a review of its impact. A photo-essay on the protests is found in Taylor, "Occupy Wall Street." And a look back on the movement several years later can be found in Levitin. The Occupy movement has a website of its own, presenting information about current protest actions and organizing. They describe themselves as a "leaderless movement," and their description of the movement's origins can be found at http://occupywallst.org/about/.

p. 284: the top 1% . . . 40% of the nation's wealth: Ingraham.

p. 284: the top 1%, only 1.7% are Black: Vega.

p. 284: Black people make up 13% of the total U.S. population: specifically, 13.4%, according to the U.S. Census Bureau, "U.S. Census Bureau QuickFacts: United States."

p. 285: "was powerful in that . . . consciousness": quoted in Shih and Williams, 99.

p. 285: Since the Occupy movement . . . income in the United States: Gold.

p. 286: Stand Your Ground (section): For an overview of the Trayvon Martin case, see "A Teen Was Shot by a Watchman 5 Years Ago."

p. 286: Black Lives Matter (section): More information about the Black Lives Matter global movement can be found at www .blacklivesmatter.com; information about the organization's origins appears in "Herstory."

p. 287: Unlike the Panthers . . . easier to target and destroy: Blacklivesmatter.com; Hall.

p. 287: Black Lives Matter: Ugorji.

p. 288: "The reason that the organizers . . . got to address": quoted in Superville.

p. 289: On August 9, 2014 . . . needing lethal force: "What Happened in Ferguson?," an interactive *New York Times* article, covers the Michael Brown shooting and subsequent protests in detail.

p. 289: In November 2014, a grand jury . . . crowd-control gear: For the Officer Wilson grand jury decision and subsequent protests, see Davey and Bosman.

p. 289: A few months later . . . a severed spinal cord: For a discussion of Freddie Gray's death and the subsequent protests, see Hermann.

p. 289: Baltimore . . . rose up in protest: Bacon and Welch reported thirty-four arrested, fifteen police officers injured.

p. 290: Freddie's death was ruled . . . eventually acquitted: Ruiz. The legal outcomes in the Freddie Gray case confused many people in Baltimore and nationwide, leading to renewed protests.

p. 290: Eric Garner . . . selling cigarettes: Carrega.

p. 291: When Black Lives Matter protestors . . . did not go their way: Associated Press, "'No Justice, No Peace.'"

p. 291: "No Justice, No Peace" is not . . . of the chant: One article that goes into more depth on the meaning of "No Justice, No Peace" is Mazie.

p. 292: The New Black Panther Party (sidebar): The Southern Poverty Law Center classified the NBPP as a hate group, which "has no connection to the original Black Panther Party, whose members have heavily criticized the group." See "New Black Panther Party."

p. 292: "There is no New Black Panther Party . . . of white people": This quote is drawn from a statement published by the Dr. Huey P. Newton Foundation. The original website is no longer active, but it is referenced in "New Black Panther Party," and archived material from the original site can be seen at Norton.

p. 293: Mass Shootings (section): Statistics on mass shootings can be found in Follman et al., "A Guide to Mass Shootings in America," and Follman et al., "U.S. Mass Shootings, 1982–2019."

p. 295: "If you had a teacher . . . gun-free zone": quoted in Merica and Klein.

p. 295: The Mulford Act . . . gun-control bill: Coleman.

p. 295: Mass Shootings in the United States graph: based on data from Mother Jones, https://www .motherjones.com/politics/2012/12 /mass-shootings-mother-jones-full-data/.

p. 297: a Black man talking on a cell phone in his backyard . . . : Levenson and Park.

p. 297: Why do police armed with tear gas . . . demonstration in Charlottesville: The difference in law enforcement response to protests led by Black citizens and those led by white citizens is made clear in numerous media images. Initially peaceful protests in Ferguson, Missouri, in 2014 were answered with tanks and tear gas. See Associated Press, "It's Been 5 Years since Ferguson." Three years later, incidents of violence by white supremacist demonstrators against counter-protestors went unanswered by police in Charlottesville. For the Charlottesville community's reaction to law enforcement failures during the Unite the Right march, held August 11–12, 2017, see Beckett, "Charlottesville Anniversary."

21. LEGACY

p. 299: "I have come to realize . . . internal revolution": Bukhari, *The War Before*, 13.

p. 299: "Frantz Fanon said . . . they can fulfill it": quoted in Shih and Williams, 171.

p. 300: "You can be inspired . . . happened back then": quoted in *Merritt College: Home of the Black Panthers.*

p. 300: "they can see past . . . really heartening": Shih and Williams, 85; Ericka made similar comments in our conversation in October 2016.

p. 301: "We who survived . . . love and sacrifice": Cleaver.

p. 301: "We worked, ate, slept . . . with that separation": quoted in Shih and Williams, 120.

p. 302: "We sincerely believed . . . we died in battle": Bukhari, *The War Before*, 82.

p. 302: "the last fifteen years . . . were tearing me apart": Joseph, 256.

p. 302: "We too are veterans . . . the ultimate shock": Bukhari, *The War Before*, 84.

p. 303: "I cried as I read . . . against one another": Joseph, 257.

p. 303: "As members of an organization . . . I've done since": quoted in Shih and Williams, 120.

p. 303: "We wanted for people . . . who have everything": quoted in *Merritt College: Home of the Black Panthers*.

p. 304: A local artist, Cheryl Parkins, designed the gravestone: Cleaver, "Statement," 10.

p. 304: "We need to pause . . . police bullets": Kathleen wrote this statement February 13, 2003, and submitted it to be shared on the occasion since she could not be in attendance. It was later printed in the Commemoration Committee of the Black Panther Party's newspaper; Cleaver, "Statement," 11.

p. 304: Fred Hampton's gravestone . . . deserve to be remembered: The gunshot marks on Fred Hampton's gravestone are visible in photographs, including one found in Riley. The anecdote about the decision not to keep replacing it comes from a Hampton family member.

p. 305: "What I'm most proud of . . . I know what I did": quoted in Shih and Williams, 91.

p. 305: "In the long struggle of blacks . . . its repression": Elaine's foreword to Newton, *To Die for the People*, xxii.

p. 306: "It was the most amazing work . . . something out of nothing": quoted in *Merritt College: Home of the Black Panthers*.

p. 306: "The Black Panther Party . . . with dignity and courage": quoted in Dr. Huey P. Newton Foundation, xi.

p. 307: "It is the power . . . for the future": Newton, *To Die for the People*, 235.

p. 307: "At this time more . . . racist world": Seale, *Seize the Time*, iii.

p. 307: "Nothing will justify . . . of the people": Newton, *To Die for the People*, 236.

p. 307: "We need activists . . . the youth of today": Seale, *Seize the Time*, iii.

AUTHOR'S NOTE: REVOLUTION IN OUR TIME

p. 309: "The revolution . . . hands of the young": "Huey Newton Talks to the Movement," 11.

p. 310: "the median age of Panthers was nineteen": quoted in Shih and Williams, 85, and Shames and Seale, *Power to the People*, 52.

p. 310: six-year-old Ruby Bridges: Anderson.

p. 314: Breonna Taylor . . . on the wrong home: Burke.

p. 314: Ahmaud Arbery, out . . . shot him to death: Fausset.

p. 314: white citizens bearing legal arms . . . social distancing orders: Cohen.

p. 314: an armed unit . . . to her office: Beckett, "Armed Black Citizens Escort Michigan Lawmaker."

Elaine Brown: Brown; Peter Walton, "Elaine Brown (1943–)," Black Past, November 24, 2007, www.blackpast.org/african-american-history/brown-elaine-1943/.

H. Rap Brown (now Jamil Abdullah Al-Amin): Daren Salter, "Hubert Brown (H. Rap)/Jamil Abdullah Al-Amin (1943–)," Black Past, April 7, 2018, www.blackpast.org/african-american-history/brown-hubert-h-rap-jamil-abdullah-al-amin-1943/.

Safiya Bukhari: Bukhari, *The War Before.*

Stokely Carmichael (Kwame Ture): Daren Salter, "Stokely Carmichael (Kwame Ture) (1941–1998)," Black Past, August 5, 2018, www.blackpast.org/african-american-history/carmichael-stokely-kwame-ture-1941-1998/.

Alprentice "Bunchy" Carter: Bloom and Martin, 143–145, 216; Ericka Huggins, "A Remembrance of John and Bunchy," Ericka Huggins website, January 17, 2019, www.erickahuggins.com/a-rememberance-of-john-and-bunchy.

Eldridge Cleaver: Victor Henry Jr., "Eldridge Cleaver (1935–1998)," Black Past, February 4, 2009, www.blackpast.org/african-american-history/cleaver-eldridge-1935-1998/.

Kathleen Neal Cleaver: Euell A. Nielsen, "Kathleen Neal Cleaver (1945–)," Black Past, January 10, 2018, www.blackpast.org/african-american-history/cleaver-kathleen-neal-1945/.

Angela Davis: Dwayne Mack, "Angela Davis (1944–)," Black Past, February 10, 2011, www.blackpast.org/african-american-history/people-african-american-history/davis-angela-1944/.

Aaron Dixon: Dixon.

Emory Douglas: Douglas; Aaron Modica, "Emory Douglas (1944–)," Black Past, November 14, 2009, www.blackpast.org/african-american-history/douglas-emory-1943/.

Fred Hampton: Dwayne Mack, "Fred Hampton (1948–1969)," Black Past, April 16, 2008, www.blackpast.org/african-american-history/hampton-fred-1948-1969/.

David Hilliard: Hilliard and Cole.

Elbert "Big Man" Howard: Howard; Brigit Katz, "Black Panther Co-Founder Elbert "Big Man" Howard Dies at 80," *Smithsonian*, July 26, 2018, www.smithsonianmag.com/smart-news/black-panther-co-founder-elbert-howard-has-died-80-180969764/.

Ericka Huggins: Ericka Huggins, "Biography," Ericka Huggins website, www.erickahuggins.com/bio.

John Huggins: Ericka Huggins, "A Remembrance of John and Bunchy," Ericka Huggins website, January 17, 2019, www.erickahuggins.com/a-rememberance-of-john-and-bunchy.

Robert James (Lil' Bobby) Hutton: Will Mack, "Bobby Hutton (1950–1968)," Black Past, April 24, 2018, www.blackpast.org/african-american-history/hutton-bobby-1950-1968/.

George Jackson: Zach Schrempp, "George Jackson (1941–1971)," Black Past, October 4, 2010, www.blackpast.org/african-american-history/jackson-george-1941-1971/.

Jonathan Jackson: Bloom and Martin, 365.

Jamal Joseph: Joseph.

Joan Tarika "Matilaba" Lewis: Veronica Wells, "Untold: Women of the Black Panther Party: Joan Tarika Lewis." Madame Noire, February 20, 2020, https://madamenoire .com/1133994/women-of-the-black-panther -party-joan-tarika-lewis/.

Sam Napier: Elbert "Big Man" Howard, "Remembering Sam Napier—My Fallen Comrade," Black Panther Alumni website, February 2012, www.itsabouttimebpp.com /Memorials/pdf/Remembering_Sam_Napier -February_2012.pdf.

Huey P. Newton: Craig Collisson, "Huey P. Newton (1942–1989)," Black Past, February 24, 2007, www.blackpast.org/african -american-history/newton-huey-p-1942 -1989/.

William O'Neal: William O'Neal, "*Eyes on the Prize* Interviews II," April 13, 1989, Washington University Libraries, Film and Media Archive, Henry Hampton Collection, http://digital.wustl.edu/e/eii/eiiweb /one5427.1047.125williamo%27neal.html.

Elmer "Geronimo Ji-Jaga" Pratt: Eric Greve, "Geronimo Pratt (1947–2011)," Black Past, April 1, 2012, www.blackpast.org/african -american-history/pratt-geronimo-1947-2011/.

Alex Rackley: Bloom and Martin, 248.

George Sams: Bloom and Martin, 248.

Bobby Seale: Seale, *Seize the Time*; Seale, *A Lonely Rage*; Craig Collisson, "Bobby Seale (1936–)," Black Past, February 24, 2007, www.blackpast.org/african-american-history /seale-bobby-1936/.

Assata Shakur: Shakur; Terry Anne Scott, "Assata Olugbala Shakur (1947–)," Black Past, February 8, 2014, www.blackpast.org /african-american-history/assata-olugbala -shakur-1947/.

Robert Webb: Bloom and Martin, 363–364.

BIBLIOGRAPHY

Alexander, Michelle. *The New Jim Crow: Mass Incarceration in the Age of Colorblindness.* New York: New Press, 2010.

Anderson, Meg. "Ruby Bridges (1954–)." Black Past, March 29, 2009. www.blackpast.org /african-american-history/bridges-ruby -1954/.

"Angela Davis Quotes: From the Radical Black Philosopher." Blackfacts.com. www.blackfacts .com/fact/angela-davis-quotes-from-the -radical-black-philosopher (accessed July 26, 2020).

"Angola, Southern Africa." South African History Online. www.sahistory.org.za/place/angola (accessed July 26, 2020).

Asbury, Edith Evans. "Black Panther Party Members Freed After Being Cleared of Charges." *New York Times,* May 14, 1971. www.nytimes.com/1971/05/14/archives/black -panther-party-members-freed-after-being -cleared-of-charges-13.html.

Associated Press. "It's Been 5 Years since Ferguson: Are Racial Tensions Even Worse Now?" August 8, 2019. https://www.usatoday .com/story/news/nation/2019/08/08/ferguson -missouri-riots-5-years-since-shooting-race -tensions-worse/1952853001/.

———. "'No Justice, No Peace, No Racist Police' Chants in Baltimore." *CBS Baltimore*, May 2, 2015. baltimore.cbslocal.com/2015/05/02/no -justice-no-peace-no-racist-police-chants-in -baltimore/.

Astor, Maggie. "'The Whole World Is Watching': The 1968 Democratic Convention, 50 Years Later." *New York Times*, August 28, 2018. www.nytimes.com/2018/08/28/us/politics /chicago-1968-democratic-convention-.html.

Austin, Curtis J. *Up Against the Wall: Violence in the Making and Unmaking of the Black Panther Party.* Fayetteville: University of Arkansas Press, 2006.

Bacon, John, and William W. Welch. "Baltimore Police, Protesters Clash; 15 Officers Hurt." *USA Today*, April 27, 2015. https://www .usatoday.com/story/news/nation/2015/04/27 /baltimore-credible-threat/26454875/.

Bausum, Ann. *Freedom Riders: John Lewis and Jim Zwerg on the Front Lines of the Civil Rights Movement*. Washington, DC: National Geographic, 2006.

Beals, Melba Pattillo. *Warriors Don't Cry.* New York: Simon Pulse, 2007.

Beck, Allan J., and Paige M. Harrison. "Prisoners in 2000." Bureau of Justice Statistics, U.S.

Department of Justice, August 2001.
www.bjs.gov/content/pub/pdf/p00.pdf.

Beckett, Lois. "Armed Black Citizens Escort
Michigan Lawmaker to Capitol after Volatile
Rightwing Protest." *Guardian,* May 7, 2020.
www.theguardian.com/us-news/2020/may
/07/michigan-lawmaker-armed-escort
-rightwing-protest.

———. "Charlottesville Anniversary: Anger
over Police Failures Simmers at Protest."
Guardian, August 12, 2018. www.theguardian
.com/world/2018/aug/12/charlottesville
-anniversary-protest-anger-police-failures
-white-supremacists.

*Black Panther/Black Panther Intercommunal
News Service.*

The Black Panthers: Vanguard of the Revolution.
Directed by Stanley Nelson Jr. 2015.

*The Black Power Mixtape, 1967–1975: A
Documentary in 9 Chapters*. Directed
by Göran Olsson. Stockholm: Sveriges
Television; MPI Media Group, 2011.

"'Black Power' Speech (28 July 1966, by Stokely
Carmichael)." *Dictionary of American
History.* Encyclopedia.com, January 24,
2020. www.encyclopedia.com/history
/dictionaries-thesauruses-pictures-and-press
-releases/black-power-speech-28-july-1966
-stokely-carmichael.

Bloom, Joshua, and Waldo E. Martin Jr. *Black
Against Empire: The History and Politics of
the Black Panther Party*. Berkeley: University
of California Press, 2016.

Bortolot, Alexander Ives. "Women Leaders
in African History: Ana Nzinga, Queen of
Ndongo." Metropolitan Museum of Art,
October 2003. www.metmuseum.org/toah
/hd/pwmn_2/hd_pwmn_2.htm.

Boyd, Herb. *Black Panthers for Beginners*.
Illustrated by Lance Tooks. New York: Writer
and Reader, 1995.

Braimah, Ayodale. "The Martin Luther King
Assassination Riots (1968)." Black Past,
November 4, 2017. www.blackpast.org
/african-american-history/martin-luther
-king-assassination-riots-1968/.

"A Brief History of the Drug War." Drug Policy
Alliance. www.drugpolicy.org/issues/brief
-history-drug-war (accessed July 26, 2020).

Brown, Elaine. *A Taste of Power: A Black
Woman's Story*. New York: Anchor, 1994.

Bukhari, Safiya. "Kamau Sadiki (formerly
known as Fred Hilton), or Injustice
Continues . . ." It's About Time. http://
www.itsabouttimebpp.com/Political
_Prisoners/Kamau_Sadiki.html (accessed
July 26, 2020).

———. *The War Before: The True Life Story of
Becoming a Black Panther, Keeping the Faith
in Prison, and Fighting for Those Left Behind*.
Edited by Laura Whitehorn. New York:
Feminist Press at the City University of New
York, 2010.

Burke, Minyvonne. "Woman Shot and Killed
by Kentucky Police in Botched Raid, Family
Says." NBC News, May 13, 2020. www
.nbcnews.com/news/us-news/black-woman
-shot-killed-after-kentucky-police-entered
-her-home-n1205651.

Carmichael, Stokely (Kwame Ture). *Stokely*

Speaks: From Black Power to Pan-Africanism. Chicago: Chicago Review Press, 2014.

Carrega, Christina. "5 Years after Eric Garner's Death, a Look Back at the Case and the Movement It Sparked." ABC News, July 16, 2019. abcnews.go.com/US/years-eric-garners-death-back-case-movement-sparked/story?id=63847094.

Churchill, Ward, and Jim Vander Wall. *Agents of Repression: The FBI's Secret Wars Against the Black Panther Party and the American Indian Movement.* Boston: South End Press, 1990.

Cleaver, Kathleen. "Statement: Placing of Headstone for Bobby James Hutton." *Commemorator*, May 2003.

Cohen, Matt. "Armed Protesters Stormed the Michigan Statehouse This Afternoon." *Mother Jones*, April 30, 2020. www.motherjones.com/coronavirus-updates/2020/04/lansing-michigan-capitol-protests-stay-at-home-order-whitmer/.

"COINTELPRO." FBI Records: The Vault. FBI. https://vault.fbi.gov/cointel-pro.

Coleman, Arica L. "When the NRA Supported Gun Control." *Time*, July 29, 2016. https://time.com/4431356/nra-gun-control-history/.

Collins, Mike. "The Big Bank Bailout." *Forbes*, July 14, 2015. www.forbes.com/sites/mikecollins/2015/07/14/the-big-bank-bailout/#3fe4ac242d83.

"Colonial Enslavement of Native Americans Included Those Who Surrendered, Too." *News from Brown*, February 15, 2017. Brown University. www.brown.edu/news/2017-02-15/enslavement.

"The Continental Association, October 20, 1774." Library of Congress. www.loc.gov/teachers/classroommaterials/presentationsandactivities/presentations/timeline/amrev/rebelln/assoc.html (accessed July 26, 2020).

Corcione, Adryan. "Who Is Karl Marx: Meet the Anti-Capitalist Scholar." *Teen Vogue*, May 10, 2018. www.teenvogue.com/story/who-is-karl-marx.

Cosgrove, Ben. "Civil Rights: Preparation and Protest, Virginia, 1960." *Life*. www.life.com/history/life-and-civil-rights-anatomy-of-a-protest-virginia-1960/ (accessed July 26, 2020).

Davey, Monica, and Julie Bosman. "Protests Flare after Ferguson Police Officer Is Not Indicted." *New York Times*, November 24, 2014. www.nytimes.com/2014/11/25/us/ferguson-darren-wilson-shooting-michael-brown-grand-jury.html.

Davis, Angela. "Masked Racism: Reflections of the Prison Industrial Complex." Color Lines. September 10, 1998. https://www.colorlines.com/articles/masked-racism-reflections-prison-industrial-complex.

Davis, David. "Olympic Athletes Who Took a Stand." *Smithsonian*, August 1, 2008. www.smithsonianmag.com/articles/olympic-athletes-who-took-a-stand-593920/.

Demby, Gene. "The Ugly, Fascinating History of the Word 'Racism.'" NPR, January 6, 2014. www.npr.org/sections/codeswitch/2014/01/05/260006815/the-ugly-fascinating-history-of-the-word-racism.

Dixon, Aaron Floyd. *My People Are Rising:*

Memoir of a Black Panther Party Captain. Chicago: Haymarket, 2012.

Donovan, K. M., and C. F. Klahm. "The Role of Entertainment Media in Perceptions of Police Use of Force." *Criminal Justice and Behavior* 42, no. 12 (2015): 1261–1281.

Douglas, Emory. *Black Panther: The Revolutionary Art of Emory Douglas.* Edited by Sam Durant. New York: Rizzoli International, 2007.

Drake, Bruce. "Incarceration Gap Widens between Whites and Blacks." Pew Research Center, September 6, 2013. www.pewresearch.org /fact-tank/2013/09/06/incarceration-gap -between-whites-and-blacks-widens/.

"Dr. Booker Taliaferro Washington: Founder and First President of Tuskegee Normal and Industrial Institute." Tuskegee University. https://www.tuskegee.edu/discover-tu/tu -presidents/booker-t-washington (accessed July 26, 2020).

Dr. Huey P. Newton Foundation. *The Black Panther Party: Service to the People Programs.* Edited by David Hilliard. Albuquerque: University of New Mexico Press, 2008.

"(1866) Mississippi Black Codes." Black Past. www.blackpast.org/african-american-history /1866-mississippi-black-codes/ (accessed July 26, 2020).

Fanon, Frantz. *The Wretched of the Earth.* Translated by Richard Philcox. New York: Grove, 2004.

Fausset, Richard. "What We Know about the Shooting Death of Ahmaud Arbery." *New York Times*, April 28, 2020. www.nytimes .com/article/ahmaud-arbery-shooting -georgia.html.

Fleischer, Matthew. "50 Years Ago, LAPD Raided the Black Panthers. SWAT Teams Have Been Targeting Black Communities Ever Since." *Los Angeles Times*, December 8, 2019. www.latimes.com/opinion/story/2019-12-08 /50-years-swat-black-panthers-militarized -policinglos-angeles.

Follman, Mark, et al. "A Guide to Mass Shootings in America." *Mother Jones*, December 29, 2019. www.motherjones.com/politics/2012/07 /mass-shootings-map/.

———. "US Mass Shootings, 1982–2019: Data from Mother Jones' Investigation." *Mother Jones*, December 18, 2019. www.motherjones .com/politics/2012/12/mass-shootings-mother -jones-full-data/.

Foner, Philip S., ed. *The Black Panthers Speak.* 3rd ed. New York: Haymarket, 2014.

"Frightening 'Army' Hits the Airport." *San Francisco Chronicle*, February 22, 1967, 1.

Ganeva, Tana. "Black Panther Fred Hampton Created a 'Rainbow Coalition' to Support Poor Americans." *Teen Vogue*, July 25, 2019. www.teenvogue.com/story/fred-hampton -black-panthers-rainbow-coalition-poor -americans.

Gates, Henry Louis, Jr. "The Truth Behind '40 Acres and a Mule.'" The African Americans: Many Rivers to Cross. PBS. www.pbs.org /wnet/african-americans-many-rivers-to -cross/history/the-truth-behind-40-acres -and-a-mule/ (accessed July 26, 2020).

Gold, Howard R. "Never Mind the 1 Percent. Let's

Talk about the 0.01 Percent." *Chicago Booth Review*, Winter 2017. review.chicagobooth .edu/economics/2017/article/never-mind-1 -percent-lets-talk-about-001-percent.

Gramlich, John. "The Gap between the Number of Blacks and Whites in Prison Is Shrinking." Pew Research Center, April 30, 2019. www.pewresearch.org/fact-tank/2019/04/30 /shrinking-gap-between-number-of-blacks -and-whites-in-prison/.

Green, Matthew. "How 9/11 Changed America: Four Major Lasting Impacts (with Lesson Plan)." KQED, September 8, 2017. www.kqed .org/lowdown/14066/13-years-later-four -major-lasting-impacts-of-911.

Haas, Jeffrey. *The Assassination of Fred Hampton: How the FBI and the Chicago Police Murdered a Black Panther.* Chicago: Lawrence Hill, 2010.

Hall, Kia M. Q. "A Transnational Black Feminist Framework: Rooting in Feminist Scholarship, Framing Contemporary Black Activism." *Meridians: feminism, race, transnationalism* 15, no. 1 (December 22, 2016): 86–105.

Hampton, Henry, and Steve Fayer. *Voices of Freedom: An Oral History of the Civil Rights Movement from the 1950s through the 1980s.* London: Vintage, 1995.

Hampton, Henry, et al. *Eyes on the Prize: America's Civil Rights Movement.* PBS Video, 2006.

Hannah-Jones, Nikole. "The End of the Postracial Myth." *New York Times*, November 15, 2016. www.nytimes.com/interactive/2016/11/20 /magazine/donald-trumps-america-iowa -race.html

Hermann, Peter. "Five Years after Freddie Gray, Baltimore Continues to Struggle." *Washington Post*, April 26, 2020. www .washingtonpost.com/local/public-safety /five-years-after-freddie-gray-baltimore -continues-to-struggle/2020/04/25/918e53ac -8636-11ea-ae26-989cfce1c7c7_story.html.

"Herstory." Black Lives Matter. https://blacklivesmatter.com/herstory/.

Herszenhorn, David M. "Congress Approves $700 Billion Wall Street Bailout." *New York Times*, October 3, 2008. www.nytimes.com/2008/10 /03/business/worldbusiness/03iht-bailout.4 .16679355.html.

Hilliard, David, and Lewis Cole. *This Side of Glory: The Autobiography of David Hilliard and the Story of the Black Panther Party.* Chicago: Lawrence Hill, 1993.

Holpuch, Amanda. "Black Patients Half as Likely to Receive Pain Medication as White Patients, Study Finds." *Guardian*, August 10, 2016. www.theguardian.com/science/2016/aug /10/black-patients-bias-prescriptions-pain -management-medicine-opioids.

Hoose, Phillip. *Claudette Colvin: Twice toward Justice.* Melanie Kroupa/Farrar, Straus and Giroux, 2009.

Horace, Matthew, and Ron Harris. *The Black and the Blue: A Cop Reveals the Crimes, Racism, and Injustice in America's Law Enforcement.* New York: Hachette, 2019.

Howard, Elbert "Big Man." *Panther on the Prowl.* N.p., 2002.

"Huey Newton Talks to the Movement about the Black Panther Party, Cultural Nationalism,

SNCC, Liberals and White Revolutionaries."
The Movement (August 1968): 8–11. Freedom
Archives. http://freedomarchives.org/
Documents/Finder/DOC40_scans/40
.Movement.August.1968.pdf.

"Huey P. Newton's Interview with *The Movement*
(1968)." Medium, January 13, 2018.
https://medium.com/@merricatherine/huey
-p-newtons-interview-with-the-movement
-magazine-1968-a328e6b78c32.

Huggins, Ericka. "An Oral History with Ericka
Huggins." Interviewed by Fiona Thompson.
Berkeley, CA: Oral History Center, Bancroft
Library, 2007. https://digitalassets.lib.berkeley
.edu/roho/ucb/text/huggins_ericka.pdf.

Ingraham, Christopher. "The Richest 1 Percent
Now Owns More of the Country's Wealth
than at Any Time in the Past 50 Years."
Washington Post, April 29, 2019. www
.washingtonpost.com/news/wonk/wp/2017/12
/06/the-richest-1-percent-now-owns-more
-of-the-countrys-wealth-than-at-any-time
-in-the-past-50-years/.

It's About Time: The Official Website of
the Black Panther Party Alumni.
www.itsabouttimebpp.com.

Jackson, George. *Soledad Brother: The Prison
Letters of George Jackson.* Chicago: Lawrence
Hill, 1994.

Jeffries, Hasan Kwame. *Bloody Lowndes: Civil
Rights and Black Power in Alabama's Black
Belt*. New York: New York University Press,
2010.

Jones, Charles E. *The Black Panther Party (Reconsidered)*. Baltimore: Black Classic, 2005.

Joseph, Jamal. *Panther Baby: A Life of Rebellion
and Reinvention*. Chapel Hill, NC: Algonquin,
2012.

Kelly, Kim. "What 'Capitalism' Is and How It
Affects People." *Teen Vogue*, April 11, 2018.
www.teenvogue.com/story/what-capitalism-is.

Kendi, Ibram X. *Stamped from the Beginning: The
Definitive History of Racist Ideas in America*.
New York: Nation Books, 2016.

Kifner, John. "F.B.I. Sought Doom of Panther
Party." *New York Times*, May 9, 1976. www
.nytimes.com/1976/05/09/archives/fbi-sought
-doom-of-panther-party-senate-study-says
-plot-led-to.html.

Lanagan, Patrick A. "Race of Individuals
Admitted to State and Federal Prisons, 1926–
86." U.S. Department of Justice, May 1991.
https://www.ncjrs.gov/pdffiles1/nij/125618
.pdf.

Lawson, James. "Training for Nonviolent
Resistance," June 23, 2009. International
Center on Nonviolent Conflict, YouTube
video, September 9, 2010. https://youtu.be
/UqlVVzyQII0.

Le Blanc, Paul. "An Introduction to Lenin and
Leninism." SocialistWorker.org, June 3, 2015.
https://socialistworker.org/2015/06/03/an
-introduction-to-lenin-and-leninism.

Levenson, Eric, and Madison Park. "Sacramento
Police Shot Man Holding Cellphone in His
Grandmother's Yard." CNN, March 22, 2018.
www.cnn.com/2018/03/22/us/sacramento
-police-shooting/index.html.

Levine, Mark L., George C. McNamee, and
Daniel L. Greenberg, eds. *The Trial of the*

Chicago 7: The Official Transcript. New York: Simon & Schuster, 2020.

Levitin, Michael. "The Triumph of Occupy Wall Street." *Atlantic*, June 11, 2015. www.theatlantic.com/politics/archive/2015/06/the-triumph-of-occupy-wall-street/395408/.

Lipsky, Jessica. "The Enduring Influence of the Black Panther Party Newspaper." *Columbia Journalism Review*, August 14, 2019. www.cjr.org/analysis/history-black-panther-newspaper.php.

Major, Reginald. *A Panther Is a Black Cat*. Baltimore: Black Classic, 2006.

Malcolm X. *The Autobiography of Malcolm X: As Told to Alex Haley*. New York: Ballantine, 1992.

———. "The Ballot or the Bullet." Speech, April 3, 1964, Cleveland. Social Justice Speeches. www.edchange.org/multicultural/speeches/malcolm_x_ballot.html.

———. *Malcolm X Speaks: Selected Speeches and Statements*. Edited by George Breitman. New York: Grove, 1990.

———. "Message to the Grassroots." November 10, 1963. Teaching American History. https://teachingamericanhistory.org/library/document/message-to-grassroots/ (accessed July 26, 2020).

Marsh, Clifton E. *The Lost-Found Nation of Islam in America*. Lanham, MD: Scarecrow, 2000.

Mazie, Steven. "What Does 'No Justice, No Peace' Really Mean?" Big Think, December 5, 2014. https://bigthink.com/praxis/what-does-no-justice-no-peace-really-mean.

McCurdy, Devon. "Congress of Racial Equality (1942)." Black Past, December 16, 2007. www.blackpast.org/african-american-history/congress-racial-equality-1942/.

McKissack, Patricia C. *Nzingha: Warrior Queen of Matamba, Angola, Africa, 1595*. New York: Scholastic, 2000.

McWhorter, John. "'Racist' Is a Tough Little Word." *Atlantic*, July 24, 2019. www.theatlantic.com/ideas/archive/2019/07/racism-concept-change/594526/.

Merica, Dan, and Betsy Klein. "Trump Suggests Arming Teachers as a Solution to Increase School Safety." CNN, February 22, 2018. www.cnn.com/2018/02/21/politics/trump-listening-sessions-parkland-students/index.html.

Merritt College: Home of the Black Panthers. Directed by Jeffrey Heyman and James Devin Calhoun. DVD. Peralta TV, 2010.

Mitchell, Mary Niall. "Rediscovering the Lives of the Enslaved People Who Freed Themselves." *Washington Post*, February 20, 2019.

Momodu, Samuel. "The Birmingham Campaign (1963)." Black Past, August 31, 2016. www.blackpast.org/african-american-history/birmingham-campaign-1963/.

"NAACP History: W.E.B. DuBois." NAACP. https://www.naacp.org/naacp-history-w-e-b-dubois/ (accessed July 26, 2020).

Nelson, Alondra. *Body and Soul: The Black Panther Party and the Fight Against Medical Discrimination*. Minneapolis: University of Minnesota Press, 2011.

Nelson, Jill. "The Soul Survivor." *Washington Post*, February 29, 1988. www.washingtonpost.com/archive/lifestyle/1988/02/29/the

-soul-survivor/fff0034c-36be-4260-ad27
-cb71af0782b7/.

"New Black Panther Party." Southern Poverty
Law Center. www.splcenter.org/fighting-hate
/extremist-files/group/new-black-panther
-party (accessed August 14, 2020).

Newton, Huey P. *The Huey P. Newton Reader*.
Edited by David Hilliard and Donald Weise.
New York: Seven Stories, 2002.

———. *Revolutionary Suicide*. Penguin, 2009.

———. *To Die for the People*. Edited by Toni
Morrison. San Francisco: City Lights, 2009.

Nodjimbadem, Katie. "The Long, Painful History
of Police Brutality in the U.S." *Smithsonian*,
July 27, 2017. www.smithsonianmag.com
/smithsonian-institution/long-painful-history
-police-brutality-in-the-us-180964098/.

"Normalizing Injustice." Color of Change
Hollywood. January 2020. https://hollywood.
colorofchange.org/crime-tv-report/.

Norton, Ben. "Huey P. Newton Foundation:
There Is No New Black Panther Party." *Ben
Norton* (blog), December 16, 2014. https://
bennorton.com/huey-p-newton-foundation
-there-is-no-new-black-panther-party/.

Oelsner, Lesley. "Charges Dropped in the Seale
Case; 'Publicity' Cited." *New York Times*, May
26, 1971. https://www.nytimes.com/1971/05
/26/archives/charges-dropped-in-the-seale
-case-publicity-cited-judge-finds-it.html.

Phillips, Mary. "The Feminist Leadership of
Ericka Huggins in the Black Panther Party."
Black Diaspora Review 4, no. 1 (Winter 2014).

Pilkington, Ed. "The Black Panthers Still in
Prison: After 46 Years, Will They Ever
Be Set Free?" *Guardian*, July 30, 2018.
www.theguardian.com/us-news/2018/jul/30
/black-panthers-prison-interviews-african
-american-activism.

Reed, Wilson Edward. "Gabriel Prosser
(1775–1800)." Black Past, February 12, 2007.
www.blackpast.org/african-american-history
/prosser-gabriel-1775-1800/.

———. "Nat Turner (1800–1831)." Black Past,
February 12, 2007. www.blackpast.org/african
-american-history/turner-nat-1800-1831/.

"Reflecting on Martin Luther King Jr.'s Legacy
50 Years after His Death." CNN, April 2, 2018.
www.cnn.com/2018/04/02/politics/gallery
/mlk-anniversary-quotes/index.html.

Riley, Ricky. "10 Outrageous Examples of
White People Vandalizing, Threatening Safe
Spaces of Black People." *Atlanta Black Star*,
December 19, 2016.

Ruiz, Rebecca R. "Baltimore Officers Will Face
No Federal Charges in Death of Freddie
Gray." *New York Times*, September 12, 2017.
www.nytimes.com/2017/09/12/us/freddie
-gray-baltimore-police-federal-charges.html.

Russell, Judy G. "Indians Not Taxed."
Legal Genealogist, March 13, 2015. www
.legalgenealogist.com/2015/03/13/9643/.

Samuel, Terence. "The Racist Backlash
Obama Has Faced during His Presidency."
Washington Post, April 22, 2016. www
.washingtonpost.com/graphics/national
/obama-legacy/racial-backlash-against-the
-president.html.

Schlosser, Eric. "The Prison-Industrial Complex."
Atlantic, December 1998. www.theatlantic

.com/magazine/archive/1998/12/the-prison
-industrial-complex/304669/.

Seale, Bobby. "*Eyes on the Prize* Interview,
November 4, 1988." Washington University
Libraries, Film and Media Archive, Henry
Hampton Collection. http://digital.wustl.edu
/e/eii/eiiweb/sea5427.0172.147bobbyseale
.html.

———. *A Lonely Rage: The Autobiography of
Bobby Seale.* New York: Times Books, 1978.

———. *Seize the Time: The Story of the Black
Panther Party and Huey P. Newton.* New
York: Random House, 1970.

Shakur, Assata. *Assata: An Autobiography.*
Chicago: Lawrence Hill, 2001.

Shames, Stephen. *The Black Panthers:
Photographs by Stephen Shames.* New York:
Aperture Foundation, 2006.

Shames, Stephen, and Bobby Seale. *Power to
the People: The World of the Black Panthers.*
New York: Abrams, 2016.

Shih, Bryan, and Yohuru Williams, eds. *The
Black Panthers: Portraits from an Unfinished
Revolution.* New York: Nation Books, 2016.

Sklansky, David Alan. "Not Your Father's Police
Department: Making Sense of the New
Demographics of Law Enforcement." *Journal
of Criminal Law and Criminology* 96,
no. 3 (Spring 2006): 1209–1244. https://
scholarlycommons.law.northwestern.edu/cgi/
viewcontent.cgi?article=7244&context=jclc

"Slavery, Within and Without." Indivisible:
African-Native American Lives in the
Americas. Smithsonian National Museum
of the American Indian. americanindian.

si.edu/exhibitions/indivisible/slavery.html
(accessed July 26, 2020).

"Slave Ship Mutinies." Slavery and Remembrance.
www.slaveryandremembrance.org/articles
/article/?id=A0035 (accessed July 26, 2020).

Snethen, Jessica. "Queen Nzinga (1583–1663)."
Black Past, June 16, 2009. www.blackpast
.org/global-african-history/queen-nzinga
-1583-1663/.

Spencer, Robyn C. *The Revolution Has Come:
Black Power, Gender, and the Black Panther
Party in Oakland.* Durham, NC: Duke
University Press, 2016.

Stultz, Spencer. "The Harlem Race Riot of 1964."
Black Past, December 4, 2017. www.blackpast
.org/african-american-history/harlem-race
-riot-1964/.

Superville, Darlene. "Obama Defends Black
Lives Matter Movement." *PBS NewsHour*,
October 23, 2015. https://www.pbs.org
/newshour/politics/obama-defends-black
-lives-matter-movement.

Sutherland, Claudia. "Denmark Vesey
Conspiracy of 1822." Black Past, March 27,
2007. www.blackpast.org/african-american
-history/denmark-vesey-conspiracy-1822/.

Taylor, Alan. "Occupy Wall Street." *Atlantic*,
September 30, 2011. www.theatlantic.com
/photo/2011/09/occupy-wall-street/100159/.

———. "The Vietnam War, Part I: Early Years and
Escalation." *Atlantic*, March 30, 2015. www
.theatlantic.com/photo/2015/03/the-vietnam
-war-part-i-early-years-and-escalation
/389054/.

Taylor, Quintard. "(1970) Huey P. Newton, 'The

Women's Liberation and Gay Liberation Movements.'" Black Past, April 17, 2018. www.blackpast.org/african-american-history /speeches-african-american-history/huey -p-newton-women-s-liberation-and-gay -liberation-movements/.

"A Teen Was Shot by a Watchman 5 Years Ago. And the Trayvon Martin Case Became a Cause." *Miami Herald*, February 28, 2017. www.miamiherald.com/news/state/florida /article135413214.html.

Tennant, Brad. "'Excluding Indians Not Taxed': 'Dred Scott, Standing Bear, Elk' and the Legal Status of Native Americans in the Latter Half of the Nineteenth Century." *International Social Science Review* 86, nos. 1/2 (2011): 24–43.

Terrell, Mary Church. "What It Means to Be Colored in the Capital of the U.S. (1906)." Black Past, September 22, 2008. www .blackpast.org/african-american-history /1906-mary-church-terrell-what-it-means -be-colored-capital-u-s/.

"3/7/91 Video of Rodney King Being Beaten Released." ABC News. https://abcnews.go .com/Archives/video/march-1991-rodney-king -videotape-9758031 (accessed August 10, 2020).

"Three Visions for African Americans." Constitutional Rights Foundation. www.crf -usa.org/brown-v-board-50th-anniversary /three-visions-for-african-americans.html (accessed July 26, 2020).

Tillet, Salamishah. "The Panthers' Revolutionary Feminism." *New York Times*, October 2, 2015. https://www.nytimes.com/2015/10/04/movies /the-panthers-revolutionary-feminism.html.

"Traveling While Muslim Complicates Air Travel." *New York Times*, November 7, 2016. https:// www.nytimes.com/2016/11/08/business/traveling -while-muslim-complicates-air-travel.html.

Ugorji, Basil. "Decrypting Encrypted Racism." *Ethnic Studies Review* 37–38, no. 1 (June 22, 2017): 27–43.

United Nations Department of Political Affairs, Trusteeship and Decolonization. "United Nations Participation in Popular Consul- tations and Elections." *Decolonization*, no. 19, December 1983. www.un.org/dppa /decolonization/sites/www.un.org.dppa .decolonization/files/decon_num_19-1.pdf.

U.S. Census Bureau. "1970 Census: Characteris- tics of the Population." United States Census Bureau. www.census.gov/library/publications /1973/dec/population-volume-1.html.

———. "US Census Bureau QuickFacts: United States." United States Census Bureau. www.census.gov/quickfacts/fact/table/US /PST045218.

"U.S. Is Dropping Action on Seale." *New York Times*, September 28, 1972. https://www .nytimes.com/1972/09/28/archives/us-is -dropping-action-on-seale-will-ask-court-to -dismiss-chicago.html.

"U.S. Public Health Service Syphilis Study at Tuskegee." Centers for Disease Control and Prevention. www.cdc.gov/tuskegee/index.html (accessed July 26, 2020).

U.S. Senate. "Senate Select Committee to Study Governmental Operations with

Respect to Intelligence Activities."
www.senate.gov/artandhistory/history
/common/investigations/ChurchCommittee
.htm (accessed July 26, 2020).

Vagins, Deborah J., and Jesselyn McCurdy.
"Cracks in the System: Twenty Years of
the Unjust Federal Crack Cocaine Law."
American Civil Liberties Union, October
2006. www.aclu.org/other/cracks-system-20
-years-unjust-federal-crack-cocaine-law.

Vega, Tanzina. "It's Lonely in the Black 1%."
CNNMoney, October 14, 2016. money.cnn
.com/2016/10/14/news/economy/black-1
-unstereotyped/index.html.

"Watts Rebellion (Los Angeles)." Martin Luther
King, Jr. Research and Education Institute,
Stanford University. https://kinginstitute
.stanford.edu/encyclopedia/watts-rebellion
-los-angeles (accessed August 14, 2020).

Wells, Ida B. *Southern Horrors: Lynch Law in All
Its Phases*, 1892. www.gutenberg.org/files
/14975/14975-h/14975-h.htm.

Wells, Veronica. "Untold: Women of the
Black Panther Party: Joan Tarika Lewis."
MadameNoire. February 20, 2020.
https://madamenoire.com/1133994/women
-of-the-black-panther-party-joan-tarika
-lewis/.

"What Happened in Ferguson?" *New York Times*,
August 10, 2015. www.nytimes.com/interactive
/2014/08/13/us/ferguson-missouri-town-under
-siege-after-police-shooting.html.

Williams, Yohuru. *Black Politics/White Power: Civil
Rights, Black Power, and the Black Panthers in
New Haven*. Malden, MA: Blackwell, 2008.

Woodham, Rebecca. "Lowndes County
Freedom Organization." Encyclopedia
of Alabama. September 25, 2008. www
.encyclopediaofalabama.org/article/h-1781.

MUSEUMS AND ARCHIVES

Allen County Public Library, Indiana

Birmingham Civil Rights Institute, Alabama

Birmingham Public Library, Alabama

Chicago Public Library, Illinois

International Civil Rights Center and Museum,
Greensboro, North Carolina

The King Center, Atlanta, Georgia

The Legacy Museum, Montgomery, Alabama

Library of Congress, Prints and Photographs
Division, Washington, D.C.

Missouri Historical Society, St. Louis, Missouri

National Civil Rights Museum at the Lorraine
Motel, Memphis, Tennessee

National Museum of African American History
and Culture/Smithsonian Institution,
Washington, D.C.

Oakland Museum of California

Oakland Public Library, California

Rosa Parks Museum, Montgomery, Alabama

Schomburg Center for Research in Black Culture/
New York Public Library, New York City

Seattle Public Library, Washington

Southern Poverty Law Center, Montgomery,
Alabama

Stanford University, California

University of California, Berkeley

Vermont College of Fine Arts Gary Library,
Montpelier

IMAGE CREDITS

p. 126: Copyright © 2021 by Emory Douglas/Artists Rights Society (ARS), New York. Image provided by Letterform Archive.

p. 130: Courtesy of the Collection of the Smithsonian National Museum of African American History and Culture, photo by Alan Copeland

p. 132: AP Photo/Charles Kelly

p. 135: MOHAI, *Seattle Post-Intelligencer* Photograph Collection, 1986.5.11579.11, photo by Doug Wilson

p. 136: Via BlackPast.org

p. 138: Copyright © The Regents of the University of California. Courtesy Special Collections, University Library, University of California Santa Cruz. Ruth-Marion Baruch and Pirkle Jones Photographs.

p. 141: Bob Fitch Photography Archive, Department of Special Collections, Stanford University Libraries

p. 142: David Fenton/Getty Images

p. 145: Courtesy of the Library of Congress, Prints and Photographs Division, LC-U9-19759- 4/4A

p. 147: Bob Fitch Photography Archive, Department of Special Collections, Stanford University Libraries

p. 148: Contraband Collection/Alamy Stock Photo

p. 151: Chicago History Museum, *Chicago Sun-Times* collection, ST-17101825-0003

p. 152: Bettmann Archive

p. 153: Angelo Cozzi (Mondadori Publishers)

pp. 154 and 156: Stephen Shames/Polaris

p. 162: Bettmann Archive

p. 163: Courtesy of It's About Time Archive

pp. 165, 166, 168, and 171: Copyright © The Regents of the University of California. Courtesy Special Collections, University Library, University of California Santa Cruz. Ruth-Marion Baruch and Pirkle Jones Photographs.

p. 172: Stephen Shames/Polaris

pp. 175, 176 (both), and 177: Copyright © The Regents of the University of California. Courtesy Special Collections, University Library, University of California Santa Cruz. Ruth-Marion Baruch and Pirkle Jones Photographs.

p. 179: Stephen Shames/Polaris

p. 180: Courtesy of It's About Time Archive

pp. 181 and 184: Stephen Shames/Polaris

p. 188: Copyright © The Regents of the University of California. Courtesy Special Collections, University Library, University of California Santa Cruz. Ruth-Marion Baruch and Pirkle Jones Photographs.

p. 190: Chicago History Museum, *Chicago Sun-Times* collection, ST-19031008-0013

p. 191: Courtesy of It's About Time Archive

p. 193: Vernon Merritt III/The LIFE Picture Collection via Getty Images

p. 195: Stephen Shames/Polaris

p. 196: David Fenton/Getty Images

p. 199: FBI COINTELPRO documents

p. 201: MPI/Getty Images

p. 202: Stephen Shames/Polaris

p. 205: AP Photo

pp. 206 (both photos) and 209: Courtesy of It's About Time Archive

p. 207: FBI COINTELPRO documents

p. 209: Courtesy of It's About Time Archive

p. 210: Roz Payne, "Panther 21 Trial (6 images)," *Roz Payne Sixties Archive*, accessed March 11, 2021, https://rozsixties.unl.edu/items/show/786

p. 212: Courtesy of the Tom & Ethel Bradley Center at California State University, Northridge

p. 214: Stephen Shames/Polaris

p. 217: Courtesy of the Howard Brodie Collection, Library of Congress, Prints and Photographs Division, LC-DIG-ppmsca-51105

p. 219: CSU Archives/Everett Collection

p. 220: *Chicago Daily News* courtesy of *Chicago Sun-Times* via AP

p. 222: AP Photo/Wally Fong (top); Bettmann Archives (bottom)

pp. 223 and 224: AP Photo

p. 226: Copyright © The Regents of the University of California. Courtesy Special Collections, University Library, University of California Santa Cruz. Ruth-Marion Baruch and Pirkle Jones Photographs.

p. 228: CSU Archives/Everett Collection

p. 229: Courtesy of the Library of Congress, Prints and Photographs Division, Howard Brodie Collection, LC-DIG-ppmsca-51107

p. 230: Roz Payne, "Rally at University of Vermont (1 image)," *Roz Payne Sixties Archive*, accessed March 11, 2021, https://rozsixties.unl.edu/items/show/825

p. 231: David Fenton/Getty Images

p. 233: Courtesy of the Library of Congress, Prints and Photographs Division, LC-USZ62-101458

p. 236: David Fenton/Getty Images

p. 238: Courtesy of It's About Time Archive

p. 242: AP Photo

pp. 245 and 247: Courtesy of It's About Time Archive

p. 251: Via Wikimedia Commons

p. 253: CSU Archives/Everett Collection

p. 254: AP Photo

pp. 256 and 258: Stephen Shames/Polaris

p. 260: Courtesy of the Collection of the Smithsonian National Museum of African American History and Culture

p. 261: Stephen Shames/Polaris

p. 263: Stanford University Libraries, Department of Special Collections, Bob Fitch Photography Archive

p. 265: Stephen Shames/Polaris

p. 267: Ron Riesterer/PhotoShelter

p. 268: Bettmann Archive

p. 269: AP Photo

pp. 272–273: Catherine Miano Johnson, CC BY 3.0, https://creativecommons.org/licenses/by/3.0

p. 274: Shereen Marisol Meraji/NPR

p. 277: Courtesy of the National Archives Catalog, 75855449

p. 279: Justin Hoch/Justin Hoch for a Hudson Union Society event, CC BY 3.0, https://creativecommons.org/licenses/by/3.0

p. 281: Courtesy of the Library of Congress, Prints and Photographs Division, LC-DIG–ppmsca-02137

p. 283: The White House

p. 284: Debra M. Gaines, CC BY 3.0, https://creativecommons.org/licenses/by/3.0

COPYRIGHT ACKNOWLEDGMENTS

INDEX